DISCOVERING
A NEW AUDIENCE
FOR THEATRE

The History of ASSITEJ
The International Association of Theatre for Children and Youth

$\mathcal{D}$ISCOVERING
A NEW AUDIENCE
FOR THEATRE

The History of ASSITEJ

The International Association of Theatre for Children and Youth
(ASSITEJ / l'Association Internationale
du Théâtre pour l'Enfance et la Jeunesse)
Volume I
(1964–1975)

NAT EEK, PhD
College of Fine Arts
University of Oklahoma
Honorary President of ASSITEJ
President, 1972–75
Norman, Oklahoma, USA
with
ANN M. SHAW, EdD
Queens College
City University of New York
Honorary Member of ASSITEJ
Vice-President, 1981–87
Santa Fe, New Mexico, USA
and
KATHERINE KRZYS, MFA
Curator, Child Drama Collection
Arizona State University
Curator, ASSITEJ/USA & ASSITEJ
1985 to present
Tempe, Arizona, USA

SANTA FE

On the Cover: Bruin the Bear, "Reynard the Fox" by Albert Fauquet (Belgium). Everyman Players (USA), directed by Orlin Corey, designed by Irene Corey. Photo courtesy of the US Center for ASSITEJ, 1977.

Book and cover designed by Vicki Ahl.

Sunstone books may be purchased for educational, business, or sales promotional use. For information please write: Special Markets Department, Sunstone Press, P.O. Box 2321, Santa Fe, New Mexico 87504-2321.

Library of Congress Cataloging-in-Publication Data
Eek, Nat, 1927-
Discovering a new audience for theatre : the history of ASSITEJ, the International Association of Theatre for Children and Youth / by Nat Eek, with Ann M. Shaw, and Katherine Krzys.
   v. cm.
Includes bibliographical references and index.
Contents: v. 1. 1964-1975
ISBN 978-0-86534-660-4 (v. 1 : pbk. : alk. paper)
1. International Association of Theatre for Children and Young People–History.
I. Shaw, Ann M. (Ann Marie), 1930- II. Krzys, Katherine. III. Title.
PN2015E45 2008
792.02'2609--dc22

2008010550

WWW.SUNSTONEPRESS.COM
SUNSTONE PRESS / POST OFFICE BOX 2321 / SANTA FE, NM 87504-2321 /USA
(505) 988-4418 / ORDERS ONLY (800) 243-5644 / FAX (505) 988-1025

This History is dedicated to ASSITEJ, to its leaders, and its National Centers and their members who gave of their time, their money, and their devotion to a firm belief in the art of the theatre for young people, making it an artistic equal to adult theatre.

CONTENTS

Volume I
(1964-1975)

FOREWORD

by
Prof. Dr. Wolfgang Schneider
President of ASSITEJ

"Children Need Theater and Theater Needs ASSITEJ"

*W*hat is ASSITEJ? Who is ASSITEJ? What does ASSITEJ do? These are questions that are constantly being asked. They are not always easy to answer. They are questions that reveal the tasks and goals of ASSITEJ. One should first explain the meaning of the Acronym, what its mission statement declares, and who, what, and where it is supported.

ASSITEJ has a website on the Internet for these answers. Also, one can learn through "The ASSITEJ Book" published every two years, or one can subscribe to the quarterly Newsletter. In addition ASSITEJ publishes a Festival Guide that lists hundreds of events all over the world where one can see many theater performances for young audiences in just a few days. On 20 March every year ASSITEJ also celebrates the International Children's and Young People's Theater Day with a prominent message and multiple activities. ASSITEJ holds a world congress every three years with an international program of theater performances and discussions.

In over forty years ASSITEJ has established an international network of more than 80 national centers on six continents devoted to the support of theater for children and young people. ASSITEJ is a youth, educational, and cultural-political initiative. It is about making theater for children and young people possible; it is about the art of theater for a young audience; it is about social communication, aesthetic education, the right to art and culture—just as the United Nations declared in Article 31 of the Children's Rights Convention.

ASSITEJ is an association of community users, and an association that has declared such honorable goals that it needs honorable members. ASSITEJ needs people who are voluntarily engaged in the subject: such people, with a convincing idea, with clever energy, with a great devotion to children, youth, and theater, are thankful for the establishment of ASSITEJ. These kinds of people have laid a foundation for an international organization that, in the era of the cold war, in times of north-south and east-west conflicts, and in times of political silence, came together, discussed together, and remained together. The adhesive was not politics—their common interest was the young audience. The theater was and is the world, in which much is possible—including the impossible.

The history of ASSITEJ is a success story: that artistic and cultural exchanges are the best politics, that cooperation and co-production require that the partners want to meet each other, want to know each other, want to to learn from each other; because they have become acquainted with each other. This mutual interest demands infrastructure, knowledge must become experience, and cooperation wants to be organized.

A few people found each other, worked together, and established ASSITEJ. It is time to document this story. Dr. Nat Eek, Honorary President of ASSITEJ, was there from the beginning. He has written his history of ASSITEJ. Painstakingly collected, chronologically organized and benevolently formulated, it was written with the assistance of Honorary Member of ASSITEJ Dr. Ann M. Shaw and Mrs. Katherine Krzys, Curator of the ASSITEJ/USA archives at Arizona State University in Tempe, Arizona. They are to be thanked for their great work, for the research that recalled important memories, for the larger story that through the telling of the smaller stories becomes understandable.

On the way to the first half century of work for ASSITEJ, we hold the documentation for the first decade in our hands. Now we all as participants in ASSITEJ know where we have come from, what is behind us, but also what the responsibility is to shape the future before us. A future without a past is unthinkable. "Here we go" is only possible when you pay attention to what has been.

Dr. Eek is our historical biographer and our biographical historian. In the name of the Executive Committee of ASSITEJ, I offer him my heartfelt congratulations, and for all people who feel the call and the connection to ASSITEJ, I express my gratitude, and I close my thanks to Dr. Eek particularly as one of those who served in the founding years of ASSITEJ. And I would like to express a wish: Dear Nat, let's read more from you very soon: In Volume 2 & 3, the history of ASSITEJ from 1975 to the present.

Prof. Dr. Wolfgang Schneider
President of ASSITEJ

The above is a translation from the original German (below) by Erik Eek and edited by Eckhard Mittelstaedt and Nat Eek

Kinder brauchen Theater

Zum Geleit für eine Geschichte der ASSITEJ
Von Wolfgang Schneider

Was, bitte schön, ist die ASSITEJ? Wer, bitte schön, ist die ASSITEJ? Und was, bitte schön, macht die ASSITEJ? Fragen, die immer wieder gestellt werden, Fragen, die nicht immer einfach zu beantworten sind, Fragen, die dem Sinn, den Aufgaben und Zielen auf die Spur kommen wollen. Es gilt zu klären, was sich hinter dem Akronym verbirgt, es gilt zu klären, was das mission statement aussagt und es gilt zu klären, wer, wo und wie dahinter steckt.

Mittlerweile kann die ASSITEJ eine website im Internet vorweisen, kann man sich alle drei Jahre im „The ASSITEJ Book" informieren und den Newsletter abonnieren, der alle drei Monate erscheint. Die ASSITEJ publiziert einen Festival-Guide, der auf Hunderte von Ereignissen in aller Welt aufmerksam macht, bei denen über wenige Tage viele Theateraufführungen zu sehen sind. Die ASSITEJ zelebriert jeweils am 20. März eines jeden Jahres den Internationalen Kinder- und Jugendtheater-Tag mit einer prominenten Botschaft und vielerlei Aktivitäten. Die ASSITEJ veranstaltet alle drei Jahre einen Weltkongress mit einem internationalen Theaterprogramm, das Kinder—und Jugendtheater zeigt und Kinder—und Jugendtheater diskutiert.

In mehr als vierzig Jahren ist die ASSITEJ in mehr als achtzig nationalen Zentren auf allen Kontinenten vertreten, ist ein internationales Netzwerk entstanden, das sich der Förderung des Kinder-und Jugendtheaters widmet. Die ASSITEJ ist eine jugend-, bildungs-, vor allem aber kulturpolitische Initiative; es geht nicht mehr und nicht weniger darum, Kindern und Jugendlichen Theater zu ermöglichen; es geht um die Theaterkunst für ein junges Publikum; es geht um soziale Kommunikation, um ästhetische Bildung, das Recht auf Kunst und Kultur—wie es die Vereinten Nationen im Artikel 31 der Kinderrechtskonvention deklarieren.

Die ASSITEJ ist ein gemeinnütziger Verein. Und ein Verein, der sich solch ehrenwerten Zielen verschrieben hat, braucht ehrenwerte Mitglieder. Die ASSITEJ braucht Menschen, die sich ehrenamtlich für die Sache engagieren. Solche Menschen, mit einer überzeugenden Idee, mit klugem Tatendrang, mit einer großen Hingabe für Kinder, Jugendliche und Theater, solchen Menschen haben wir die Gründung unserer Assoziation zu verdanken. Diese Menschen haben den Grundstein gelegt für eine internationale Organisation, die in Zeiten des Kalten Krieges, in Zeiten von Nord-Süd- und Ost-West-Konflikten und in Zeiten von politischer Sprachlosigkeit, zusammenkamen, zusammen redeten und zusammenhielten. Die Klammer war nicht die große Politik, das Verbindende waren die kleinen Zuschauer. Das Theater war und ist die Welt, in der vieles möglich ist—auch das Unmögliche.

Die Geschichte der ASSITEJ ist eine Erfolgsgeschichte; denn der künstlerische und kulturelle Austausch ist die beste Politik, das Kooperieren und Koproduzieren setzt voraus, dass sich die Partner kennen wollen, sie wollen sich kennen lernen, sie lernen voneinander, weil sie sich kennen. Das Interesse bedarf der Infrastruktur, Kenntnisse müssen erfahren werden, das Zusammentun will organisiert sein.

Ein paar Menschen haben sich zusammengefunden, haben sich zusammengetan, haben zusammen die ASSITEJ erfunden. Es ist Zeit, diese Geschichte zu dokumentieren. Dr. Nat Eek, Ehrenpräsident der ASSITEJ, war von Anfang an dabei. Er hat sie geschrieben, seine Geschichte der ASSITEJ. Akribisch zusammengetragen, chronologisch geordnet und wohlwollend formuliert, mit dem Ehrenmitglied der ASSITEJ, Dr. Ann M. Shaw und unter Mithilfe von Katherine Krzys, die das Archiv der ASSITEJ USA an der Arizona State University in Tampa (USA) leitet. Ihm und ihnen ist zu danken: Für eine großartige Arbeit, für eine Recherche, die wichtige Erinnerungen hervorgebracht hat, für eine Geschichte, die auch durch das Erzählen kleiner Geschichten nachvollziehbar wird.

Auf dem Weg zu einem halben Jahrhundert Werk und Wirken der ASSITEJ halten wir die erste Dekade in Dokumenten in Händen. Jetzt wissen alle an der ASSITEJ Beteiligten, wo sie herkommen, was hinter uns liegt, aber auch Verpflichtung sein kann, zu gestalten, was vor uns liegt. Zukunft ist ohne Geschichte nicht denkbar, ein ‚weiter so' ist nur machbar, wenn man sich gewahr wird, was bisher war.

Dr. Nat Eek ist unser historischer Biograph und unser biographischer Historiker. Im Namen des Executiv-Komitees der ASSITEJ beglückwünsche ich ihn aus tiefem Herzen, ich gratuliere im Auftrag aller Menschen, die sich derzeit der ASSITEJ verpflichtet und verbunden fühlen und ich schließe in meinen Dank an Dr. Nat Eek all jene mit ein, die sich insbesondere in den Gründungsjahren der ASSITEJ verdient gemacht haben. Und einen Wunsch möchte ich noch abschließend äußern: Lass recht bald, lieber Nat, wieder von dir lesen: In Band 2 fff—die Geschichte der ASSITEJ ab 1975 bis heute.

Prof. Dr. Wolfgang Schneider
President of ASSITEJ

«Les enfants ont besoin du théâtre et le théâtre a besoin de l'ASSITEJ»

du professeur Wolfgang Schneider
Président de l'ASSITEJ Internationale

Qu'est-ce que c'est l'ASSITEJ? Qui compose l'ASSITEJ? Que fait l'ASSITEJ ? Voici des questions que l'on me pose souvent et auxquelles il n'est pas toujours facile de répondre. Ce sont des questions qui se rapportent aux buts et aux objectifs de l'ASSITEJ. Je devrais d'abord expliquer la signification de l'acronyme, rappeler la déclaration de sa mission et mentionner par qui l'Association est soutenue.

L'ASSITEJ a une page web pour répondre à ces questions. Les annuaires de l'ASSITEJ paraissent tous les deux ans, il y a la lettre d'information, le guide des festivals, festivals où l'on peut voir plusieurs spectacles pour jeunes publics en l'espace de quelques jours. Le 20 mars, elle célèbre la journée internationale de théâtre pour les enfants et la jeunesse. Tous les trois ans, elle organise le Congrès et le Festival de l'ASSITEJ Internationale.

Grâce à son action, déployée sur plus de quarante ans, L'ASSITEJ est devenue un réseau international dont le nombre de ses «centres membres» s'étend sur plus de 80 pays répartis sur les six continents. L'ASSITEJ est une initiative socioculturelle en direction de la jeunesse et de l'éducation. Son objectif est de donner la place qu'elle mérite au théâtre pour les enfants et la jeunesse, autrement dit, l'art scénique pour les jeunes spectateurs; mais aussi la communication sociale, l'éducation esthétique, le droit de tous à l'art et à la culture, conformément à la Déclaration des Droits de l'Enfant, article 31, des Nations Unies.

L'ASSITEJ est une association composée de personnes issues des différentes communautés ainsi que de membres honoraires, volontairement engagés dans le travail. L'ASSITEJ a besoin de gens comme eux pour réaliser ses «nobles objectifs»; des personnes idéalistes, énergiques, dévouées aux enfants, aux jeunes et au théâtre. Ces personnes ont créé une organisation internationale qui n'a cessé de se réunir, de discuter, maintenir une union, même pendant les périodes difficiles: la guerre froide, les conflits entre le nord et le sud, l'est et l'ouest et en dépit du silence politique qui a entouré ces évènements.

Ce qui les rassemblait c'était le jeune public, non pas la politique. Le théâtre est un monde où tout est possible, même l'impossible.

L'Histoire de l'ASSITEJ est une histoire couronnée de succès; car quels meilleurs outils politiques que les échanges artistiques et culturels?: la coopération et la co-production exigent des partenaires une volonté réelle de se rencontrer, de se connaître et ainsi d'apprendre l'un de l'autre. La rencontre peut devenir une expérience. Cet intérêt mutuel a besoin d'une infrastructure...la co-opération doit être organisée. C'est cet encadrement qui fait la force d'ASSITEJ.

Quelques personnes se sont rencontrées, elles ont travaillé ensemble et elles ont fondé l'ASSITEJ. Le docteur Nat Eek, président honoraire de l'ASSITEJ était parmi ces fondateurs. Il a écrit l'histoire de l'association. Consciencieusement il a collecté, organisé dans l'ordre chronologique les documents et enfin écrit son œuvre avec l'assistance de docteur Ann Shaw, membre honoraire de l'ASSITEJ et Mme Katherine Krzys, curatrice des archives de l'ASSITEJ USA à L'Arizona State University à Tempe, Arizona. On veut les remercier pour leur travail acharné, pour les recherches qui ont mis à jour des souvenirs fondateurs grâce auxquels on a pu construire une plus grande histoire remontant des petites anecdotes.

Après presque un demi-siècle de travail, l'ASSITEJ a maintenant en main la documentation des dix premières années de l'association. Aujourd'hui, nous, les membres de l'ASSITEJ, savons d'où nous venons, ce qui a été fait avant nous, mais aussi ce qu'il faut faire demain. Un avenir sans passé n'est pas pensable. «On y va» n'est possible que si on fait attention à ce qui a été avant.

Docteur Nat Eek est notre biographe historien et notre historien biographe. De la part du Comité exécutif de l'ASSITEJ, je le félicite chaleureusement. Je suis reconnaissant à tous ceux qui sont attachés à L'ASSITEJ et travaillent pour ses objectifs. Je remercie de tout mon coeur Nat Eek et les autres fondateurs pour le travail sur ces débuts de notre association et j'espère pouvoir bientôt lire les tomes 2 et 3 qui racontent l'histoire de l'ASSITEJ jusqu'à nos jours.

Professeur Wolfgang Schneider
Président de l'ASSITEJ

Translation in French by Katarna Metsälampi, revised by Noémi Tiberghien

"Детям нужен театр, а театру нужна АССИТЕЖ"

Д-р Вольфганг Шнайдер,
Президент АССИТЕЖ

Что такое АССИТЕЖ? Кто входит в АССИТЕЖ? Чем занимается АССИТЕЖ? Такие вопросы задают постоянно. И не всегда легко на них ответить. В этих вопросах - желание узнать о целях и задачах АССИТЕЖ. Чтобы ответить на них, надо прежде всего объяснить, что скрывается за этой аббревиатурой, затем рассказать о целях, заявленных ассоциацией и о том, где, как и кто ее поддерживает.

Ответы на эти вопросы можно получить на сайте АССИТЕЖ в Интернете. Также можно узнать об АССИТЕЖ из издания «Книга АССИТЕЖ», которое выходит каждые два года. Или можно подписаться на информационный бюллетень АССИТЕЖ, выпускаемый раз в квартал. Помимо этого, АССИТЕЖ издает фестивальный справочник, где дает информацию о сотнях фестивалей во всем мире, на которых можно всего за несколько дней посмотреть много разных спектаклей для юных зрителей. Ежегодно, 20 марта, специальным обращением и разнообразными акциями, АССИТЕЖ отмечает Международный День Театра для Детей и Молодежи. Раз в три года АССИТЕЖ проводит свой Всемирный Конгресс и международный фестиваль театров для детей и молодежи, сопровождающийся обсуждениями и дискуссиями.

АССИТЕЖ существует более 40 лет. За это время она открыла на всех шести континентах 80 своих национальных центров, преданно поддерживающих театр для детей и молодежи. АССИТЕЖ - это молодежная, образовательная и культурно-политическая инициатива. АССИТЕЖ - это поддержка театра для детей и молодежи; это развитие искусства театра для детей и молодежи; это общественное взаимодействие, эстетическое воспитание, право на доступ к искусству и культуре, подтвержденное статьей 31 Конвенции о правах ребенка Организации Объединенных Наций.

АССИТЕЖ - это общественная ассоциация, ставящая перед собой очень благородные задачи, поэтому ей нужны достойные члены. АСИТЕЖ нужны люди, которые на добровольной основе помогают ей. Это люди с твердыми убеждениями, умные и энергичные, преданные детям, молодежи и театру, понимающие, зачем была создана АССИТЕЖ. Такие люди заложили основу этой международной ассоциации еще во времена холодной войны, во времена конфликтов севера и юга, запада и востока. Во времена политического безмолвия, они, тем не менее, собирались вместе, обсуждали совместные дела и оставались вместе, несмотря ни на что. Их объединяла не политика, их общим интересом были юные зрители. Театр был и будет особым миром, где многое возможно, в том числе и невозможное.

История АССИЕТЖ - это история успеха, подтверждающая, что творческие и культурные обмены есть самая лучшая политика. Сотрудничество и создание копродукций влечет за собой желание встречаться друг с другом, знать больше друг о друге, учиться друг у друга. Таким обоюдным интересам нужна инфраструктура, нужно знание, переходящее в опыт, нужна кооперативная организованность.

Несколько людей, нашли друг друга и начали работать вместе над созданием АССИТЕЖ. Пришло время документально подтвердить эти события. Д-р Нэт Ик, Почетный президент АССИТЕЖ, стоявший у истоков ассоциации, написал историю АССИТЕЖ. Проведя кропотливые исследования, он хронологически воссоздал и ее. Ему помогала Почетный член АССИТЕЖ д-р Энн Шоу и г-жа Кэтрин Кржис., куратор архивов АССИТЕЖ /США в Университете штата Аризона в г. Темпе. Нам нужно поблагодарить их за проделанную большую работу, за исследования, которые вызывают в памяти очень важные эпизоды, за то, что с помощью маленьких воспоминаний общая большая история становится более понятной.

В преддверии своего пятидесятилетия мы держим в руках документальную историю нашего первого десятилетия. Теперь мы все в АССИТЕЖ будем знать, откуда мы пришли, какой путь пройден, а также какая ответственность лежит перед нами в будущем. Будущего без прошлого не существует. Можно сказать «Пошли дальше!» только тогда, когда стало понятным, что было в прошлом.

Д-р Нат Ик - наш исторический биограф и биографический историк. От имени Исполкома АССИТЕЖ я горячо поздравляю его. Я поздравляю его от имени всех, кто ощущает свою связь с АССИТЕЖ и кто работает на благо АССИТЕЖ. Я выражаю свою глубокую благодарность д-ру Нэту Ику как человеку, который принес большую пользу в годы создания АССИТЕЖ. И я бы хотел высказать пожелание - дорогой Нэт, мы будем ждать от тебя продолжения истории АССИТЕЖ, начиная с 1975 года и до наших дней!

Д-р Вольфганг Шнайдер,
Профессор,
Президент АСИТЕЖ

Translated by Galina Kolosova

SE NECESITA EL TEATRO PARA LOS NIÑOS
Y SE NECESITA EL TEATRO PARA ASSITEJ

por Prof. Dr. Wolfgang Schneider
Presidente, ASSITEJ

¿Qué es ASSITEJ? ¿Quién es ASSITEJ? ¿Qué hace ASSITEJ? Siempre se pregunta estas preguntas. No es fácil responderlas todo el tiempo. Son preguntas que muestran las misiones y los motives de ASSITEJ. Primero hay que explicar el sentido de las letras "ASSITEJ", lo que presenta su declaración de missión, y quien, que y donde esta sostenido.

Se puedo hallar estas respuestas en el sitio de ASSITEJ en el "Internet". También, se puede descubrirlas en "El Libro ASSITEJ", publicado cada tres años, o se puede subscribir a la publicación trimestral. También, ASSITEJ publíca un Guiá Festival que lista cientos de eventos por todas partes del mundo donde se puede ver muchas obras del teatro de juventud en unos pocos días. Cada año en el 20 de marzo, ASSITEJ también celebra el Día Internacional del Teatro de Niños y Jovenes. Cada tres años, ASSITEJ tiene un congresso mundial con un programa internacional de obras del teatro y discusiones.

En más de cuarenta años, ASSITEJ has establecido una malla internacional de más de 80 centros nacionales en seis continentes dedicados a sostener el teatro para los niños y la juventud. ASSITEJ es un iniciativo dedicado a la juventud, educación y cultura/política. Es de hacer posible el teatro para los niños y la juventud; es del arte del teatro para el audencia joven; es de comunicación social, educación estética; el derecho al arte y la cultura así como está declarado por las Naciones Unidas en el artículo 31 de la Convención de Derechos para los Niños.

ASSITEJ es una asociación de los que emplean de la comunidad y una asociación que ha declarado misiones tan honorables que necesita a miembros honorables. ASSITEJ necesita a los que están comprometidos voluntariamente en el sujeto; tal gente, con un concepto convincente, con energía avisada, con una gran devoción a los niños, a la juventud y el teatro, quien está agradecido para el establecimiento de ASSITEJ. Esta clase de gente ha abrido las zanjas para una organización internacional que se juntaron, discutieron juntos uno con uno, y se quedaron juntos, aún durante la época de la Guerra Fría; de los conflictos entre el norte y el sur y el este y el oeste; y del silencio político. Lo que se unieron no fué lo político sino su interés común en el audencia joven. El teatro era y es el mundo en que mucho es posible, incluyendo lo imposible.

La historia de ASSITEJ es un cuento de éxito: que las experiencias artísticas y culturales entre la gente de todas partes es lo mejor político; que la cooperación y coproducción requieren que los compañeros quieren encontrar y conocer el uno al otro y parender de cada uno, porque se hicieron conocidos el uno al otro. Este interés mutual require una estructura internal, el saber tiene que hacerse experiencia, la cooperación quiere estar organizada.

Pocas personas se hallaron el uno al otro y establecieron ASSITEJ. Ahora, hay que documentar este cuento. El Dr. Nat Eek, el presidente honorario de ASSITEJ, ha estado con la asociación desde el principio. El ha excrito su historia de ASSITEJ. La historia fué escrito por recoger laboriosamente, organizer cronológicamente y formular benévolamente. Le ayudaron al Dr. Eek, al Dr. Ann M. Shaw, un miembro honorario de ASSITEJ, y la Sra. Katherine Krzys, la conservadora de los archivos de ASSITEJ/EU a la Universidad del Estado de Arizona en Tempe, Arizona. Hay que darles gracias por su gran esfuerzo, por la investigación que hizo volver memorias importantes, por la historia más grande que hizo más entendido debido al contar los cuentos pequeños.

En nuestros manos tenemos la documentación para ASSITEJ de la primera decena de la primera mitad del siglo. Ahora, todos nosotros como participantes en ASSITEJ, sabemos de donde venimos, lo que está detrás de nosotros, pero también la responsabilidad para formar el porvenir enfrente de nosotros. No se puede creer en el porvenir sin el pasado. "Aquí vamos" solamente es posible cuando presta atención a lo que ha sido.

El Dr. Eek es nuestro biógrafo histórico y nuestro historiador biográfico. En el nombre del Comité Ejectivo de ASSITEJ le ofrezco mis felicitaciones de corazón, y para todos que sienten llamados y juntados a ASSITEJ, expreso mi gratitud. Termino mis gracias al Dr. Eek particularmente como uno de esos que sirvió en los años expósitos de ASSITEJ. Y también quiero expresar un deseo: Querido Nat, vamos a leer muy pronto más de Ud. por la historia de ASSITEJ de 1975 al presente en volumenes 2 y 3.

Prof. Dr. Wolfgang Schneider
Presidente de ASSITEJ

Translated by Anneke Chittim

"BARN BEHÖVER TEATER OCH TEATERN BEHÖVER ASSITEJ"

av Prof Dr Wolfgang Schneider,
president, ASSITEJ International

Vad är ASSITEJ? Vem är ASSITEJ? Och vad gör ASSITEJ? Dessa frågor är ständigt återkommande. De är inte alltid enkla att svara på. De är frågor om ASSITEJs uppdrag och målsättning. Vad gömmer sig bakom förkortningen? Vad är målsättningen? Vem vänder man sig till? Vad stöder organisationen och var?

ASSITEJ:s hemsida på Internet kan svara på dessa frågor. Man kan också få svar genom "The ASSITEJ Book" som publiceras vartannat år, eller så kan man prenumerera på Newsletter som publiceras kvartalsvis. ASSITEJ publicerar också en festivalguide som innehåller hundratals evenemang över hela världen där man på festivaler under några få dagar kan se mängder av barn- och ungdomsteaterföreställningar. Den 20 mars varje år firar ASSITEJ "the International World Day of Theatre for Children and Young People" med ett årligt uttalande och många aktiviteter. Var tredje år arrangerar ASSITEJ sin världskongress med ett inernationellt program av barn- och ungdomsteaterföreställningar och diskussioner.

I över 40 år har ASSITEJ varit ett nätverk med mer än 80 nationella center på sex kontinenter tillägnat barn- och ungdomsteater. ASSITEJ är ett kulturpolitiskt initiativ baserat på teater för barn och unga och på deras utbildning. Det är om att möjliggöra barn- och ungdomsteater, det är om barn- och ungdomsteater som konst, det är om social kommunikation, estetisk utbildning, om rätten till konst och kultur – precis som i artikel 31 i Förenta Nationernas konvention om barnens rättigheter.

ASSITEJ är en medlemsorganisation, och som sådan också en organisation med hedersmedlemmar. ASSITEJ behöver människor som ideellt engagerar sig, människor med en övertygande idé, med uppfinningsrik energi, med en stor passion för barn, ungdomar och för teater. Dessa människor har etablerat en internationell organisation som, under det kalla kriget, i tider av konflikt mellan nord-syd, öst-väst, i tider av politisk tystnad, samlades, diskuterade och förblev tillsammans. Sammanhållningen var inte politisk – det gemensamma intresset var den unga publiken. Teater var och är världen där mycket är möjligt – också det omöjliga.

ASSITEJ:s historia är en framgångshistoria: att konstnärlig och kulturell utväxling är den bästa politiken, att samarbete och samproduktion kräver att de inblandade vill träffas, vill lära känna varandra, vill lära från varandra; för att de lärt känna varandra. Det gemensamma intresset kräver en infrastruktur, kunskap ska bli erfarenhet och samarbete kräver organisation.

Några människor fann varandra, arbetade tillsammans och grundade ASSITEJ. Nu är det är dags att dokumentera historien. Dr Nat Eek, hederspresident i ASSITEJ, var med från början. Han har skrivit sin ASSITEJ:s historia. Samvetsgrannt samlat, kronologiskt organiserat och generöst formulerat, har historien blivit skriven med assistans av Dr Ann Shaw, hedersmedlem i ASSITEJ och mrs Katherine Krzys, föreståndare för ASSITEJ USA:s arkiv vid Arizona State University i Tempe, Arizona. Tack för ett enastående arbete, för forskningen som gav viktiga minnen, som gjorde den större historien begriplig genom mindre berättelser.

På väg mot ASSITEJ:s första halvsekel håller vi nu det första årtiondet i vår hand. Nu vet vi alla, som medlemar i ASSITEJ, varifrån vi kom, vad som ligger bakom oss och vi känner ansvaret att skapa vad som ligger framför oss. En framtid utan historia är otänkbar. Framtiden blir bara begriplig när vi vet vad som varit.

Dr Eek är vår historiska biograf och vår biografiska historiker. På ASSITEJ:s exekutiv kommittées vägnar vill jag framföra mina hjärtliga gratulationer, och för alla som känner sig kallade och som känner ASSITEJ uttrycker jag min tacksamhet. Jag vill avsluta med att i synnerhet tacka Dr Eek och i allmänhet tacka alla som medverkade i ASSITEJ:s tidiga år. Jag vill också uttrycka en önskan: Kära Nat, låt oss snart få läsa mer från dig: i volym 2 & 3, i ASSITEJ:s historia från 1975 till idag!

Prof Dr Wolfgang Schneider
ASSITEJ:s president

Translated by Niclas Malmcrona

INTRODUCTION

by
Nat Eek

My 40-year involvement in ASSITEJ

In 1965 when I was President of the Children's Theatre Conference in the United States, Sara Spencer, publisher of the Children's Theatre Press, author, and a leading advocate of theatre for young audiences, asked me if I would go with her to the Founding Congress of a proposed international organization of theatre for young audiences. Spencer, an important delegate (USA), had returned recently from the Preparatory Committee meeting in Venice, Italy in September 1964, where the Statutes of the new organization were written.

As an astute woman, Spencer had observed that men predominated in the Venice Meeting, so she told me it would be important for a man to represent the USA in Paris along with herself. I was honored to be chosen by her, and I agreed immediately to join her at the Paris conference.

This appointment began my lifelong involvement with ASSITEJ, and one that opened up my professional life to vistas and commitments that I never would have envisioned possible. I moved from a mere delegate (1965-68), to a member of the Executive Committee (1968-75), to a Vice-President (1968-72), to President (1972-75), and ultimately to an Honorary President (1981). In 1996 I established the ASSITEJ International Award for Artistic Excellence in gratitude.

During those first ten years I personally witnessed and participated in the events, conflicts, and achievements that made ASSITEJ a highly regarded international association dedicated to the theatrical art of theatre for young people. I have attended every International Congress from 1965 to 2005, with the exception of the VIIIth Congress in Moscow, USSR in 1984, and I kept seeing the need for a complete history of ASSITEJ to be written.

When I stepped down from the Presidency of ASSITEJ in 1975, events in my own professional life prevented me from doing anything more than amassing a personal archive, and depositing it in the Child Drama Collection at Arizona State University, Tempe, Arizona, USA.

Finally, when I retired from the University of Oklahoma in 1993, a Regents Professor Emeritus of Drama, and Dean Emeritus of Fine Arts, the opportunity for my writing such a history became a possibility. As one of the few surviving members of ASSITEJ's early years, I found the writing of this History of paramount importance.

Ann M. Shaw's 31-year involvement in ASSITEJ

Once the organization ASSITEJ became a reality in 1965, it was important that the United States of America create a national center that could then join the new organization. Since I was currently President of CTC, it was logical that this national organization should become the new national center for ASSITEJ.

Accordingly, the US Center for ASSITEJ was created in 1965 after the Paris Constitutional Conference of ASSITEJ, and members of CTC were able to join the new US Center. Since CTC was a division of the American Educational Theatre Association (AETA), all the organizational details and decisions had to go through the Board of AETA for approval.[1]

Ann M. Shaw (EdD) is a retired Associate Professor from Queens College of the City College of New York, a research historian of ASSITEJ, and an authority in creative dramatics and theatre for the disabled. She was a member of the US Center since its founding in 1965. She was elected Executive-Secretary-Treasurer of the US Center in 1977-1978, and was elected President of the US Center in August 1978. In 1979 Shaw and other members of the US Center saw the need for the Center to become totally independent of any other organization, to develop its own national constituency, and to drive its own destiny which included championing the development of the professional theatre for young audiences in the USA.

ASSITEJ/USA, as the new US Center was called, was incorporated in 1981, and Shaw was elected as its Founding President, and was re-elected by the membership twice, serving from 1981-1986. ASSITEJ/USA has continued to grow with a significant membership of professional, non-professional, and educational theatre members. In 2007 ASSITEJ/USA changed its name to Theatre for Young Audiences/USA, but continued to represent the USA to ASSITEJ International.

From 1978-1987 Shaw was able to speak directly to ASSITEJ International as the official voice of the US Center and then of ASSITEJ/USA, ultimately becoming a Vice-President of ASSITEJ (1981-84 and 1984-87) who served as a USA voting delegate at eight Congresses from Madrid, Spain in 1978 through Tromsö, Norway in 1999. As a highly respected delegate and officer, in 2002 at the XIVth World Congress in Seoul, Korea she was made an Honorary Member of ASSITEJ. She has attended every International Congress from 1972 to 2005, with the exception of the Vth Congress in Berlin, GDR in 1975.

The ASSITEJ/USA Archives at Arizona State University

During the development and growth of ASSITEJ/USA, its Board designated the Child Drama Collection of the Hayden Library at Arizona State University as the official repository for the Archives of the US Center for ASSITEJ and ASSITEJ/USA as well as the Archives for anything to do with the USA relationship with ASSITEJ International. The major sources for this history reside in the ASSITEJ International Collection, the Gerald Tyler Collection, the Ann Shaw Collection, and the ASSITEJ/USA Collection, Child Drama Collection, Department of Archives and Manuscripts, University Libraries, Arizona State University, Tempe, Arizona.

Katherine Krzys (MFA) is Curator of the Child Drama Collection and Theatre Specialist for the Arizona State University Libraries. She received her MFA in Theatre with a Concentration in Theatre for Youth from ASU in 1988, and has been Curator since 1985. She has directed plays and stage managed for professional theatres and community recreational programs. She has curated many theatre exhibits, served as Editor of ASSITEJ/USA's journal *TYA Today* for two years, and served on the Board of the American Alliance for Theatre and Education for 13 years. Her archival training includes the Modern Archive Institute at the National Archives in Washington, DC. She has been of invaluable assistance in the writing of this History with her knowledge of the archives, the people, and her personal knowledge of the field.

Since the time of the establishment of these archives in 1979, many members of ASSITEJ have contributed their personal files, correspondence, and memorabilia to them. The authors have been able to draw freely on these archives for this history, and most of these have been primary sources.

The Speeches at One Theatre World Symposium

ASSITEJ celebrated its thirtieth birthday on 10 May 1995 at the Seattle Children's Theatre in Seattle, Washington, USA. The celebration was the opening event of the ONE THEATRE WORLD Symposium hosted by ASSITEJ/USA. Both Mme. Rose-Marie Moudoués (France) and Dr. Ilse Rodenberg (Germany) were in attendance as guests of ASSITEJ/USA, and the 1995 ASSITEJ Executive Committee met there as part of the Symposium.[2]

The program concluded with members of the ASSITEJ Executive Committee presenting birthday wishes to ASSITEJ for its next decade. These wishes were presented in the native language of the speaker and were ably accompanied by Secretary-General Michael Ramløse at the piano. Following are some of these tributes:

Congratulations ASSITEJ for reaching 30 years. We very well know that to raise a child to maturity requires many guardians, guardians with love for children and a heart for commitment. To the Guardians of ASSITEJ, congratulations and do not give up, but go up to fifty years, ninety, and even a hundred, and we from Tanzania wish you luck.
Presented by Penina Mlama on behalf of ASSITEJ/Tanzania.

In a world of war and hunger it is important to remember the importance of culture in the struggle to survive in a possible future. My hope is that ASSITEJ will work to make theatre a medium for children and young people for their impressions and expressions—offering them the possibility to serve as human beings and a chance to influence their surroundings in a positive way. It is also my hope that the member countries will support each other in these efforts.
Presented by Helge Endersen on behalf of ASSITEJ/Norway:
With dedication and respect for human beings we can achieve

a better world. Proud of our differences, ASSITEJ is working to bring us together. We all are ASSITEJ and I just want to invite us to keep on walking forward, taking the hand of whoever is on my right or left side.

Presented by Jacqueline Russo on behalf of ASSITEJ/Venezuela.

HAPPY BIRTHDAY ASSITEJ

If somebody applauds your songs, you can be glad.

If some applauds your poems, you can be happy.

If someone applauds your performance, you can say—I am
successful.

But if somebody applauds your soul, you can be sure,
you are very, very useful on our planet.

And that is all I wish ASSITEJ—a soul to applaud.

Presented by Marian Lucky on behalf of ASSITEJ/Slovakia.[3]

ASSITEJ Annual 1996/97

In 1994 Dr. Wolfgang Schneider of the German National Center asked Shaw to write a history entitled "The Formation of ASSITEJ", a short history of ASSITEJ from 1965-1994 to celebrate the first thirty years. This was the first written document that attempted to chronicle completely these important events from 1965-95, and it was published in the ASSITEJ Annual 1996/67. Much of Shaw's original writing and research has been incorporated in this document, and this author expresses immense gratitude for the fact that her document was the final event that prompted him to start writing this history.

Shaw comments in her short history: "That the Publications Commission entrusted the writing to me is an honor; that my perspective on the pulse points of these thirty years may differ radically or in part from those others is to be expected. As Pieter Geyl, the great Dutch historian wrote, 'History is indeed an argument without end.' "[4]

Sources

Shaw wrote in her original document: "Writing the history of the first thirty years in the life of an international organization is a daunting task. Much of the documentation needed has either vanished or rests in the files of individuals and national centers. Many of my own records are awaiting cataloguing into the ASSITEJ/USA archives.

"Special thanks are due to ASSITEJ President Michael FitzGerald (Australia) and Secretary-General Michael Ramløse (Denmark) for information about recent ASSITEJ history. Katherine Krzys, Archivist of the Child Drama Collection at the Hayden Library, Arizona State University, USA, has generously faxed me copies of important catalogued materials from the Archive of Gerald Tyler (Great Britain) and the records of ASSITEJ/USA.

"Much of this history was written while visiting the Archives in the Library for accurate information. Recollections and/or written accounts from ASSITEJ founders have been particularly helpful: Gerald Tyler (Great Britain), Rose-Marie Moudoués (France), Vladimir Adamek (Czechoslovakia), Nat Eek (USA), and Ilse Rodenberg (GDR). In addition, I have also drawn on personal experiences and available records as well as on those of Harold Oaks, USA representative to the ASSITEJ Executive Committee since 1988."[5]

Of particular significance is the fact that between Eek and Shaw they have personally observed and participated in all of the Assemblies and Congresses of ASSITEJ International from 1965-2005.

There are two early histories that partly cover the formation of ASSITEJ. The first written was: Janice C. Hewitt, "The Development of the International Association of Theatre for Children and Young People with Particular Emphasis on the United States Participation". Her MA Thesis for the University of Kansas essentially gives excellent coverage of the very first years of the founding of ASSITEJ by reviewing the documents available at that time, as well as making and recording personal interviews.

An equally excellent source is: Frederick Scott Regan's "The History of the International Children's Theatre Association From Its Founding to 1975." Regan's Dissertation for the University of Minnesota covers those first ten years in greater detail, and only misses out on the Berlin Congress in April of 1975 as a result of time constraints in its writing deadline.

In addition, the following people, who were involved significantly in ASSITEJ, have both contributed to and helped edit the manuscript: Orlin

Corey, Jed Davis, Joyce Doolittle, Michael FitzGerald, Moses Goldberg, Agnes Haaga, Ann Hill, Christel Hoffmann, Galina Kolosova, Kim Peter Kovac, Niclas Malmcrona, Barbara McIntyre, Michael Ramløse, Harold Oaks, and Wolfgang Schneider. The authors owe them a great debt of gratitude. I am also very grateful to Konrad Eek for technical assistance with the preparation of photographs in this book.

Organizational Pattern of the History

Overview: This History is in three volumes. Volume I covers the first 11 years of the formation of ASSITEJ, the time when Eek was an officer and most active in the organization. Volume II is projected to cover the years from 1976 to 1990 when Shaw was an officer and most involved. Volume III covers the years from 1991 to 2005, and both the latter two volumes are yet to be completed. All three have been written in chronological order starting with the early informal meetings of 1957. They continue on through 2005, the first forty years of the existence of ASSITEJ, and will conclude in 2005 with the Canadian Congress in Montreal.

This History covers all the major meetings as well as the World Congresses. The major agenda items and the ensuing discussions at each gathering are included, a list of the conference activities, and the election results of each Congress are listed in detail where possible.

There is a narrative of all the Executive Committee and Bureau meetings over the years, as well as the results of those meetings. Anything significant that occurred between meetings is also listed, which includes major world events that affected the tenor of the meetings and the activities of ASSITEJ.

At the end of every few years is a Summary listing the salient points, achievements, failures, and disappointments of that time in the progressive history of the Association. Comments on historic events and personal experiences and observations are added whenever pertinent, interesting, and appropriate. If the reader wishes to get a complete but simplified overview of the History of ASSITEJ, it is recommended that he or she go from Summary to Summary, thus avoiding many of the finer details. Hopefully the reader will then want to go back and read this History in greater detail.

This History concludes with a summing up of the past and future of ASSITEJ, its current status, and its possible future direction.

Appendices: In Volume I separate Appendices list the dates of meetings, locations, biographies of the major individual participants, and a listing history of the national centers participating. Also in the Appendices is a copy of the original 1965 Constitution of ASSITEJ, plus other items too lengthy to include in the body of the History. Usually there are interim sections between major meetings that describe the activities of the Association. Conclusions that take note of achievements, failures, growth, and development of the organization are always written at the end of major sections.

Conference Titling: Consistency in terminology has been difficult in that many different terms were used interchangeably and in some cases indiscriminately. Many times this was a result of improper translation. In terms of titling, the archives show a mixture of terms—conference, general assembly, congress, world congress. The initial meetings to form ASSITEJ were called conferences. Since the organizational structure of ASSITEJ was patterned after the United Nations, the word General Assembly began being used for the proposed future gatherings. That in turn was abandoned for the term International Congress by the Prague meeting in 1966. For clarity in this History, the Paris meeting is called the Constitutional Conference. Meetings after Paris are designated as International Congresses and numbered accordingly, and then World Congresses after 1990. The term World Congress emerged after the Stockholm meeting in 1990, undoubtedly prompted by the incredible increase of national centers around the world promoted by the Scandinavian Centers. The governing rules of the Association are called both the Statutes and the Constitution.

The meetings within a Congress have been called Plenary Sessions, General Assemblies, Discussion Sessions, etc. For the sake of clarity the term General Assembly has been used whenever all the delegates at the Congress met together.

Abbreviations: To avoid writing out the term Executive Committee each time, the abbreviation EXCOM has been used. The abbreviations FGR for the Federal Republic of Germany. GDR for the German Democratic Republic, USSR for the Union of Soviet Socialist Republics, and USA for the United States of America have been used. As countries were consolidated, separated, and/or changed in name, the new name has always been used with a single identification of the old name at the time of the change. Then the new name is used consistently. For example: USSR became Russia, Georgia, Ukraine, etc.; Czechoslovakia became the Czech Republic and Slovakia; FGR and GDR became Germany; Ceylon became Sri Lanka; and part of Yugoslavia became Croatia. Participants are first mentioned by their full name, and after that the narrative uses only their last name. Usually no formal titles are used, only the titles of the elected officers of the ASSITEJ Association.

Meeting Narrative: Each meeting's narration begins with a listing in bold type of dates, locations, officers, participants, countries represented, members absent, and special items of information. The notes on the meeting itself usually follow this order: agenda, discussion, motions or decisions, special presentations, special events or performances seen, and finally a brief evaluation.

Summaries: Personal brief biographies, anecdotes, historic notes, observations, comments, and evaluations on the meetings and performances presented are all given in the Summaries to put the actions taken in proper perspective.

Notes: Notes which identify sources of the written information are placed at the end in the Appendices to avoid interrupting the narrative.

Authors' Caveat: Lastly, it must be mentioned that this History is written from the perspective of citizens of the United States of America, and should be judged accordingly. However, the authors have tried to be as objective as possible in their observations and judgments, while keeping an international perspective. Also, we have tried to keep the narrative human and personal, and any errors of fact are certainly not deliberate but those of the authors.

The authors hope that this document will prove to become a rich and accurate resource of the history of an important international theatre organization, and they are grateful for the privilege of attending the actual events and recording this history in writing.

USA and Russian Delegates at the Preparatory Meeting, London, Great Britain. May, 1964. Among the delegates were: USA : Rita Criste, Jed Davis, Ann Hill, Agnes Haaga, Sara Spenser; Russia : Konstantin Shakh-Azizov, Victor Rosov; Sweden: Dan Lipshitz. Courtesy of the British Children's Theatre Association.

PART I:

THE EARLY YEARS OF ACHIEVEMENT
(1964-1972)

Background

*W*ith a sense of achievement and survival from the devastation of World War II, the brave new world began to put itself back together in 1945. After years of colonialism, new nations in the third world were emerging, many sharing socialistic ideologies. After six years of deprivation, violence, and making "do", world trade had soared in an atmosphere of monetary stability. Repairs of the devastation, new housing, consumer goods, world-wide travel led the march to prosperity in which the revitalized world shared.

WWII had made the peoples of the world conscious of the rest of the world, and many returning home from the devastation of the war at home or elsewhere brought with them new ideas, new experiences, new tastes. In the eastern European countries there was a great thaw in the repression of scientific and cultural life, and artists were eager to learn what other artists outside their borders were doing. Cultural exchange became important to all countries.

Tragically the "cold war" of East and West emerged within the three years after the end of WWII, but fortunately that did not defeat the sense of optimism, renewal, and experimentation that the arts around the world were witnessing. Despite these new fears, suspicions, and ideological conflicts that the building of the Berlin Wall in 1961 symbolized, the 1960s were years of rising expectations along with the longest sustained economic boom on record. And there was no major war going on between the end of the Korean conflict and the start of the war in Vietnam.

Television, film, easily available air travel, Pop art, the mod-style revolution, new kinds of music, and increasingly rapid communication all worked towards making the arts available to many more people around the world, and the world seemed to have more leisure time in which to enjoy them.

How did the idea of a world organization composed of theatres that presented plays for children and young people begin? First, theatre was experiencing a burst of activity and creativity, and it was only natural that the children's theatres around the world were experiencing this same renewal. Second, as a result of the deaths in the war, children were a precious commodity and deserved special attention. Third, with the conflicts in political ideologies in the adult world, children's theatre proved to be an excellent national teaching device in terms of history, political philosophy, and cultural identity.

The Formation of ASSITEJ

Rosamund Gilder (USA), Honorary President of the International Theatre Institute, traces ASSITEJ's roots to the United Nations Educational Scientific and Cultural Organization's (UNESCO) founding of the International Theatre Institute (ITI) in 1947 amidst the rubble and festering wounds of WWII. She wrote: "The ITI saw theatre as one, whether for children or adults alike . . . Following up on this ideal, the ITI devoted its 5th Congress at The Hague to children's theatre, developed a Children's Theatre Committee, and published several international bibliographies of children's plays."[6]

This first meeting which included delegates interested in theatre for children and youth on an international level was held in 1952 in Paris, and consisted exclusively of adult professional people. Subsequent meetings were held in Dubrovnik (1955) and Cologne (1958), and two publications were prepared, "The International Bibliography of Children's Theatre Plays" and "A Survey of Children's Theatres Across the World." This ITI Committee on Youth was abandoned in 1960 for financial reasons,[7] and was not revived until 1973, when it changed its focus.

However, ITI seemed to have relegated theatre for children to "committee" status, and "adult theatre" seemed to be the focus of most of its Congresses. Obviously, "children's theatre" was to be given separate but unequal treatment. ITI, perhaps unwittingly, had furthered the "ghetto-ization" of theatre for young audiences as well as of theatre artists, pedagogues, and managers who were committing their professional lives to that theatre art.

The world of the 1960s did not augur well for the founding of an international theatre organization concerned with young audiences. Rose-Marie Moudoués (France-ASSITEJ Secretary-General, 1965-1990) stated: "If we are to appreciate ASSITEJ's early days and understand how significant the founding was, we should remember that historically speaking we were living in the so-called 'cold war' period and that politically the world was split in two."[8]

It was also a world in which the majority of the professional children's theatres (adults earning their living by creating/performing theatre for audiences of children and young people) were located in Eastern Europe. The creation of a professional international association was of particular interest to them. They, as well as theatre leaders from any countries who took various approaches to theatre for young audiences, were eager to learn about theatre work around the world from each other.

It was clear that an independent, international organization devoted to the art of theatre and its role in young lives and peace among nations was urgently needed. To its credit ITI became a willing and valuable advisor to those persons developing the new organization, as was the International Union of Marionette Artists (UNIMA). ASSITEJ's statutes and structure parallel many of those of ITI, and a number of national centers of ITI have given valuable assistance to the national centers of ASSITEJ.

Who is most responsible for the formation of ASSITEJ? Moudoués gives pride of place to Léon Chancerel of France, pointing out that he founded the first performing theatre for young audiences in Paris, and in 1957 created in France l'Association du Théâtre pour l'Enfance et la Jeunesse (ATEJ). He advocated an international organization for children's theatre, and was actively involved in the formative meetings of ASSITEJ. Chancerel provided office space in Paris for ATEJ, which was made available to the French National Center of ASSITEJ, and this became the base of operations for the ASSITEJ Secretary-General from 1965-1990.[9]

There is some confusion over the time and place of the earliest meetings, but Vladimir Adamek (Czechoslovakia) and Léon Chancerel (France) were the prime movers. In March, 1960 Adamek met with people from the USSR, Bulgaria, and the GDR. A subsequent meeting was held on 3 October 1960 with consultations about a possible children's theatre organization among Konstantin Shakh-Azizov (USSR), M. Grigorov (Bulgaria), Rolf Buttner (GDR), and Vladimir Adamek (Czechoslovakia). Then in 1962 there were consultations in Paris among Chancerel, Moudoués, Michael Pugh (Great Britain), and José Géal (Belgium) related to the same topic. Moudoués recalls that:

> Chancerel wished for the birth of an international association because he believed that to have its full significance children's theatre needed to become an international field of action, permitting to those involved in the theatre and to the educators a constant exchange of experience and information.[10]

At this time Shakh-Azizov (USSR, later ASSITEJ President—1968-72), a former highly regarded and talented actor and later a theatre manager, was Artistic Director of the Moscow Children's Theatre. He was a man of the professional theatre, who held a strong political position in the cultural hierarchy of the Soviet Union. He was a short, square, balding man, usually with a serious countenance, which concealed a quick mind and a great sense of humor.

Adamek (Czechoslovakia, later ASSITEJ President—1975-78) was a highly respected member of the children's theatre community by both the East and West. His Jiri Volker Theatre did plays from both the East and the West with impeccable casts, and imaginative design, giving a theatrical experience to young people that was professional in every sense. As a person he was quiet, modest, but dedicated to the sense of the "art" in theatre. From the Western viewpoint he was able to skate the differences in the opposing "cold war" philosophies extremely well.

Ilse Rodenberg (GDR, ASSITEJ President, 1978-87) was a short, stocky, energetic grey-haired woman with a quick smile and a ready laugh which belied a sharp mind and a strong political acumen. She was appointed Director of the prestigious Theater der Freundshaft in the GDR in 1959, remaining in that position until she retired in 1987. She answered the question of how did ASSITEJ begin as follows: "Yes, yes. Of course Chancerel was very important. But also we must remember the hard work of Vladimir Adamek. Vladimir was very wise for us, and he was a great artist in the children's theatre. Of course Shakh-Azizov was also very important." Then with an engaging smile and a quick nod she would add: "And, of course, I was also very active to form ASSITEEY, . . .and you were there, too, Rose-Marie, from the beginnings." Certainly both Moudoués and Rodenberg each deserve the title: founder.[11]

Nat Eek (USA, ASSITEJ President, 1972-75) agrees that *all* of the above mentioned persons played a large role in the formation of ASSITEJ, adding: "But we must not forget the very early and indispensable contributions of Gerald Tyler and Michael Pugh, both from Great Britain. They initiated and took part in many of those first meetings in the early 1960s. The British Children's Theatre Association (BCTA) hosted the International Theatre Conference and Festival in 1964 which was the first and most important meeting for the formation of ASSITEJ. Tyler chaired the Preparatory Committee charged with drawing up the Constitution in 1964-5, and he became ASSITEJ's first president, serving from 1965 to 1968."[12]

On 21 August 1962 Tyler and Adamek had consultations related to the proposed organization in Prague, Czechoslovakia. Tyler commented many times to Eek how he admired Adamek's sense of theatre and its art.

On 26-30 January 1963 in Brno, Czechoslovakia there were further consultations among Tyler, Shakh-Azizov, Adamek, Miguel Deuynck (France), Kakos, and Schmidt. That same year in 15-16 November there were consultations in Paris among Chancerel, Moudoués, Alain Recoing, Gabriel Vessigault (France); José Géal, Maedard Tytgart (Belgium); Gerard Binet (Canada); Jan Malik (Czechoslovakia); Ilse Rodenberg (GDR); A.R. Philpott, Michael Pugh (Great Britain); Don Rafaello Lavagna, Maria Signorelli (Italy); Hans Snoek, Erik Vos (Netherlands); Margareta Barbutza, Dumitri Issac (Romania); and Serge Mikhalkov (USSR) to explore the advantages of an international children's theatre association. Out of this meeting the first draft of a possible constitution was drawn up.[13]

At this time the working acronym for the projected organization was UNITEJ (International Union of Theatre for Children and Young People). For this Paris meeting Pugh stated: "The BCTA invited the representatives of those countries which had been particularly interested in the development of a permanent union to Paris [in Novenber 1963] to meet and discuss possibilities."[14]

Later a number of the London delegates viewed this Paris meeting as an attempt by a few to design and control the "union", and present it as a *fait accompli* for the majority to ratify in London. Pugh and others vehemently denied this. Whatever the full intent may have been, there can be no doubt that the November 1963 Paris deliberation of issues involved in creating an international organization expedited decision making in London.[15]

Finally there were more discussions on 1-4 April 1964 in Brussels, Belgium among Pugh, Mikhalkov, Géal, Malik, Barbutza, and others. A few changes were made in this first draft at this meeting, and then it was to be distributed at the London Conference.[16] Obviously the London Preparatory Meeting had been well discussed and prepared for by May of 1964.

The Preparatory Meeting / London / 13-21 May 1964

The initial conference/festival plan of the BCTA was to gather together the British Commonwealth members interested in children's theatre on the occasion of the celebration of the 400th anniversary of Shakespeare's birth. At the November 1963 meeting in Paris Pugh had discussed the plans of a London Preparatory Meeting with Géal, Chancerel, and Jean Dacante (France), then General Secretary of ITI. At that time they had agreed ". . . that the London conference should become fully international and not be restricted to just English speaking countries."[17]

Thirty-two countries responded to the invitation of the BCTA. Countries represented were: Australia, Austria, British Guiana, Canada, Czechoslovakia, Denmark, France, GDR, Great Britain, Greece, Netherlands, Hungary, India, Israel, Jamaica, Japan, Malaysia, Mexico, New Zealand, Norway, Poland, Romania, South Africa, Spain, Sweden, Uganda, the United Arab Republic, USA, USSR, the Vatican, and Yugoslavia.[18] There were over 200 delegates plus observers in attendance.

The Conference was conducted in the multiple languages of the delegates, since there were no official translators present. However, the delegates ate together in the official dining room, and they assisted each other as translators, although they tended to stay with their delegations. French and English were the dominant languages. However, during the sessions it was very easy for any delegate to stand and talk about whatever was of concern.[19]

A Constitutional Draft: At this conference the edited Draft of a possible constitution was presented. In addition, a second proposed constitution had been created and distributed informally by members of the French delegation.[20] This was patterned after their constitution of ATEJ, many of whose details were included as part of the final Constitution.

The UNITEJ Interim Committee and BCTA had put together an excellent Festival and Conference Program for the 1964 conference. The Committee was truly international and consisted of: Margareta Barbutza (Romania), Léon Chancerel (France), José Géal (Belgium), Don Rafaello Lavagna (Vatican, Italy), Serge Mikhalkov (USSR), A.R. Philpott (Great Britain), Ilse Rodenberg (GDR), Maria Signorelli (Italy), Medard Tytgat (Belgium), Gerard Binet (Canada), Miguel Deuynck (France), Dumitru Isac (Romania), Jan Malik (Czechoslovakia, and Secretary-General of UNIMA), Rose-Marie Moudoués (France), Michael Pugh (Great Britain, and Chairman of the Committee)), Alain Recoing (France), Hans Snoek (Netherlands), Gabriel Vessigault (France), and Erik Vos (Netherlands).

The overall program assembled by BCTA was impressive. Dame Sybil Thorndike opened the Festival on 13 May, and on 16 May Sir Edward Boyle, Minister of State for Education and Science, and Mr. Michel Saint-Denis, Director of the Royal Shakespeare Theatre, opened the Conference part. Géal presented the report on the Brussels Meeting on Repertory; Samar Chatterjee (India) on the Calcutta Children's Little Theatre; Barbara McIntyre (USA) on Creative Dramatics and Children's Theatre; Konstantin Shakh-Azizov (USSR) on Actor Training for Children's Theatre; and John Allen (Great Britain) on Theatre and the Adolescent. Gerald Tyler (Great Britain) outlined what he hoped was the delegates' common ground:

> ...cooperation and mutual respect for one another's cultures, and belief in the desire to be of service to children are what we here look for in Children's Theatre.[21]

Discussions followed each of the presentations, as well as open critiques of the productions seen. Most importantly, intermingled among the sessions were discussions on the possible forming of an international children's theatre association. In addition there were film and TV viewings, book and exhibit displays, and cultural side-trips.

On 17 May 1964, Pugh opened the "Preparatory Meeting of ASSITEJ". Representatives of thirty-two (32)—some accounts list forty (40)—countries attended. "During the week of stimulating speeches, provocative productions, dynamic discussions and enjoyable extracurricular exchange of ideas, it became apparent indeed that there was a desire and a need for continual communication and cooperation."[22]

Another Constitutional Draft: Unbeknownst to the BCTA a small group led by the GDR, Hungary, and Czechoslovakia in anticipation of the upcoming Conference had held a preliminary caucus in Paris to draft a constitution for the proposed association. They intended presenting this at the London conference as a *fait accompli* and inviolate. However, the shear size of the conference and its many attendant countries quickly destroyed any such intention. Also, the French delegation presented a draft of a proposed constitution which had been drawn up in Paris modeled on their ATEJ Constitution, and had it distributed to the delegates at the conference. This and its English translation would become the model upon which the final constitution in Paris would be based.

Tension charged the meetings. Heated exchanges began immediately; chaos seemed imminent; Pugh struggled to maintain parliamentary order. There were four areas of disagreement: 1) the status of amateurs in a professional organization; 2) the use of child actors in performance; 3) the inclusion of creative dramatics as part of the association's focus; and 4) what was considered suitable repertory for children and youth.

The French position regarding amateurs and child actors was clearly stated by Pugh:

> ...no the French do not insist on UNITEJ being strictly professional. They are quite happy to include amateurs. They are only standing out against child actors.[23]

This concern about the use of child actors would emerge again and again as an international sore point, and has never been resolved satisfactorily. The "against" attitude was particular difficult for Third World countries, many of whom use children in their casts extensively, and could be denied admission to membership accordingly.

The battle lines were quickly drawn between those holding extremely different points of view. One rigidly exclusive group wanted only professional theatre companies made up of full time adult artists whose sole purpose was creating theatre for young audiences to be admitted as members. The other rigidly inclusive group wanted any group or individual concerned with any form of theatre for/with children and young people, whether professional, amateur, or educational, to be admitted as members. Individual opinions ranged between these two

Performances: For the Festival, plays were presented by the British Dance-Drama Theatre, Scottish Children's Theatre, Western Theatre Ballet, Calcutta Children's Little Theatre, Belgium's Le Théâtre de l'Enfance, De Nieuwe Komedie of the Netherlands, University of Kansas Children's Theatre of the USA, Rose Buford College of Speech and Drama Children's Theatre of Great Britain, and Carousel Mime Theatre Company of the Netherlands.

Tyler had asked Sara Spencer if the USA could bring over a production. Although Spencer did not attend this London meeting, she had appealed to Jed Davis, Director of the University of Kansas Children's Theatre, to bring his company to perform *Johnny Moonbeam and the Silver Arrow* by Joseph Golden to the conference. It was presented on 19 May 1964 at the Commonwealth Institute in London.

The actors were students at the University where Davis taught, and they had been touring Europe for six weeks presenting other plays. They arrived in London and began rehearsal of the play. Davis commented that "...the production situation was a nightmare, when the facilities staff showed up three hours late for the scenic setup in a miserable venue."[25]

The production was probably under-rehearsed with very limited design aspects. It proved to be highly controversial. At the end when Johnny is asked what he will do with the silver arrow of power, the delegates, especially from the Eastern countries, were outraged, attributing the conclusion to just another demonstration of the USA's thirst for power and domination. This response was totally unexpected by the USA delegation, since they felt the title with its Native American theme was quite appropriate, and Johnny's response was one of accepting responsibility, not achieving domination.

Also, the production *The Crowned Boot* of De Nieuwe Komedie of the Netherlands directed by Erik Vos aroused great concern. Its Director, Erik Vos, explained that his group produced classics for young people above the age of thirteen. The play contained "earthy language", drunkenness, male frontal nudity, and in one scene a character vomited into a barrel, threw another character into the barrel, and then rolled him around the stage. While most of the delegates were delighted with the hearty humor of the play and its excellent production, it contained bawdy elements that were unheard of in children's theatre.[26] One delegate walked out of the performance.

On 19 May the conference delegates unanimously approved resolutions agreeing that "...it is advisable that an international children's theatre association of some kind should come into being..." and "...that a Preparatory Committee should be set up to consider how this should come about . . . taking into account documents and opinions presented and expressed at the London Conference and opinions expressed through correspondence after that conference." The Resolution further instructed the Preparatory Committee to "...first of all concern itself with the formation of a constitution and secondly study important questions such as translation and exchange of plays, texts, etc."[27]

In the discussion of possible countries to include on the Committee, Barbutza (Romania) urged the inclusion of the GDR on the basis that it was one of the first countries to advocate an international association. Debate followed concluding with the delegate from the FGR offering to resign his seat in deference to the GDR. However, the GDR was added to the Committee on its own merits.[28]

Unfortunately the GDR representative Ilse Rodenberg had been unable to participate due to past problems of obtaining Western visas. She was the administrative head of the GDR's leading children's theatre—the Theater der Freundschaft, and she had proved herself an excellent administrator with a strong sense of the art of the theatre. Since she was married to the GDR Minister of Culture, she was obviously high up in government circles. Also, it was documented in Great Britain, USA, Italy, and France that she carried money with her for support of groups in the country being visited who approved of the GDR. Consequently, for many years it was difficult if not impossible for Rodenberg to get Western visas.

Selection of the Preparatory Committee: According to Tyler's notes, twenty-one countries were chosen to be represented on the Preparatory Committee: Australia, Belgium, British Guiana, Canada, Czechoslovakia, Egypt, FGR, France, GDR, Great Britain, Netherlands, India, Italy, Japan, Mexico, Romania, Sweden, USA, USSR, the Vatican, and Yugoslavia.[29]

Each country was to name its delegates within 28 days of the end of the London Conference. However, this made for an unwieldy committee, so the following 12 countries were selected by mutual agreement: Belgium, Canada, Czechoslovakia, FGR, France, GDR, Great Britain, Italy, Netherlands, Romania, USA, and USSR, a comprise that included representation from the East and West as well as a split of six to six in political philosophy, with several of the smaller excluded countries asking the USA delegates to represent their concerns at the meeting of the Committee. This Committee agreed to meet in Venice, Italy in mid-September of 1964, and as a final decision the conference accepted the French invitation to have its next conference in Paris in June 1965.

The conference ended with a tremendous sense of achievement. Despite the turmoil and arguments, a Preparatory Committee had been formed, a possible Constitution had been distributed for revision by the Committee, and the Committee was to meet in Venice, Italy on 20 September 1964, only four months from this conference. The creation of ASSITEJ was definitely on its way with the blessings of all concerned.

The Preparatory Committee

Perhaps ASSITEJ has never fully appreciated the work of the Preparatory Committee that met in Venice, Italy, 20-24 September 1964 to complete the nearly impossible task of preparing a constitution which was responsive to all aspects of the London debate. Chairman Gerald

Tyler reported that the matter of membership, voting privileges, name for the organization, and languages required lengthy debate and a spirit of compromise.[30]

Ten of the twelve appointed members attended: José Géal (Belgium), Olivia Hasler (Canada), Vladimir Adamek (Czechoslovakia), Hanswalter Gossmann (FGR), Rose-Marie Moudoués (France), Gerald Tyler (Great Britain), Maria Signorelli (Italy), Hans Snoek (Netherlands) Margareta Barbutza (Romania), and Sara Spencer (USA). Ilse Rodenberg (GDR) and Konstantin Shakh-Azizov (USSR) were unable to attend. Tyler had been selected by the members as their Chairman.

The Committee's sanity was probably saved by the opportunity to see the work of outstanding, fully professional theatre companies performing in the Children's Theatre Festival at the Venice Biennale. The delegates were able to attend five different productions: *Ambrosio Tue L'Heure* by Arthur Fauquez (Géal's Theatre de L'Enfance, Belgium), *Frontiere Fiorite* by Raffaello Lavagna (Carrodi Respi per il Teatro dei Ragazzi), *Phouft* and *Le Petit Fantome* by Maria Clara Machado (Compagnie Ahouva Lion-Theatre pour la Jeunesse, Paris, France), *Le Aventure di Pinocchio* by Carlo Collodi (Teatro per Ragazzi Angelicum, Milan, Italy), and *Biberce* by Ljubiša Djokič (Zagrebacko Pionersko Kaliste, Zagreb, Yugoslavia).

When the Committee finished its deliberations, it had a proposed Constitution in hand to be distributed in its final version to its members for approval in Paris. Its task had been accomplished well ahead of schedule.

Nine months later the Preparatory Committee met for the last time in Paris, 3-4 June 1965, just prior to the Constitutional Conference. Sara Spencer represented the USA, and this was the first time that Eek attended any of the preparatory meetings.

At Paris during these two days, the Committee codified the Statutes of the new organization as created, developed, and approved in Venice. The Committee's meeting in Paris was coming to a close "...when Konstantin Shakh-Azizov announced through his interpreter that his country felt it could not ratify the document unless Russian became the third *official* language of ASSITEJ. There was a stunned silence at which point Sara Spencer (USA) said 'SO BE IT! A country with the high quality of professional children's theatre which the Soviet Union has must be a full member of our new organization.' "[31]

In the discussion following the USSR's pronouncement, Moudoués pointed out that it was recognized " . . . that the 11 Soviet satellite countries had thriving theaters for children and young people, and that at the time Russian was the *lingua franca* between these countries."[32]

The Preparatory Committee unanimously approved Russian as the third official language, and it was recognized that any country hosting an event could add its own language to the official three. This final version was distributed in the three languages—French, English, and Russian—to the Committee members for their final perusal prior to the Founding Conference.

The Preparatory Committee adjourned with its job well done, and the new Constitution was ready for ratification by the delegates at the ensuing conference. As a neophyte to international conferences, Eek's first assignment was then to type up the English version of the new Constitution on a French typewriter, a formidable task when confronted by at least three different "e" keys (e, é, è) and "a" keys (a, à, â), but one that was accomplished by the time of the General Assembly.

Dame Sybil Thorndike (Gerald Tyler behind and right) opens the Preparatory Meeting,. London, Great Britain. May, 1964. Courtesy of the British Children's Theatre Association.

1965
THE CONSTITUTIONAL CONFERENCE OF ASSITEJ
Paris, France / 4-9 June 1965

*O*n 7 June 1965 Léon Chancerel, Founder of the French Children's Theatre Association (ATEJ), by then enfeebled and living his final year, presided over the opening session of the Constitutional Conference, a fitting tribute to his leadership. In fragile health he concluded the first session with this challenge to the delegates: "Work hard, do right, and keep a happy spirit. May joy, which St. Francis of Assisi counted as a cardinal virtue, go with us."[33]

187 representatives from 23[34] countries voted unanimously to found the organization under the name ASSITEJ (l'Association International du Théâtre pour l'Enfance et la Jeunesse—The International Association of Theatre for Children and Young People.) This name was an acronym to separate it as a concept from the names of ATEJ and UNITEJ. They affirmed the intention of ASSITEJ to work for peace and understanding between nations within the NGO (Non Governmental Organization) framework and to establish links with UNESCO.

The French minutes listed the following countries as attending: Belgium, Brazil, Bulgaria, Canada, Czechoslovakia, Denmark, FGR, France, Hungary, India, Israel, Italy, Netherlands, Norway, Poland, Portugal, Romania, Spain, Sweden, Uruguay, USA, USSR, and Yugoslavia.

According to Tyler and Eek[36] at the Paris Conference the Constitution was accepted by 183 delegates from 24 countries. Egypt, Great Britain, and Switzerland were added, and Hungary and Uruguay were omitted. The French version had omitted Egypt, Great Britain, and Switzerland. Between the two versions it would be safe to include all the countries listed bringing the attendance to a total of 26 countries participating. The four person difference in the number of delegates is insignificant.

Aims: The approved aim of ASSITEJ was to encourage the development of fine theatre for children and young people with particular emphasis given to the art of theatre and its presentation by adult professional actors. Recognizing the important place of amateur theatre in many countries, ASSITEJ made provision in the Statutes to include them in the national centers. Each national center, eligible to participate in an ASSITEJ General Assembly, was allowed a maximum of 3 votes—2 votes to represent the professional theatre and 1 vote to represent the amateur theatre. Official meetings of ASSITEJ would include deliberation on the business of the organization as well as artistic activity: festivals, symposia, and workshops.

Membership: Members would only be national centers who would honor the international Statutes. The Statutes obligated the national centers to make membership available to all people and groups involved in the work of theatre for young people in their country. The French Center of ATEJ (Moudoués) offered their Paris address to be the official international headquarters. The annual dues for each national center were set at 25 USD.

The Provisional Committee: A "Provisional Committee" (Tyler referred to it as the first Executive Committee) was elected to take charge of the new organization until a formal election could be held at the first General Assembly which was scheduled to be held in Prague, Czechoslovakia, on 28 May to 1 June 1966. [This date was later changed.] The 12 countries elected to be on this Provisional Committee were: Belgium, Canada, Czechoslovakia, FGR, France, GDR, Great Britain, Italy, Netherlands, Romania, USA, and USSR. The officers elected to the Provisional Committee were: President—Gerald Tyler (Great Britain), Vice-President—Konstantin Shakh-Azizov (USSR), Secretary-General—Rose-Marie Moudoués (France), and Treasurer—José Géal (Belgium). The other elected members of the Provisional Committee were: Olivia Hasler (Canada), Vladimir Adamek (Czechoslovakia), Hanswalter Gossmann (FGR), Ilse Rodenberg (GDR), Maria Signorelli (Italy), Hans Snoek (Netherlands), Margareta Barbutza (Romania), and Sara Spencer (USA).[37]

"The conference consisted of four working sessions where various papers were presented, performances of five children's plays, and three discussion sessions devoted to the modification and final passing of the Constitution."[35]

Performances: There were five official productions. A French production of *Don Quixote* by le Théâtre d'Animation du Manifole utilized enormous puppets and live actors. *My Black Brother* presented by the Teatro Dei Ragazzi and written by Don Rafaello Lavagna from Italy proved to be a mish-mash involving racism. *The Golden Apples* from José Géal's theatre in Belgium was well done but too mature for a child audience. *The Lost Wedding Ring* written by Jan Staal and performed by the Toneelgroep from the Netherlands had highly imaginatImaginativee and artistic décor. A musical review called *La Feria (The Fair)* was performed by Spain's National Children's Theatre "Los Titeres", which consisted of a compendium of individual acts, songs, and dances, similar to a zarzuela which presented theatre to the children "...in one bright, streaming flow of highly charged theatre."[38]

ASSITEJ was born! But unlike Athena, ASSITEJ did not spring fully armed from the head of Zeus or that of any one theatre leader. Its creation was a long, often dramatic process in which a few dedicated people played key roles and representatives from twenty-six countries took part.[39]

Its purpose was clearly stated in the new Constitution under the heading—Creation:

> Since theatrical art is a universal expression of mankind, and possesses the influence and power to link large groups of the world's peoples in the service of peace, and considering the role theatre can play in the education of younger generations, an autonomous international organization has been formed which bears the name of the International Association of Theatre for Children and Young People.[40]

Sara Spencer, the head USA delegate, a playwright and publisher of children's plays, stated as follows:

> An International Children's Theatre Association has been formed, and its implications are large, fascinating, and appalling. Large, because this development obliges us to take ourselves seriously, for the first time in our happy, carefree young lives. Fascinating, because international interchange opens up a thousand new facets

of children's theatre work that fire the imagination. Appalling, because all at once we are thrust into the midst of international politics.[41]

Spencer had grave concerns about an ensuing East-West conflict. She felt that the USA delegates were regarded as mere amateurs and were not authorities in the field. She felt that the West was excluded, citing these facts: Russian was chosen as a third official language; the USSR delegate was appointed as Vice-President; the next two meetings were scheduled in the East—Berlin and Prague; and Moudoués as the new Secretary-General was a strong supporter of leftist causes. However, she ignored the facts that Adamek, Moudoués, Rodenberg, and Shakh-Azizov had earned their places by being some of the first ones involved in the creation of an international association.

Delegate Ann Hill (USA) commented:

It has been a real lesson in human nature, with dynamic and forceful people from many nations discussing their common problems, arguing their differences, but all bound together by one ideal—bringing the very best to their children.[42]

Delegate Muriel Sharon (USA) wrote that the Americans were overly concerned about the effects of the cold war:[43]

Americans seemed unable to consider, without ambivalence, the forest of possibilities of international exchange the moment they confronted the Russian tree. A general fear existed that the Russians were attempting to dominate the proceedings...not wholly unfounded...

The problem is admittedly a ticklish one and the temptation to become concerned with the political ramifications must not take precedence over theatrical objectives of international exchange. I am of the opinion that the situation will relax as our country can produce professional children's theatre of which we are proud. For the Russians are very proud of their children's theatre, which has existed as a professional achievement since 1918.

In a personal interview with Scott Regan, Eek said:

...how impressed he was by the variety of personalities involved, their dedication to children's theatre, and the fact that they were all mature artists in their various countries.

Immediately following this conference Spencer and Eek as well as many of the other delegates returned to their countries with the need to establish a National Center which could belong to the new international organization—ASSITEJ.

Léon Chancerel (France). Founder of ATEJ and Founder of ASSITEJ, Member of Honor of ASSITEJ. Photo courtesy of Maryline Romain, Société d'Histoire du Théâtre, Paris, France.

Gerald Tyler (Great Britain).
Founder of ASSITEJ, First
President of ASSITEJ (1965-1968),
Honorary President of ASSITEJ.
Photo by A. Wolf, Potsdam, GDR,
1968.

1966
EXECUTIVE COMMITTEE MEETING
Berlin, GDR / 19-26 February 1966

The Provisional Executive Committee of ASSITEJ met in Berlin, GDR on 19-26 February 1966. Gerald Tyler (Great Britain) presided as Acting President, with Konstantin Shakh-Azizov (USSR) as Acting Vice-President, Rose-Marie Moudoués (France) Acting Secretary-General was ill and was replaced by George Vessigault (France), and José Géal (Belgium) as Acting Treasurer.

Other members of the EXCOM attending were: Vladimir Adamek (Czechoslovakia), Hanswalter Gossmann (FGR), Ilse Rodenberg (GDR), Maria Signorelli (Italy), Hans Snoek (Netherlands), Margareta Barbutsa (Romania), and Nat Eek (USA).

Members absent: Canada.

New members and their centers who were welcomed included: Thais Bianchi (Brazil), Inga Juul (Denmark), Orna Porat (Israel), Halfdan Scaanland (Norway), Wanda Kolziewska (Poland), and Maria Sunyer (Spain).[44]

*T*his was the first meeting of ASSITEJ following the Paris Constitutional Conference, so much of the organization's business and discussions pushed into new territory.

At the time records indicated that there were a total of 16 active national centers. Of these 8 had paid their dues. Finance was a constant problem, but the French Center continued its most welcome subsidization. Pugh presented a report on the translation of plays bibliography which requested the appointment of a Translation Committee, and for each center to nominate an active contact for information about plays in that country. Géal was appointed Acting Treasurer until the Prague Assembly. The program of the Prague meeting was discussed and set. The theme became "Plays for Children—7 to 12 Years of Age." The plays presented would concentrate on this, and only local companies would be featured. After each play, discussions would be held with all casts and artistic staffs who were present.

Publications: For the first time the concept of an ASSITEJ publication was aired. It was proposed that the *Review* published by the French association ATEJ become the literary organ of ASSITEJ, in accordance with the resolution made at the Paris Conference. The proposal was accepted with thanks.

The Elections: There was considerable discussion about the nomination process for the upcoming election of officers in Prague, since this would be the first official General Assembly. Eek sensed that all the current twelve members would be considered as nominated, and possibly three more would be elected, which would make up the maximum fifteen as detailed in the Statutes. He also indicated that Tyler would undoubtedly be elected the first president.

Performances: Plays seen included: *La Farola, Tom Sawyer's Great Adventure, Hansel and Gretel, The Miracle Hat, Princess Turandot, Sombrero, Twelfth Night,* and Felzenstein's celebrated production of Jacques Offenbach's *Bluebeard.* After the presentation of the plays, there was usually a discussion of their artistic, social, and psychological merit. The West German theatre's very traditional production by Hanswalter Gossmann of *Hansel and Gretel* was roundly criticized for the cruelty of the step-mother, and the burning of the witch in the oven which "was reminiscent of the holocaust!" This production sparked the greatest controversy of the EXCOM!

The meeting concluded with President Tyler thanking Dr. Rodenberg and her theatre for their gracious hospitality, the open discussions, and the excellent receptions.

Brandenburg Gate, Berlin, GDR. February, 1966. Personal photograph.

Dr. Ilse Rodenberg, Intendant, Theater der Freundschaft. Host of ASSITEJ EXCOM Meeting in Berlin, GDR. February, 1966. Personal photograph.

Dr. Nat Eek (USA Member of EXCOM) and Dr. Ilse Rodenberg (GDR Member of EXCOM and host of meeting). Personal photograph.

1966
IST INTERNATIONAL CONGRESS OF ASSITEJ
Prague, Czechoslovakia / 26-30 May 1966

The Ist International Congress of ASSITEJ met in Prague, Czechoslovakia on 26-30 May 1966. Gerald Tyler (Great Britain) presided as Acting President, with Konstantin Shakh-Azizov (USSR) as Acting Vice President, Rose-Marie Moudoués (France) as Acting Secretary-General, and José Géal as Acting Treasurer. All four held these administrative positions as members of the Provisional Committee. A meeting of this Executive Committee was scheduled for 25 May to review and set the Agenda.

Other members of the Provisional EXCOM attending were: Victor Georgiev (Bulgaria), Betty Anderson (Canada), Vladimir Adamek (Czechoslovakia), Inga Juul (Denmark), Hanswalter Gossmann (FGR), Ilse Rodenberg (GDR), Don Rafaello Lavagna (Vatican, Italy), Hans Snoek (Netherlands), Margareta Barbutsa (Romania), Maria Sunyer (Spain), Nat Eek (USA), and Ljubiša Djokič (Yugoslavia).[45]

Members absent: Maria Signorelli (Italy).

The balmy spring weather augured a good meeting, and there was a wonderful sense of expectancy as this was the first official Congress of the new organization with 29 countries represented. According to the roster printed by the Czech Center, 99 persons attended representing the following countries: Argentina, Austria, Belgium, Bulgaria, Canada, Chile, Columbia, Cuba, Czechoslovakia, Denmark, Ecuador, FGR, France, GDR, Great Britain, Iraq, Italy, Mexico, Netherlands, Norway, Poland, Romania, Spain, Sweden, Tunisia, Uruguay, USA, USSR, and Yugoslavia.

The opening session featured welcomes by host Vladimir Adamek, the Czech Vice-President of Education and Culture, the Czech Union of Theatre Artists, and ASSITEJ President Gerald Tyler. Don Lavagna gave a brief eulogy of Léon Chancerel (France) who had recently died, and who was considered a major founder of the organization. Moudoués presented her annual Report Morale of the organization ASSITEJ, and

Géal gave the Treasurer's Report. Of interest is the fact that ASSITEJ had received a total of 4,909 French Francs as income and spent a total of 3,525 French Francs, and seemingly was solvent.

At this time a total of 17 National Centers belonged to ASSITEJ, but only 8 were paying their dues. Obviously most of the organization's costs were being born by the members and their various governments. As a result of this report they decided to raise dues to 50 USD as a minimum subscription, with the hope that wealthier countries would pay up to 150 USD a year.

Publications: The publication of the new ASSITEJ journal, *Theatre, Childhood and Youth: The Quarterly Review* (hereafter referred to as the *Review*), was approved, and it would be compiled, printed, and distributed by the French Center. Centers were encouraged to send in articles of a theoretical nature, which in turn would be printed in one of the three official languages, with summaries in the other two. At the same time Adamek announced the publication of the *Czech Bulletin* which would provide international information on activities, productions, new plays, and other events submitted by the national centers.

The second session concentrated on suitability of plays for the various ages of children. The discussion was prefaced by a paper presented by Adamek. In the third session discussion shifted to a particular theatre's approach toward plays for young people, along with a discussion of the plays seen. At the Jiri Volker Theatre delegates saw Czech productions of *The Sun, The Moon, and The Wind; Outwitting the Devil;* and *Aladdin's Magic Lamp.* In addition there were Czech productions of Chekhov's *The Three Sisters,* the opera *Prince Igor,* a jazz opera, and the world-reknowned.Laterna Magica which could be viewed in its own specially designed theatre.

The Elections: Most important on the Agenda was the first official election of officers to replace the members of the Provisional Committee. The election pattern established at this meeting continued for many years. There were no nominations: the Centers indicated verbally or in writing whether they were willing to serve on the Executive Committee or not. A paper ballot was taken with the national center's representative receiving a ballot for each of the up-to-three votes of the national center (2 for professional theatres, 1 for amateur theatres). Three tellers were appointed to count the ballots and give the totals to the Secretary-General who then announced the results. This election established the Executive Committee. Candidates for election as officers were chosen from among the newly elected members of the EXCOM, at first by a show of hands. Later this was all done by paper ballot.

At this election the following countries were chosen to serve on the EXCOM for the next two years: Belgium, Canada, Czechoslovakia, FGR, France, GDR, Great Britain, Italy, Netherlands, Romania, USA, and USSR. Eek remembers Rodenberg giggling in amusement when Moudoués announced that no Center had been nominated to the EXCOM. Accordingly, the sitting EXCOM decided by acclamation that the current twelve countries be re-elected to continue for the next two years. Although the Statutes stated that there could be a maximum of fifteen centers elected, only twelve were chosen at this time, evenly divided between East and West in political sympathies. Two countries were co-opted to sit on the EXCOM as non-voting members: Scandinavia, a single delegate to represent Norway, Sweden, and Finland (Inga Juul was already representing Denmark as an observer), and Yugoslavia.

The EXCOM then selected the following officers: Gerald Tyler (Great Britain) as President; Konstantin Shakh-Azizov (USSR) as 1st Vice-President; Vladimir Adamek (Czechoslovakia) as 2nd Vice-President, Rose-Marie Moudoués (France) as Secretary-General, and José Géal (Belgium) as Treasurer. Moudoués was to handle the duties and written reports of the Treasurer for several years with Géal presenting the Financial Reports. The EXCOM also approved the next year's budget at 25,700 French Francs (approximately 5,140 USD)! The Netherlands extended an invitation to host the next General Assembly in 1970, and the FGR to host the next EXCOM meeting.

During the various business discussions the Czech Center proposed to provide a new publication which would list international activities of the membership based on reports from the Centers. Then consideration of a place for the next Assembly was raised. The Netherlands, Denmark, Venice, and the Gold Coast of Africa were mentioned, but Hans Snoek (Netherlands) offered to hold the next Congress in Amsterdam in 1968 (it was later changed to The Hague), and her offer was accepted with great thanks. At this time it was planned to have a Congress every year, but because of high costs as well as the problems of organization, the interval was changed officially to every two years at the meeting in The Hague in 1968.

Centers: At the end of the Congress the named centers of ASSITEJ were: Belgium, Brazil, Canada, Czechoslovakia, Denmark, FGR, France, GDR, Great Britain, Israel, Italy, Netherlands, Poland, Romania, Spain, USA, USSR, and Yugoslavia, a total of 18 National Centers.

The normal pattern for each conference became as follows:
- Opening ceremonies with official welcomes
- 1st Meeting of the Old Executive Committee
- General Assembly of the delegates of the ASSITEJ Centers
- Discussions and presentations related to the theme
- Meetings of the Special Committees (Play, Artistic, Publications, etc.)
- General Assembly and elections
- 1st Meeting of the New Executive Committee
- Closing ceremonies

The election pattern for each conference became as follows:
- Centers indicated verbally or in writing if willing to serve on the EXCOM.
- Election was held by paper ballot. Each dues-paying national center's representative received a ballot for each of the up-to-three votes of the national center (2 for professional theatres, 1 for amateur theatres).
- Three tellers were appointed to count the ballots and give the totals to the Secretary-General who then announced the results.
- This election established the EXCOM. Candidates for election as officers were chosen from among the newly elected members of the EXCOM, at first by a show of hands, later by recommendation of a slate from the EXCOM, which was then voted upon by the General Assembly.

The host country always included a one day excursion to a place of unusual interest to the visiting delegates. Delegates were responsible for their own meals and housing. However, the opening and closing ceremonies usually had elaborate hors d'oeuvres and beverages provided gratis to all delegates. This Congress closed with a great sense of achievement and goodwill.

City Gates, Old Town, Prague, Czechoslovakia. May, 1966.
Personal photograph.

Karlschtejn Castle, Prague,
Czechoslovakia. May, 1966.
Personal photograph.

"The Sun, The Moon, and the Wind", produced by the Jiri Volker Theatre,
Prague, Czechoslovakia. February 1966. Personal photograph.

A SUMMARY OF 1965-1966

*A*SSITEJ (l'Association Internationale du Théâtre pour l'Enfance et la Jeunesse – The International Association of Theatre for Children and Young People) would never have been founded if it hadn't been for a dedicated international group of leaders in the profession of children's theatre. These primarily European men and women had been meeting informally since the late 1950s discussing mutual problems and concerns as well as the art of the theatre, with France, Great Britain, Czechoslovakia, Germany, and the USSR being the most involved.

1964

After Preparatory Meetings in London, England in May of 1964 and then in Venice, Italy in September of 1964, a group of children's theatre professionals created a proposed Constitution of a new association. This group expanded to 187 individuals in the profession who agreed to meet in June of 1965 in Paris, France at a conference to give birth to the new organization of ASSITEJ!

1965

On 4 June 1965 in Paris, France Léon Chancerel (France) presided over the opening session of the Constitutional Conference, a fitting tribute to his previous constant leadership. Ailing at the time, he would die the next year. 187 representatives from 26 countries voted unanimously to found the organization, affirming their intention to work for peace and understanding between nations.

Countries: Countries in attendance were: Belgium, Brazil, Bulgaria, Canada, Czechoslovakia, Denmark, Egypt, FRG, France, Great Britain, Hungary, India, Israel, Italy, the Netherlands, Norway, Poland, Portugal, Romania, Spain, Sweden, Switzerland, USSR, USA, Uruguay, and Yugoslavia.

Aim: The approved aim of ASSITEJ was to encourage the development of fine theatre for children and young people with particular emphasis given to the art of theatre and its presentation by adult professional actors. Recognizing the important place of amateur theatre in many countries, ASSITEJ made provision in the Statutes to include them in the national centers.

Membership: Members would only be national centers who would honor the international Statutes. The Statutes obligated the national centers to make membership available to all people and groups involved in the work of theatre for young people in their country. Paris was to be the official international headquarters. French and English would be the official languages. The annual dues were set at 25 USD.

Official Languages: At a preliminary meeting in Paris the day before the conference began, the Preparatory Committee reviewed the entire Constitution as it was to be presented to the delegates. The Committee's meeting was coming to a close when the Soviet delegate "....announced through his interpreter that his country felt it could not ratify the document unless Russian became the third *official* language of ASSITEJ. Sara Spencer (USA) said 'SO BE IT! A country with the high quality of professional children's theatre which the Soviet Union has must be a full member of our new organization.' "[46] The Preparatory Committee unanimously approved Russian as the third official language, and it was recognized that any country hosting an event could add its own language to the official three.

Later in a private conversation Gerald Tyler (Great Britain) said to Spencer that she did not have to capitulate to a third language. He felt that the Soviets were too committed to joining the organization, and while perhaps walking out at first, they would have eventually joined. Unfortunately accepting the third language made translation at World Congresses more complex, and all publications had to be printed in the three official languages.

Translations: At these early meetings the sessions had a French-English and English-French interpreter, who would translate the text at the end of several paragraphs of each speech or presentation. The USSR delegation always brought its own interpreter. As ASSITEJ became increasingly global in scope, host countries of the Executive Committee (EXCOM) or Congress frequently provided an "elbow interpreter" who sat beside or behind small delegations who had difficulty understanding the official languages. Soon simultaneous translation with individual headsets replaced the individual interpreters, but still many times countries would bring their own translators, either for accuracy in translation or because of the uniqueness of their country's language.

By the time of the Seattle EXCOM Meeting in 1995, English had become the most common working language in the world. Under the Presidency of Michael FitzGerald at the XIIth Congress in Rostov-on-Don, Russia in 1996, a statute was approved making English the working language of the Association. In the future the 1+1 principle would be applied to the languages of the Congresses: English plus the language of the host country. This decision simplified the working business and reduced the costs of the countries hosting ASSITEJ considerably.

The Provisional Committee: At the end of the Paris Conference in June of 1965 a "Provisional Committee" was elected to take charge of the new organization until a formal election could be held at the first General Assembly which was scheduled to be held in Prague, Czechoslovakia in 1966. The 12 countries elected to be on this Provisional Committee were: Belgium, Canada, Czechoslovakia, FGR, France, GDR, Great Britain, Italy, Netherlands, Romania, USA, and USSR. The officers elected to the Provisional Committee were: Gerald Tyler (Great Britain) as President with Konstantin Shakh-Azizov (USSR) as Vice-President, Rose-Marie Moudoués (France) as Secretary-General, and José Géal (Belgium) as Treasurer.

Performances: During the conference there were 5 official productions, establishing the concept that there would always be performances at each conference featuring the best of theatre for children and youth. Sometimes the Congress would be in conjunction with a national or international festival.

At the Paris Conference a French group presented a play based on *Don Quixote* which utilized giant puppets and live actors, and the professional national Spanish company Los Titeres brought a musical revue called *La Feria (The Fair)*, which consisted of a compendium of individual acts, songs, and dances, similar to a zarzuela. It was the hit of the conference for its quality, exuberance, and pacing, and in talking with the company members later, it was discovered that it had only been put together four days before the conference.

The creation of ASSITEJ was a long, often dramatic process in which a few dedicated people played key roles and representatives from many countries took part, and as of June 1965 it was officially a live entity!

Development of the National Centers: Immediately following this conference many of the delegates returned to their countries with the immediate need to establish a National Center which could belong to the new international organization—ASSITEJ.

The development of centers varied from country to country depending on the theatre leadership and the involvement of national governments in that country. However, a center evolved as it grew in strength of membership and professional stature depending on its individual leadership with or without governmental support.

Most of the Eastern bloc centers received governmental support from the beginning, while many Western centers were self-supporting until their activity had earned governmental recognition. Though very active in the association the US Center received no governmental subsidy from 1965 to 1977, although agencies of individual states and cities had assisted in funding international ASSITEJ events held in that state/city. For example the 1972 ASSITEJ Congress held in Albany, NY was hosted by the State University of New York.

US Center for ASSITEJ: As Director (President) of the Children's Theatre Conference (CTC) in the USA, Eek met with his colleagues at their annual conference in August of 1965 in Miami, Florida. An Executive Committee was appointed, statutes were drawn up, and the US Center for ASSITEJ was created. Its founding members were Eek as President (University of Oklahoma), Sara Spencer (Anchorage Press, Inc.), James Popovich (University of South Florida), Jed H. Davis (University of Kansas), and Muriel Sharon (Producer of the Pocket Players in New York City), the only professional theatre representative. With the establishment of ASSITEJ/USA in 1981 replacing the US Center for ASSITEJ, the Executive Committee changed radically with the majority coming from professional theaters.

The US Center was first under CTC (which was a division of the American Theatre Association – ATA) and it submitted the name of a correspondent (Eek who was elected to the EXCOM in 1966), a mailing address (Eek's address at the University of Oklahoma in Norman, Oklahoma which remained the official address for the next ten years with the University providing the necessary financial subsidization), and the US Center statutes, drafted at the August CTC meeting in accordance with the new international constitution. From 1975-1981 the address became that of the US Member of the EXCOM of the time, but in 1981 with the creation of ASSITEJ/USA the US Center was located with its President or Secretary.

With her election as the first Secretary-General of ASSITEJ, Rose-Marie Moudoués (France) was undoubtedly the strongest and most visable of the early leaders of ASSITEJ. She was a worldly attractive blond woman in her late thirties at the time of the Founding Congress, multi-lingual, and an energetic politician. As a dedicated partner of Leon Chancerel, founder of the French center for youth theatre (ATEJ), she was pledged to the development of regional alternate theatre and young playwrights, as well as to the furthering of professional theatre for young people. She was an accomplished speaker and writer.

As the Secretary-General of ASSITEJ, she was in a position of considerable power, and she used it accordingly. A dedicated leftist in her political sympathies, she at first kept a careful balance between East and West, but by the late 70s and early 80s she primarily favored the Eastern bloc.

With the death of Chancerel in 1966, she shouldered the responsibilities of both the Presidency of ATEJ and the ASSITEJ Secretariat. In the latter position she provided a stable center for the young organization, used the financial resources of the French Center to support ASSITEJ generously, traveled extensively to promote the formation of new centers, and proved to be a skilled diplomat among the centers.

Dedicated to keeping the organization Euro-centric she consciously delayed the international growth of the organization through personal manipulation. When she was not able to accommodate the younger national centers around the world who were joining, she was not re-appointed as Secretary-General at the Stockholm Congress in 1990 by a decisive majority. She had served that office under six different Presidents for a total of 25 years. Whatever archives there are of those 25 years reside in Paris with her. Only two boxes of records have been transferred to the German archives, and whatever remains is unavailable or missing.

Despite her biased politicking she gave ASSITEJ an international office, a permanent address for correspondence, and an important stability and financial support. The young organization should forever be grateful for that contribution.

1966

ASSITEJ's first Provisional Committee Meeting (EXCOM) was held in Berlin, GDR in February, 1966.

Checkpoint Charlie: Visiting Berlin (GDR) for the first time, found Eek in an uncomfortable position. The GDR and the USA were in a hostile relationship. The Berlin wall was up, and anyone visiting had to go through Checkpoint Charlie—a Passport Control location jointly monitored by the GDR and the USA—a scene that had witnessed captures and slaughters of citizens attempting escape into West Berlin.

Eek checked with Rosamund Gilder (President of the USA's ITI), and she both explained the process as well as assured him that there was no personal danger.

Dragging his luggage, after landing in West Berlin, Eek took the subway to its termination at the Checkpoint Charlie underground station monitored by the GDR. Everyone got out, and were ushered by armed guards into a bare grey-painted room with a long wooden bench on one side. Opposite was a walled cubicle with a single slot in the middle of the wall—no window. To its side was a half-wall with a long table butted up against it, where several armed soldiers in full uniform sat or stood. Pistols were on their counter.

Eek was given a newspaper thin piece of paper with a many digited number to be placed in his passport. He was given the top half containing the same number which was torn off, and the guard pointed towards the slot in the wall. Everyone lined up and inserted their passports or papers accordingly, and then sat or stood and waited.

Since Eek did not speak German, Gilder had told him to find an English speaking person going through to let him know when his number was called. The man seated next to him graciously did so. The wait seemed interminable, but eventually Eek's number was called. He went to the counter where he was interrogated first in German and then in English as to why he was coming to the GDR, although he had the proper visa. The soldier was quite young, spoke good English, and with a smirk passed Eek's passport to him.

Eek went up a stairway which emerged onto the bridge over the river Spree which separated the two halves of Berlin. Walking across, he could see Klaus Urban of the Theater der Freundschaft waving in welcome on the GDR end of the bridge—freedom!

The EXCOM: At the Provisional EXCOM's initial meeting as a result of their discussion of the coming election process, they recommended to the General Assembly that the current 12 provisional members be retained as the new Executive Committee with Gerald Tyler (Great Britain) as its first President.

Performances: As part of the Berlin Conference 7 different plays were presented. After the presentation of the plays, there was usually a discussion of their artistic, social, and psychological merit. The children's theatre of Hanswalter Gossmann of the FGR presented a traditional production of *Hansel and Gretel* which was roundly criticized for the cruelty of the step-mother, and the burning of the witch in the oven as "reminiscent of the holocaust!" Gossmann defended the production by saying that cruelty is a part of all fairy tales, and it shouldn't be eliminated since it is an integral part of life. The arguments con and pro easily fell into the East-West camps.

In his report to the US Center of ASSITEJ Eek wrote: "The Czech *The Wonderful Hat* was probably the best all-round show, vital, lively, lots of fun, and marvelous acting. The Moscow *The Little Kid* and *The Little Hut* were like 30-year-old fairy tales come to life—magnificent color, brilliant acting, and a traditional mixing of mime, music, and dance. The East German productions showed a highly competent company held down by turgid and serious scripts, such as a drama taking place in Brazil [with children living in cardboard boxes on the beach front], and a *Tom Sawyer* with the Ku Klux Klan involved, but their musical version of *Twelfth Night* was first rate. If they just had our scripts, and we—their companies."[47]

1st Congress: The First International Congress of ASSITEJ was held in Prague, Czechoslovakia in May of 1966. 99 delegates from 29 countries participated. New countries present were: Argentina, Austria, Chile, Columbia, Cuba, Ecuador, Iraq, Mexico, and Tunisia. At this time a total of 17 National Centers belonged to ASSITEJ, but only 8 were paying their dues. Obviously most of the organization's costs were being born by the French Center, as well as the individual members and their various governments.

Creation of the Bureau: To set the Agenda before the conference opened there was a meeting of the Bureau. The Bureau is not mentioned in the Statutes by name. However, Article XI, Section 2[48] states: "In the case of any urgent matters not foreseen by the Executive Committee, the Officers are given power to act at their discretion and will take the first opportunity to report on these matters to the Executive Committee." Using this as legal permission, Tyler adopted the word Bureau, and used it while Acting President and President as a means of getting administrative business organized for the membership without the open discussion and wrangling that would occur if the entire EXCOM was involved. The Bureau Members were the President, the Vice-Presidents, the Secretary-General, and the Treasurer. The Bureau could also be convened by the President to meet at any time during the interim between Meetings and International Congresses to deal with problems that might arise demanding immediate attention.

The Elections: The delegates at the Prague Congress elected 12 countries to serve on the EXCOM for the next two years: Belgium, Canada, Czechoslovakia, FGR, France, GDR, Great Britain, Italy, Netherlands, Romania, USA, and USSR. Although the Constitution stated that there could be a maximum of 15 centers elected, only 12 were chosen, evenly divided between East and West in sympathies. Two countries were co-opted to sit on the EXCOM as members: Scandinavia (a single delegate to represent Norway, Sweden, and Finland) and Yugoslavia. [Denmark, normally considered part of Scandinavia, was already represented by Inga Juul.]

Co-option: The EXCOM used the concept of co-option (the Constitution states a maximum of two persons[49]) to allow the representatives of new or forming national centers to sit in on the EXCOM meetings with or without vote to learn about ASSITEJ and its functions, while at the same time representing their center and advising the EXCOM about matters which might affect their centers. The appointments could be motivated by political expediency, a desire to keep the East-West balance, a sincere desire to train and inform a new center, and/or a need for that center's continuing advice. It could be particularly helpful in opening up new countries and territories to the concepts of theatre for young people. Unfortunately many times a center continued to be co-opted long after its training period and usefulness were over, when it should have moved on to be elected at the next Congress on its own merits.

In Prague Gerald Tyler (Great Britain) was elected President: with Konstantin Shakh-Azizov (USSR) as 1st Vice-President, Vladimir Adamek

(Czechoslovakia) as 2nd Vice-President, Rose-Marie Moudoués (France) as Secretary-General, and José Géal (Belgium) as Treasurer. Moudoués was to handle the business details and write the Financial Report for the Treasurer to present to the General Assembly.

Centers: At the end of the Congress the 18 official centers of ASSITEJ were: Belgium, Brazil, Canada, Czechoslovakia, Denmark, FGR, France, GDR, Great Britain, Israel, Italy, Netherlands, Poland, Romania, Spain, USA, USSR, and Yugoslavia.

In the business meeting the General Assembly accepted the Netherlands invitation to hold the next Congress in that country in 1968. The Hague would be finally selected as its site. Dues were raised to 50 USD as a minimum subscription, with the hope that wealthier countries would pay up to 150 USD a year. Next protocols for the creation of Agendas and the Elections were established. The concept of the Bureau was also established.

Tours and Performances: There was a tour of Prague and of the Karlstejn Castle with its impressive audience chamber paneled in marble and semi-precious agates, and the evenings were open for the delegates to attend Czech company productions of *Prince Igor, Crime and Punishment,* and *The Three Sisters.*

Probably the most important achievement of this first Congress was that it met at all and had so many nations attending. There was a sense of euphoria in the air, and Prague seemed to be relaxing and opening up to the West. Controls were easing. ASSITEJ had truly become an international association. It was alive and well and continuing with an important role in the future of the theatre. It now had a constitutionally elected Executive Committee, a slate of officers, a modest budget, a home office in Paris, and a place and plans for the next International Conference. It also had established a pattern for future conferences and elections.

***Sherpas* and Agents:** In these early years of foreign travel, when Eek returned to the University of Oklahoma, he would occasionally be visited in his office by an unannounced federal agent asking questions about his visit to East Berlin, Prague, or the Soviet Union. The visits were short, friendly, and the questions related to what Eek had observed of the current political climate in the country which he had just visited. No names were ever mentioned or inquired about. Obviously the information gathered would be fed into the federal maw to get an overall sense of what was going on abroad among the opposition in the Cold War. Eek was surprised that his obscure trips for an unknown organization were of that significance to his government.

Considering the East-West divisions and the constant felt need for intelligence of every country, many countries would have covert agents, nick-named *sherpas*, placed within a particular delegation or organization which traveled to foreign countries. This was undoubtedly true of both sides of the iron curtain, but some were more blatant than others. It was assumed that someone in an Eastern delegation would report the activities at the Congress and of the delegates to their governments on the return home. Nothing was secret, even though the organization was supposed to be non-political.

At the Albany Congress in 1972 the *sherpa* traveling with the Soviet theatre company of thirty plus was easily recognized, because in performance he was the one out of step in all the dance numbers, and the other USSR members avoided him.

One of the most blatant examples of spying occurred at a strategy meeting of the USA and British delegations in the corner lounge at the conference hotel in East Berlin (Hotel Beroliner) in 1966 when a nearby seated man was reading a newspaper without turning the pages, obviously eaves-dropping. In indignation when the British delegate raised his voice announcing the outrage, the man quietly folded his newspaper, put it under his arm and left, only to be replaced by another newspaper toting man who sat down in exactly the same place.

Obviously all organizations, foreign or national, become political, despite their noble intents and their statements to the contrary.

"The Little Kid" by Marshak, Moscow Central Children's Theatre. Presented at the Ist International Congress of ASSITEJ in Prague, Czechoslovakia. May, 1966. Courtesy of USSR ASSITEJ Center, Moscow, USSR, 1968.

1967
EXECUTIVE COMMITTEE MEETING
Nuremberg, FGR – 6-11 May 1967

The Executive Committee of ASSITEJ met in Nuremberg, FGR on 6-11 June 1967. Gerald Tyler (Great Britain) presided as President, with Konstantin Shakh-Azizov (USSR) as 1st Vice President, Vladimir Adamek (Czechoslovakia) as 2nd Vice President, and Rose-Marie Moudoués (France) as Secretary-General.

Other members of the EXCOM attending were: Victor Georgiev (Bulgaria), Florence James (Canada), Hanswalter Gossmann (FGR), Ilse Rodenberg (GDR), Benito Biotto (Italy), Hans Snoek (Netherlands), Margareta Barbutsa, (Romania), and Nat Eek (USA). Also attending were Inga Juul (Denmark), Michael Pugh (Great Britain), Orna Porat (Israel), Maria Sunyer (Spain), and Ian Cojar (Romania) and Lubisa Djokič (Yugoslavia).

At the Prague Congress (1966) the EXCOM had decided to continue Canada on the committee for two more years, and Florence James was appointed by her country to succeed Myra Benson. At this meeting Bulgaria was appointed to the EXCOM.[50]

Members absent: José Géal (Belgium) as Treasurer, and was replaced for this meeting by George Vesigault (France). Scandinavia had been co-opted in Prague, but apparently was not in attendance.

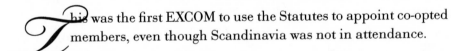 his was the first EXCOM to use the Statutes to appoint co-opted members, even though Scandinavia was not in attendance.

Agenda: The standard agenda for the business meetings of the EXCOM included:
- the Report Morale of the Secretary-General
- a financial report
- a publications report
- reports of sub-committees
- the selection of a site for the next EXCOM meeting
- a discussion of the next General Assembly

Miscellaneous subjects usually closed the meeting. At the same time the host city and country provided many planned diversions in theatre and in sight-seeing for the delegates.

Centers: Secretary-General Moudoués announced that new centers were forming in Poland, Portugal, and Cuba, and that ones in Switzerland and Bulgaria were definitely established. Since its representative Victor Georgiev was attending this EXCOM Meeting assuming it was a Congress, the EXCOM decided to appoint him to membership, although President Tyler stated it was a bad precedent.

Publications: Adamek presented the first issue of the Czech Bulletin. This was to come in mimeographed form from the Czech Center gratis three to four times a year with information on various events and festivals in children's and youth theatre, plus news of the individual National Centers of ASSITEJ. The Secretary-General also announced the new *Review* of ASSITEJ, whose first issue would be labeled 1966 and distributed to the centers as paid subscriptions. Both the *Review* and the *Czech Bulletin* were discussed with recommendations made regarding distribution and content. There was a strong plea from Adamek for National Centers to contribute more fully to both publications.

Performances: Since the Nuremberg meeting was in conjunction with the 4th International Festival of Youth Theatre in Germany, the following plays were presented: *Captain Piplfox* (Bulgaria) with Victor Georgiev performing in a pirate play which utilized a constantly readjusted unit-setting and an excellent acting ensemble, *The Robbers of Kardemomme* (Nuremberg) was a bouncey musical story of the town's reforming three delightfully villainous thieves. *The Pasha and the Bear* and *Street Games* (Scapino Ballet of Amsterdam) was a visually exciting and well-danced double bill. *Pao and Pao* (Italy) was a charmingly wistful story of a sad-sack clown finding true love with a ballerina. *Sinziana and Pepelia* (Romania) involved two children in a circus setting, well-acted with the actors wearing over-sized Styrofoam heads on top of their own which gave them child-like proportions, imaginatively conceived and directed by Ian Cojar, and *To My Fellowmen* presented by the Theater der Freundschaft (GDR).[51]

Decisions were made that the EXCOM would next meet in Moscow in March 1968 pending an official invitation, and that the next General Assembly would be held in Amsterdam (though this was switched later to The Hague) towards the end of May 1968. Eek indicated that the USA might be interested in hosting either the EXCOM in 1971 or a General Assembly in 1972. The EXCOM felt a General Assembly would allow greater participation.

George Vessicault gave the Financial Report which was accepted without change. Pugh was in attendance with a report on translations, and there continued to be a discussion of dissemination of new plays in translation, since every theatre was constantly seeking new works. Lastly, there was general discussion of an official ASSITEJ exhibit to go to theatres around the world, but the costs seemed to keep putting its creation off. A committee of three was appointed to investigate and make a recommendation to the EXCOM.

The meeting concluded with President Tyler thanking Herr Gossmann and the Nuremberg Theatre for Children and Youth for the excellent conference and their kind hospitality.

"Twelfth Night", a musical based on the play by William Shakespeare. Photo: Hans-Joachim Kuka and courtesy of the Theater der Freundschaft, Berlin, GDR, 1972.

1968
EXECUTIVE COMMITTEE MEETING
Moscow, USSR / 1-10 March 1968

The Executive Committee of ASSITEJ met in Moscow, USSR on 1-10 March 1968. Gerald Tyler (Great Britain) presided as President, with Konstantin Shakh-Azizov (USSR) as 1st Vice President, Vladimir Adamek (Czechoslovakia) as 2nd Vice President, Rose-Marie Moudoués (France) as Secretary-General, and José Géal (Belgium) as Treasurer.

Other members of the EXCOM attending were: José Géal (Belgium), Hanswalter Gossmann (FGR), Ilse Rodenberg (GDR), Benito Biotto (Italy), Hans Snoek (Netherlands), Ian Cojar (Romania), and Nat Eek (USA).

Also attending were: Victor Georgiev (Bulgaria) who had been appointed to the EXCOM at the Nuremberg Meeting, Inga Juul (Denmark), Don Raffaelo Lavagna (Vatican, Italy), Elizabeth Gording (Norway), Maria Sunyer (Spain), and Ljubiša Djokič (Yugoslavia). Joyce Doolittle (Canada) attended as an observer.

Members absent: none

There were now thirteen official members of EXCOM (with the Nuremberg appointment of Bulgaria), but there were always several co-opted delegates and members of ASSITEJ who headed sub-committees and various special interests. Sometimes there were many spectators who just sat and observed the meetings. There was no attempt to keep the meetings private, but those attending usually had an item of business to conduct.[52]

New Canadian Delegate: Canada had sent no official representative to the Moscow meeting, although the EXCOM at the Prague Congress in 1966 had voted to continue them on the EXCOM. Joyce Doolittle was attending The Festival of Soviet Children's Theatre on a government grant, and attended the ASSITEJ meetings. While there she was designated an official observer.[53]

The EXCOM then asked Doolittle to look into regularizing

the Canadian representation. She agreed, and promised to circulate a report on the Moscow meetings to the Canadian Child and Youth Drama Association (CCYDA) and to Canada's professional theatres for children.[54]

The Moscow meeting was held in conjunction with The Festival of Soviet Children's Theatre, Moscow and Leningrad, so delegates were treated to a variety of plays presented by the Moscow Central Children's Theatre, the Moscow State Musical Theatre for Children, the Leningrad Theatre for Young Spectators, plus the national children's theatre companies from Latvia, Estonia, and Georgia, USSR. There were 150 delegates from 25 nations.

Shakh-Azizov welcomed the delegates, followed by a welcome by Gregory Vladikin, Deputy Minister of Culture, who gave the background of Soviet children's theatre. It began with the October Revolution of 1917, and currently consisted of 43 companies and 100 puppet theatres. Vsevolod Ostalsky, Deputy Chairman of the All-Russian Theatre Society, spoke briefly thanking the delegates for their dedication and wished all a successful conference. Adamek responded on behalf of ASSITEJ since President Tyler had not yet arrived.

Report Morale: The Secretary-General presented her Report Morale indicating centers forming in Hungary, Poland, Japan, and possibly Portugal. The Japanese delegate guest presented his report on forming a national center to the EXCOM the next day. As of 1950 adults had begun participation in children's theatre in Japan, and although there was no national center yet, they hoped to have one in the near future. Japan was finally accepted as a Member of ASSITEJ with a national center in 1969.

Moudoués reiterated that ASSITEJ was an association of theatres *for* children, not *by* children, and consisted of professionals, not amateurs. When the question of Spain's current political situation was raised, Tyler stated that by statute ASSITEJ was a non-political organization, and that each national center was responsible for determining their status in relation to the ASSITEJ statutes. Ultimately the general election every two years would decide a center's popularity and eligibility, he added.

There was no official Treasurer's Report, even though the Treasurer was present. However, in the past the Secretary-General had provided a Financial Report which indicated all the official centers, and who had and who had not paid their dues. This was always a part of her Report Morale. Moudoués continued by stating that France would continue to subsidize the Association. Only twelve centers had paid their annual dues, and ASSITEJ needed to seek money from various foundations.

Future Meetings: There was considerable discussion related to the next EXCOM meeting, as well as the Netherlands General Assembly which would now be held in The Hague. "The Dramatic Shaping of Topical Events" was selected as the theme of the Assembly. Biotto and Lavagna requested confirmation of the next Assembly in Venice at the time of the Biennale in 1970. Djokič inquired about having the next EXCOM meeting in June 1969 at the time of the Youth Festival in Šibenik, Yugoslavia. Eek stated that the USA hoped to host the IIIrd International Congress, possibly in Washington, D.C. at the John F. Kennedy Center for the Performing Arts.

Performances: While in Moscow the delegates saw productions of *Tales of Pushkin* (performed by the Moscow Central Children's Theatre that was later brought to Canada and the USA for the IVth International Congress in 1972), *King Matius I* (a strong anti-war play which pitted innocent children against scheming politicians and diplomats), *Warsaw Alarm* (which dealt with children being exterminated in the Treblinka concentration camp during WWII), *The Three Fat Men* (a delightfully melodic opera), and *Uncle Stiopa* "...who is always on hand for the rescue."[55]

In Moscow there were sighting-seeing tours of the Kremlin, including Lenin's personal office for the Westerners, and the Tretiakov Art Gallery.

Leningrad Tour: On 5 March after a performance, the delegates took the Red Arrow train to Leningrad at midnight, arriving the next morning for two days of plays and discussion. The Leningrad Theatre for Young Spectators of Zinovy Korogodsky was a contemporary open-staged theatre designed strictly for young audiences, and they presented *The Little Hump-Backed Horse* and *Tren Bren*, one from a new genre called "today" plays. Today Plays dealt with contemporary problems of young people, which concept since then has become an accepted and effective direction for contemporary plays for child audiences.[56] Though Korogodsky was world-renowned, this was the first time that many

Westerners were able to see the work of one of the USSR's best directors of youth theatre. In Leningrad there were also tours of the Hermitage and the Russian Museum.

After returning to Moscow for the closing ceremonies, the delegates and the Moscow Center were thanked by President Tyler, for their excellent hospitality and arrangements, the remarkable festival, and the great success of their meetings. A final performance in the Palace of Congresses was followed by a reception given by Mme. Furtseva, the Minister of Culture.

In retrospect the warm welcome in the Soviet Union, the excellence of the productions seen, the positive results of the EXCOM's deliberations, the reality of The Hague Congress to come with Venice in the offing, and a distinct softening of the East-West tensions made this meeting most successful. This sense of euphoria would be shattered within the next few months!

Vishnevsky Statue, Soviet Square, Moscow, USSR. March, 1968. Sign celebrating the 50th Anniversary of the Soviet Union. Personal photograph.

Saint Basil Cathedral, Soviet
Square, Moscow, USSR. March,
1968. Personal photograph.

Cathedral of the Annunciation, The
Kremlin, Moscow, USSR. March,
1968. Personal photograph.

Delegates to the EXCOM of ASSITEJ, The Kremlin, Moscow, USSR, March 1968.
Members present (in part): Milka Natcheva (Bulgaria), Hanswalter Gossman
(FGR), Ian Kojar (Romania), Rose-Marie Moudoués (France), Don Rafaello
Lavagna (Vatican), Emily Tyler (Great Britain), Joyce Doolittle (Canada), Sara
Spencer (USA), Gerald Tyler (Great Britain), Ljubiša Djokič (Yugoslavia). Personal
photograph.

The Soviet Palace of Congresses, Moscow, USSR. March 1968.

Formal Dinner at the EXCOM of ASSITEJ, Moscow, USSR. March 1968. (Seated left to right) Mrs.Gerald Tyler (Emily) and President of ASSITEJ Gerald Tyler (Great Britain), Mme Furtseva (USSR Minister of Culture), Konstantin Shakh-Azizov, Vice-President of ASSITEJ (USSR).

(Left to right) Nat Eek (USA Delegate) congratulates Konstatin Shakh-Azizov, Vice-President of ASSITEJ (USSR) on the success of the EXCOM Meeting, Moscow, USSR. March 1968. (In center background) Sara Spencer (USA

Auditorium of the Theater for Young Spectators, Zinovy Korogodsky, Director, Leningrad, USSR. March 1968. Personal photograph.

"Tren Bren", a Today play, directed by Zinovy Korogodsky, Leningrad Theater for Young Spectators, Leningrad, USSR. March 1968. Personal photograph.

1968
IInd INTERNATIONAL CONGRESS OF ASSITEJ
The Hague, Netherlands / 27-31 May 1968

The IInd International Congress of ASSITEJ met in The Hague, Netherlands on 27-31 May 1968. Gerald Tyler (Great Britain) presided as President, with Konstantin Shakh-Azizov (USSR) as 1st Vice President, Vladimir Adamek (Czechoslovakia) as 2nd Vice President, Rose-Marie Moudoués (France) as Secretary-General. Treasurer José Géal was absent, and Moudoués appointed Ian Cojar (Romania) to act in his stead.

Other members of the EXCOM attending were: Victor Georgiev (Bulgaria), Volker D. Laturell (FGR), Ilse Rodenberg (GDR), Benito Biotto (Italy), Hans Snoek (Netherlands), and Nat Eek (USA). Also attending were Joyce Doolittle (Canada) as an official observer, Bjorn Endreson (Norway) and Ljubiša Djokič (Yugoslavia) as co-opted members.

Countries attending were: Austria, Belgium, Bulgaria, Canada, Czechoslovakia, Denmark, FGR, France, GDR, Great Britain, Ireland, Israel, Italy, Japan, Netherlands, Norway, Poland, Portugal, Romania, Spain, Sweden, Switzerland, USA, USSR, and Yugoslavia.[57]

Members absent: José Géal (Belgium).

The Old EXCOM Meeting—25-26 May 1968

*P*rior to the Congress, the EXCOM met on 25-26 May 1968 for a general discussion of business and in preparation for the upcoming Congress. After an opening statement of welcome by the Dutch ITI Representative Max Wagoner, Moudoués presented her Report Morale: the *Czech Bulletin* listing national activities had been very well received; there was a great need of articles for the *Review*, especially in English. An animated discussion ensued on plays to be published in the *Review*, which was referred to the Translation Committee.

The ASSITEJ Exhibit: At the meetings in Berlin and Moscow there had been considerable discussion about an ASSITEJ Exhibit which could be sent to various countries for display at the time of a major festival or conference. A committee had been appointed in Moscow, and Moudoués announced that there would be such an exhibit in Paris in January and February of 1969. She requested that centers send her materials, such as photos, play programs, designs, etc., as soon as possible for inclusion.

The French Center would put the exhibit together at its own expense. However, the costs of shipping the exhibit elsewhere remained a major problem. Rodenberg volunteered to cover shipping expenses to Moscow, Prague, and Berlin. Tyler appointed a new exhibit committee of Rodenberg, Laturell, Enderson, and Eek to deal with these problems.

New Centers: The EXCOM then considered the eligibility of the Canadian Center and the Norwegian Center for full status in the organization. Upon query by Tyler, Doolittle (Canada) and Enderson (Norway) replied that each had a Center, were in conformity with the ASSITEJ Statutes, and that their dues were either paid or in process of payment. For the moment the Norwegian Center would represent Scandinavia, with hopes of centers in Sweden and Denmark. Finland had told him they were not interested. Canada and Scandinavia were welcomed accordingly.

Bjorn Endreson, who was the Director of the Rogaland Theater of Stavanger, Norway, raised the question that Inga Juul did not officially constitute the Danish Center since she was the only member. Tyler said this question must be discussed directly with Juul.

Election Discussion-EXCOM: There had been no self-nominations received by the international office, but also there had been no resignations. The Bureau, consisting of the Officers of the Association, recommended retention of the current twelve members. A motion was made by Eek and seconded by Rodenberg to that effect. It passed unanimously. The Bureau had also recommended that Norway, representing Scandinavia, and Yugoslavia be nominated since they had been co-opted for membership previously. (The EXCOM by the Constitution is allowed to appoint representatives of 2 national centers to sit on the EXCOM with vote.) The EXCOM approved their nominations, and a slate of 14 was to be presented to the Congress.

The Bureau also recommended the reappointment of Moudoués as Secretary-General and Ian Cojar (Romania) as Treasurer. Further they recommended Shakh-Azizov as President, Adamek, Eek, and Rodenberg as Vice-Presidents, and Tyler as Honorary President. Upon motion by Enderson, seconded by Snoek, the EXCOM passed the slate unanimously.

Italy proposed that the next Congress be held in their country at the time of the Venice Biennale. Biotto promised a forthcoming invitation in four to six months. The Congress would be in Venice or Milan. Tyler informed Biotto to tell his government that ASSITEJ would be honored to have the next Congress in his country if invited officially. Moudoués then announced that she had received an official invitation from Yugoslavia to have the next meeting of the EXCOM in Šibenik. This ended the meeting.

The Opening General Assembly—27 May

On Monday 27 May, Her Excellency Dr. M. Klompé, the Dutch Minister of Culture, welcomed the delegates at the Opening Session urging them to "explore new directions, new works, and new methods." There were approximately 150 delegates representing at least 25 countries. An official welcome was given by the Burgomaster of The Hague, Dr. H.A.M.T. Kilfshoten, and Snoek welcomed the delegates on behalf of the Netherlands Center for ASSITEJ.[58]

Tyler responded with thanks, and then addressed the membership bringing them up to date on the progress of ASSITEJ since its inception in Paris in 1965. He also raised these questions:

Are we preparing the child for independent thought and action, or are we shaping him in our own image? We must rediscover the child audience. What is our theatre doing to help the child discover and develop himself? Theatre should help him discover life. We must discover more of the personal world of the child.[59]

The theme of the Congress was "The Portrayal of Present Day Problems in Children's Theatre." At this first General Assembly session Erik Vos, former Director of the Netherlands Central Theatre, gave the keynote address. He spoke of the confusion felt by children in an adult world over words and attitudes and apparent contradictory behavior:

> The task of the theatre is to raise questions, not to give answers. It is important for theatres to be different. They must develop respect and understanding. There is the current problem of chaos and change in our contemporary theatre.
>
> Don't offer an audience a finished product as a teacher to a student. The Audience must feel that they participate in the creation. The main aim is to allow the audience to handle reality, rather than life handling the person.
>
> You can do anything on the stage as long as there is sense in what you are doing. The play is a classic, not because it is old, but because it always has a new sense. Actual problems on stage are dangerous, because they show truth vividly, but this should be the responsibility of the theatre.[60]

He also lay to rest the conflicts between the professional and the amateur by stating:

> It might therefore be well for ASSITEJ, as we become strong and more sure of ourselves, to turn our attention to the study of these [new] forms, and seek to build more bridges in our national centers. Bridges between the amateur and the professional. Between the theatre art and the classroom drama.

In the discussions that followed in the next few days there was great concern about the pessimism and ugliness in the current plays for young audiences. There was no resolution or consensus. Basically it was agreed that theatre can and should show the ugliness in the world, but the theatre must decide what and how much to show.

Rodenberg gave the second major speech on the educational aspects of the theme. She suggested that all problems were suited to children's theatre, because children's theatre like the adult theatre dealt with the whole of life itself and therefore with all its problems. It was not a matter of the problem and its topicality but of the manner in which the basic issues could be presented to children.[61]

General Assembly—Business Session—28 May

The General Assembly session to handle the business of the Association was held on Tuesday, 28 May 1968.

New Centers: The Secretary-General in her Report Morale stated that more centers were forming; most recently: India, Japan, Hungary, Sweden, Ireland, Cuba, Portugal, and Poland.

Exhibit: Moudoués also discussed the current status of the exhibit, apologizing that it wouldn't be ready for The Hague Congress. She discussed the status of the *Review* and the *Czech Bulletin,* and asked for more articles.

The Elections: Tyler then explained the voting process: each center would have three votes—2 for professional companies, and 1 for amateur. Ballots would be distributed by country in alphabetical order, to be marked, and then placed in the ballot box in the same order. Tyler would select 3 tellers to count the ballots and report the results to the Secretary-General.

Financial Report: Moudoués presented the Treasurer's Report, since Géal had resigned and was not present. After its presentation Tyler commented that "In 1967 our balance was 3,736 French Francs. In 1968 the balance is 6,000 French Francs. There is still not enough money for great projects, and we continue to rely very heavily on the French Center."[62]

General Discussion: In general business Tyler said that the EXCOM wanted to know what activities the membership wished them to undertake. Spain asked each center to send copies of two well selected plays to each of the other Centers. Eek on behalf of his Center proposed an annotated bibliography of no more than 50 plays from each country, to be mailed to each National Center. Tyler asked the US Center to create the form for such a listing.

Pugh announced that the Third Edition of his Bibliography contained 200 titles, and it would soon be available. Georgiev (Bulgaria) requested that the EXCOM consider meeting in Sophia on 21-31 October 1968, which would be concurrent with a youth festival. The budget was approved for the next two years with the suggestion that each Center give a special performance whose proceeds would go to ASSITEJ.

General Assembly Session—The Elections

While there was little controversy in the elections, the process did not run smoothly. Tyler began by commending the dedication of the EXCOM, and recommended that Moudoués be re-appointed as Secretary-General, and that Ian Cojar (Romania) be appointed to succeed Géal as Treasurer. The banking would continue to reside in Paris, but Cojar would handle the paper work. These items were approved by the General Assembly.

Tyler then explained that no one had sent in nominations by the deadline, but also that there had been no resignations. He said the Bureau and the EXCOM recommended the re-election of the current twelve members plus the two new members—Scandinavia and Yugoslavia. Eek nominated Shakh-Azizov, Spain nominated Snoek who declined, and Shakh-Azizov was elected unanimously. Then confusion erupted over the whole election process. Ballots were prepared but wrongly distributed. There was a miscount of results, so finally a single ballot was given to the Head of each National Center's delegation.

The EXCOM: The following 12 countries were elected to serve on the EXCOM for the next two years: Belgium (Géal), Canada (Doolittle), Czechoslovakia (Adamek), FGR (Gossmann), France (Moudoués), GDR (Rodenberg), Great Britain (Tyler), Italy (Biotto), Netherlands (Snoek), Romania (Cojar), USA (Eek), and USSR (Shakh-Azizov). Scandinavia (Bjorn Endreson) and Yugoslavia (Zvjezdana Ladika) were co-opted to sit on the EXCOM. Then from the floor Natalia Sats (USSR) nominated Bulgaria (Georgiev) also to be co-opted, which was done.

The Bureau: Of the officers, Konstantin Shakh-Azizov (USSR) was elected President, and Vladimir Adamek (Czechoslovakia) and Nat Eek (USA) as Vice-Presidents. Rose-Marie Moudoués and Ian Cojar were elected to continue as Secretary-General and Treasurer respectively.

The election with its lack of proper nominations as well as its co-opting of 3 additional members was in complete conflict with the Statutes, but the results made a proper total of fifteen members on the EXCOM. As a result of the confusion, Tyler warned the delegates that in the future all nominations must be made by letter three months ahead of the election.

General Discussion: In a special discussion session following the election Natalia Sats presented a paper urging that good children's theatre must be used for building not destroying; the world has enough problems (Viet-Nam), and we should create hope, and give a beautiful aesthetic, not a newspaper (a veiled criticism of the Scapino production of *De Krant* at the Congress. Victor Rosov (USSR) stated that good theatre should be medicine for the soul, not an irritant. There is too much rationalism and not enough fantasy in today's children's theatre. A Dutch delegate felt that children's theatre could either indoctrinate youth or give them a philosophic ethic for judgment. Teach the child not to hide from ugliness, but learn to live with it. Elizabeth Gording (Norway) wanted a depiction of true life that is a blend of good and bad. Bob Alexander (USA) said keep up with the kids, or they will leave the theatre. Zvjezdana Ladika (Yugoslavia) wanted us to give a realistic picture of the world but still a hopeful picture. Rosov also commented that "The child audience is an unlisted author for each play." Finally Peter Mitchell (Great Britain) said that the 11 to 25-year-old age group wanted life not fantasy, and they wanted violence.

As a result of this very animated discussion, it was requested that at the next Congress there be more free form discussions such as this one for the universal exchange of ideas and philosophies. The session ended.

The New EXCOM Meeting

President Shakh-Azizov presided at the final EXCOM session, nominated Gerald Tyler as Honorary President, asked for comments to be sent to the Secretary-General, and effusively thanked Snoek and the Netherlands Center for an excellent Congress, its organization, and their superlative hospitality.

Performances: As the person in charge of program planning for the Congress, Snoek personally was able to bring many of the Netherlands dance companies to the Congress to perform. Delegates were able to see the following performances: a visit to the Puppet Centre of Mr. Van Deth for a demonstration and his collection of historic puppets, prints, and documents; *Het Laatste Loverbos* by Jan Staal by the Theatre Company, Arena; *De Krant (The Newspaper)* by the Ballet Group Scapino; *Surprise*, a group of ballets by the Ballet Group Scapino; and the National Ballet Company performed *Romeo and Juliet* to the musical score of Prokofiev.

Kasjtanka, based on a Chekhov story, was performed at the Stadsdoelen in Delft. There were also planned excursions to Delft, Madurodam, and Rotterdam.

Dame Hans Snoek (Netherlands Delegate and host of IInd International Congress) at the Moscow, USSR EXCOM Meeting. March 1968. Courtesy of USSR ASSITEJ Center, Moscow, USSR, 1968.

A SUMMARY OF 1967-1968

1967

*T*he first meeting of the new EXCOM in Nuremberg, Germany in May of 1967 occurred exactly one year after the remarkable Congress in Prague, Czechoslovakia. During the previous year the Association primarily had solidified its borders.

Publications: The Paris office concentrated on keeping contact with its Centers, and began publishing a new *Review: Theatre Childhood and Youth* that would feature articles of national activities as well as topics for discussion about children's and youth theatre. Its first issue made its debut in 1966, and was financed by the French Center. Subscriptions were handled through the Paris office. Rose-Marie Moudoués was the Editor.

At the same time the Czechoslovakia Center had volunteered publication of the *Czech Bulletin* which was being sent to all the national centers free of charge. In mimeographed form it came out three to four times a year and featured lists of festivals, play schedules of various international theatres, and other current information among the participating centers. Vladimir Adamek was the Editor.

The National Centers were responsible for the distribution of both publications to their members. Of the two the *Czech Bulletin* was regarded as the most reliable and helpful, and it was delivered on time. Often the *Review* was over a year behind in publication. Publications were always a major item of discussion at all the international meetings. The editors of both publications were always pleading for more materials from the Centers. Publications were important, not just to keep the membership up to date in the field, but good publications were always a mark of prestige to be recognized by other professional associations.

Nurenberg EXCOM: 11 of the 12 members of the EXCOM were present at the Nuremberg meeting: Canada, Czechoslovakia, FGR, France, GDR, Great Britain, Italy, Netherlands, Romania, USA, and USSR. Belgium was absent. The Prague Meeting in 1966 was the first EXCOM Meeting to use the Constitution to appoint co-opted members. Scandinavia and Yugoslavia had been selected, but Scandinavia did not attend the Nuremberg Meeting.

Since this was the second official EXCOM Meeting to be held since the Constitutional Conference of 1965, a standard form of Agenda was created and followed afterward for many years. The topics and their order usually were:

- the Report Morale [the state of the Association] of the Secretary-General
- a financial report
- a publications report
- reports of sub-committees
- the selection of a site for the next EXCOM meeting
- a discussion of the next General Assembly or Congress
- miscellaneous discussion

The Nuremberg meeting was in conjunction with the 4th International FestIVal of Youth Theatre in Germany, so 6 international plays were seen by the members. The companies came from the Netherlands, Italy, the FGR, the GDR, and Bulgaria.

At the request of several members of the EXCOM, Bulgaria was appointed to the Committee although President Tyler reminded them that this was an exception rather than a precedent. The Committee continued to be a delicate balance of East and West. Victor Georgiev (Bulgaria), a distinguished actor in his country as well as head of his national center, was performing during the conference at Nuremberg, and this undoubtedly helped promote his appointment.

The EXCOM approved their next meeting to be in Moscow in March 1968 pending an official invitation, and the next General Assembly (Congress) would be held in Amsterdam towards the end of May 1968. This was later moved to The Hague with the same dates.

1968

Moscow EXCOM: The Moscow EXCOM Meeting was the first time that many Western members officially had visited the USSR. The Soviet hosting of the meeting was part of a warming of relations between the East and the West, and at the end of the ten days the delegates felt that it had been an extremely satisfactory meeting.

For several years Canada had been kept on the EXCOM more out of recognition of its involvement in the creation of ASSITEJ than in its consistency. Its Center had had four different representatives since its beginning, and no representative had shown up in Moscow. Joyce Doolittle, who was on a government grant to visit the Soviet Union, attended the meetings and asked to be an "observer" for Canada. She was instructed by the EXCOM to formalize an appointment as an official representative of Canada with her National Center. Upon her return home, this was done, and Doolittle officially represented Canada until 1979.

Center Leadership: Appointment of a national center's representative was the responsibility of the center. Countries with no center were usually represented by an individual from a theatre or organization that produced or promoted theatre for young people. These persons usually proved to be quite dedicated, and were responsible for their own expenses. Many times they would return to their countries and establish a new center which in turn they would represent. In order to apply for membership, each center had to have professional theatres for children as members (good for two votes), and while not required, many had amateur theatres for children as members (good for one vote). There could be no official centers of amateur theatre members only. The three requirements for establishing a national center were that: 1) they had an official representative with an official address for all correspondence; 2) they had statutes in conformity with those of the Association; and 3) they had or were paying their dues. Regrettably, faces and countries would come and go with regularity, but usually in the well established centers the same person represented his or her country for an extended period of time. This familiarity created a sense of security, and gave a consistency to the decisions of the EXCOM.

In the EXCOM's discussion of co-opting Scandinavia, Bjorn Endreson (Norway) raised the question that Inga Juul did not officially constitute the Danish Center. Tyler said this question must be discussed directly with Juul, and closed the discussion. For several years Juul, as a conservative, represented Denmark on a personal basis. She continued as Denmark's official representative until 1983 when a separate official Center was formed under Michael Ramløse's leadership. As a Social-Democrat and a more liberal individual, he opened the Danish Center to admitting many new members regardless of political persuasion.

In his opening welcome the Soviet Deputy Minister of Culture gave a brief background of Soviet children's theatre. It had begun with the October Revolution of 1917 and now fifty years later there were 43 children's theatre companies and one 100 puppet theatres, an enviable achievement.

New Centers: The Secretary-General indicated that centers were forming in Hungary, Poland, Japan, and possibly Portugal. The Japanese delegate as a guest presented his report on forming a national center to the EXCOM the next day. For several years Japan had tried to get its national center accepted as a member, but for some reason this never came to a vote of acceptance. It was finally received as a center in 1969, and from that time forward, it has been an active and contributing center of ASSITEJ, continuing to this day as of 2005.

Since Japan had both extensive professional theatres and amateur theatres which used child actors, the Secretary-General reiterated that ASSITEJ was an association of theatres *for* children, not *by* children, and consisted of professionals, not amateurs. When the question of Spain's current political situation was raised, Tyler responded that by statute ASSITEJ was a non-political organization, and that each national center was responsible for determining their status in relation to the ASSITEJ statutes, and ultimately the general election every two years decided a center's popularity and eligibility. This concern over theatre *for* children, not *by* children, would be raised again and again over the years, since performing children were not regarded as *professional*.

Financial Report: There was no official Treasurer's Report, even though the Treasurer was present. However, in the past the Secretary-General had provided a Financial Report which indicated all the official centers, and who had and who had not paid their dues. This was always a part of her Report Morale. For many years Moudoués would provide the Financial Report for the Treasurer to present. Not until she was replaced as Secretary-General twenty-five years later was the Treasurer and his Report presented independently.

Performances: Perhaps the most memorable of the many excellent performances in the USSR was that of the Leningrad Theatre for Young Spectators. Its Director was Zinovy Korogodsky. His theatre was a contemporary open thrust-stage auditorium designed strictly for young audiences, and they presented *The Little Hump-Backed Horse* plus another one from a new genre called "today" plays. Today Plays dealt with contemporary problems of young people, and since then have become an accepted and effective type of contemporary play to be written for child audiences. Though Korogodsky was world-renowned, this was the first time that many Westerners were able to see the work of one of the USSR's best youth theatre directors. Tragically much later his theatre was taken away from him, but eight years later he returned to directing, although not as the head of a theatre. Later he was totally exonerated, and he died in 2004.[63]

Eek had taken his wife and three sons to the meeting since he felt it was an unusual opportunity for all of them. Mrs. Patricia Eek had even taken two years of Russian at their University in preparation. Eek had not realized that taking his entire family to the Soviet Union was a mark of respect and acceptance that pleased the Russians immediately and this was announced many times by Shakh-Azizov at various public gatherings.

After seeing the plays, the delegates would meet in a large room in the theatre with the actors, designers, and staff, and critique the play just seen. In Leningrad in the discussion following *The Little Hump-Backed Horse*, Eek's 14-year-old son Robert was asked for his comments for the microphone that was making the rounds. He thanked the Soviet Union for their excellent hospitality, and stated that he had greatly appreciated the opportunity "...to see how the other half lives!" Eek and his wife winced at the gaff, but were saved by Valentina their interpreter who translated "...to see how *the people in your country live!*"

Tours: In Moscow delegates were given sighting-seeing tours of the Kremlin, including for the Westerners Lenin's personal office, Lenin's Tomb, and the Tretiakov Art Gallery. In Leningrad the Hermitage and the Russian Museum were visited by the delegates, and then back in Moscow they were treated to a farewell performance in the Palace of Congresses followed by a reception given by Mme. Furtseva, the Minister of Culture.

While in Lenin's Office in the Kremlin, Emily Tyler, wife of the British President, noted a photograph on the wall of Léon Trotsky with other officials. Turning to Patricia Eek, she said "Wasn't Trotsky assassinated with an axe in Mexico City?" Mrs. Eek agreed, and then they noted that their interpreter, a delightful Russian woman who had been abroad many times and spoke excellent English, was strangely silent. In a small quiet voice she said "We were told that he had died of disease in Mexico!"

While in the Soviet Union a visitor always assumed he was being "bugged". Colleagues mentioned seeing a Soviet agent step out of a large mirrored four-sided pillar in the lobby of the Metropole Hotel (built in 1905) who had obviously been observing the comings and goings of people there. In another case friends were shown with pride to the floor where all the monitoring equipment was harbored.

Eek's wife and he assumed their room at the Metropole was wired, and they enjoyed the occasion's indirect way of getting things done. Once when the toilet was running constantly all night, they commented to each other about the noise and inconvenience. The next day it was repaired. The same occurred about a stuck window. All the time they and their family were in the Soviet Union, they were treated with great courtesy and consideration. Tragically as soon as they flew out of Moscow on their way to Prague, they felt a tremendous sense of relief and loss of tension. Friends reported exactly the same feelings despite the warm hospitality.

In retrospect the warm welcome in the Soviet Union, the excellence of the productions seen, the positive results of the EXCOM's deliberations, the reality of The Hague Congress to come, with Venice in the offing in 1970, and a distinct softening of the East-West tensions made this meeting most successful. Unfortunately this sense of euphoria would be shattered within the next few months!

IInd Congress: Two months after the Moscow meeting the IInd International Congress was held in The Hague in the Netherlands. Mme. Hans Snoek, Dame of the Society—one of her country's highest awards, was trained as a dancer and a choreographer, and headed the Ballet Group Scapino. She had been active in ASSITEJ since its founding, and single-handedly she had put a remarkable program together for the delegates.

The EXCOM: In the business sessions the Bureau agreed to recommend the reappointment of Rose-Marie Moudoués (France) as Secretary-General and Ian Cojar (Romania) as Treasurer. Further they recommended Shakh-Azizov as President, Adamek, Eek, and Rodenberg as Vice-Presidents, and Tyler as Honorary President. The EXCOM passed the slate unanimously.

Natalia Sats: There was one surprising appearance out of the mists of time at the Congress. Natalia Sats, a world renowned major theatrical director and entrepreneur from the 1930s, who as a child had had Prokofiev dedicate *Peter and the Wolf* to her, had just recently been rehabilitated from a gulag by Premier Nikita Krushchev, and attended the Congress as a Soviet delegate. Later she was named head of the Moscow Musical Theatre for Children, had a new theatre built and named for her, and was an honored and active participant in ASSITEJ in her later years. She died in 1993 at the age of 100.[64]

The Elections: In the General Assembly the current EXCOM of 12 was re-elected for the next two years: Belgium (Géal), Canada (Doolittle[65]), Czechoslovakia (Adamek), FGR (Gossmann), France (Moudoués), GDR (Rodenberg), Great Britain (Tyler), Italy (Biotto), Netherlands (Snoek), Romania (Cojar), USA (Eek), and USSR (Shakh-Azizov). 3 nations were co-opted for membership. The EXCOM named Scandinavia (Bjorn Endreson representing Norway, Sweden, and Finland), and Yugoslavia (Zvjezdana Ladika). Natalia Sats (USSR) nominated Bulgaria (Victor Georgiev) from the floor for co-option, which was accepted. Since Bulgaria had been appointed to the EXCOM at the Nuremberg Meeting irregularly, this co-option made its sitting on the EXCOM legitimate. However, the Statutes specified only two co-options. This author felt that Bulgaria's presence was benign, but it continued the East-West balance.

The election with its lack of proper nominations as well as its co-opting of 3 additional members was in complete conflict with the Statutes, but the results made a proper total of 15 members on the EXCOM for the first time. As a result of the confusion, Tyler warned the delegates that in the future all nominations must be made by letter three months ahead of the election.

Centers: The creation and acceptance of a new national center was always of interest and sometimes considerable discussion. The current status was closely guarded by the Secretary-General. Supposedly, to become an official national center, the country had to have a set of statutes in agreement with the Constitution, a correspondent and an address within the country for the conducting of all official business and correspondence, and a payment of dues. The number of members within a center was never questioned.

Information on the status of a current, new, or forming center was provided verbally by the Secretary-General as part of her Report

Morale at the EXCOM meetings or International Congresses. To Eek's knowledge, no documentation was ever provided to anyone, except whether a center had paid its dues; the Secretary-General's word was sufficient. Consequently small centers came into being and then disappeared equally easily, usually depending on political persuasion. Representatives came and went, but as Doolittle commented much later "Active participation in ASSITEJ by individual centres depends a great deal upon having a committed individual at the head of a national centre."[66]

Performances: As the person in charge of program planning for the Hague Congress, Snoek personally was able to bring many of the Netherlands dance companies to the Congress to perform. Delegates were able to see the following performances: a visit to the Puppet Centre of Mr. Van Deth for a demonstration and his collection of historic puppets, prints, and documents; *Het Laatste Loverbos* by Jan Staal by the Theatre Company, Arena; *De Krant (The Newspaper)* by the Ballet Group Scapino; *Surprise*, a group of ballets by the Ballet Group Scapino; and *Kasjtanka*, based on a Chekhov story, at the Stadsdoelen in Delft. There were also planned excursions to Delft, Madurodam, and Rotterdam. Also, the National Ballet Company performed *Romeo and Juliet* to the musical score of Prokofiev.

De Krant was the most interesting piece, and it had been created specifically for the Congress. It was performed by an excellent large group of accomplished dancers who moved and danced against a black and white backdrop of the front page of a large newspaper surrounded by black drapes, with the choreography commenting on items of interest to a young audience.

This was the first Congress held in the West since the Paris Founding Conference in 1965, and the third Congress of the fledgling organization. The three previous EXCOM's had been held in the East— Berlin, Prague, and Moscow. Consequently there was a sense of total artistic freedom in discussion that had not been present since Paris. Despite the openness and charm of Prague in 1966, there still had been a sense of guarding your spoken thoughts and ideas. The openness and accessibility of the Netherlands and Amsterdam contributed to many Western delegates attending, and one was conscious of many young people being present. Discussions were wide open and sometimes quite confrontational.

In attitude and demeanor the Netherlands was very liberal in its arts, which came as a shock to many from the Eastern countries. This expressed itself in the discussions of good versus evil, beauty versus ugly, kind versus wicked. All the centers were now witnessing some of the results of the 60s, the "cold war" era, "the decade of peace, love, and harmony". The ugliness of Viet-Nam was ever present politically, socially, and culturally. However, ASSITEJ was growing up, and in the process, perhaps unknowingly, was accomplishing its goal of constant and free exchange of artistic information and ideas.

Anatoly Schukin (Old Man) and Valentina Sperantova (Old Woman) in "Fairy Tales by A. Pushkin", performed by the Moscow Central Children's Theatre, Moscow, USSR, at the IVth International Congress of ASSITEJ, SUNY, Albany, New York, USA, June 1072. Photo courtesy of SUNY Dept. of Theatre, Albany, New York.

"Fairy Tales by A. Pushkin", performed by the Moscow Central Children's Theatre, Moscow, USSR, at the IVth International Congress of ASSITEJ, SUNY, Albany, New York, USA, June 1072. Photo courtesy of SUNY Dept. of Theatre, Albany, New York.

1968
EXECUTIVE COMMITTEE MEETING
Sophia, Bulgaria / 20-28 October 1968

The Executive Committee of ASSITEJ met in Sophia, Bulgaria on 20-28 October 1968. President Konstantin Shakh-Azizov (USSR) presided, Orlin Corey (USA) acting for 2nd Vice-President Nat Eek (USA) who was absent, Ilse Rodenberg (GDR) as 3rd Vice-President, Rose-Marie Moudoués (France) as Secretary-General, and Ian Cojar (Romania) as Treasurer.

Other members of the EXCOM attending were: Benito Biotto (Italy), Hans Snoek (Netherlands), Victor Georgiev (Bulgaria) as a co-opted member, and Christo Stefanovski observing for Ljubiša Djokič (Yugoslavia).

Members absent: Belgium, Canada, Vladimir Adamek (Czechoslovakia) as 1st Vice-President, FGR, Great Britain, and Scandinavia.

*J*n August of 1968, two months before the EXCOM Meeting of ASSITEJ in Bulgaria, members of the Warsaw Pact Nations (USSR, GDR, Hungary, Poland, and Bulgaria) sent troops into Czechoslovakia to restore order in a situation and in a country that was becoming dangerously Westernized and liberal under the "Prague Spring" leadership of Alexander Dubcek. After securing the country, they deposed Dubcek in 1969. The new Czech leaders then agreed to restrain their liberal policies in return for gradual withdrawal of the occupational forces.

The Statutes of ASSITEJ state that ASSITEJ was non-political[67], but this action affected the discussions and the decisions of the Association for many years to come. However, those "dedicated to ASSITEJ acted continually with a calm determination to make the best of difficult situations and to strive for constant progress."[68]

The Bureau Meeting-20 October

Prior to the EXCOM meeting, the Bureau met on 20 October 1968 in the office of the Bulgarian National Youth Theatre to prepare the Agenda. Shakh-Azizov presided at the meeting, and present were Moudoués, Shakh-Azizov, Rodenberg, Cojar, Georgiev, Stefanovski, and Corey.

Moudoués presented the following proposed Agenda:
- plan for the work of the Bureau and EXCOM for 1969
- report of the Bulgarian Center
- examine the Budget for 1969
- discussion of the Exposition for 1969
- report of Publications—*The Review* and *Czech Bulletin*
- plan for the EXCOM to meet in Yugoslavia in June 1969
- plans for the Venice Congress in autumn of 1970

Members were free to add other items to the Agenda. Also, she announced there would be a Bureau Meeting in Paris in late March or early April of 1969, and Djokič and Biotto would explain the details of their individual proposed Association meetings. Moudoués added that Switzerland and Hungary definitely, and Egypt and Central America possibly, would be candidates as Centers at the Venice Congress.

The 1ˢᵗ EXCOM Meeting—21 October

The opening session of the EXCOM Meeting of ASSITEJ was held at 11 am in the conference room of the Sophia City Hall on 21 October 1968. Present were Shakh-Azizov, Moudoués, Corey, Cojar, Georgiev, Inga Juul (Denmark), Ilse Rodenberg (GDR), Hans Snoek (Netherlands), and Ljubiša Djokič (Yugoslavia). In addition Peter Mitchell (Great Britain) was present representing the London Speech and Drama Association in place of Gerald Tyler, plus many guests.

Absent: Belgium, Canada, Czechoslovakia, FGR, Italy, and Scandinavia.

Georgiev gave a brief welcoming address and introduced the Committee members, which was followed by a greeting on behalf of the City of Sophia and the Minister of Culture. The Committee was given blue and red kerchiefs by four boys and four girls of the Young Pioneers of Sophia. Shakh-Azizov responded with thanks, and talked briefly about the history of ASSITEJ, which was only four years old. The purpose of its work was "...to aid children and to enable them to forget the meaning of the word war, and to know the meaning of the words peace and friendship." The meeting was then adjourned for a reception in those offices by the Mayor of Sophia.[69]

The 2nd EXCOM Meeting-22 October

The first item of discussion was attendance. Adamek had sent word that he could not attend "...because I am concerned night and day with events in Czechoslovakia." According to Corey, at the time of this meeting, the Prague Airport was ringed with tanks from the Soviet Union.

Tyler reported he wished to attend, but could not because of illness and appointed Peter Mitchell in his stead, and the British Drama League sent a letter to ASSITEJ protesting the meeting in Bulgaria following the invasion of Czechoslovakia, and stating that they would not send a representative. A similar letter came from Norway, and Enderson was not in attendance. Eek had appointed Orlin Corey to serve in his stead since Eek was in production, and Géal could not attend because he was in production. Joyce Doolittle (Canada) sent regrets, but indicated they were working with the US Center regarding co-hosting the 1972 Congress, and that she would definitely attend the June Meeting in Yugoslavia. There was no mention of FGR in the minutes. Only 8 out of the 15 elected EXCOM members were in attendance.[70]

Shakh-Azizov stated that "...this association is free of every political restriction since its founding in 1964, and so I cannot understand these letters from London and Norway. The one matter of prime importance to us is our work with children, not such matters. We should write to know if they will still cooperate or will quit ASSITEJ." To which Moudoués replied "I do not believe it is the intention of the English to withdraw from ASSITEJ."[71]

Corey proposed seating Juul as an "observer", but Moudoués protested saying that Denmark had no Center, and only Scandinavia (Norway) had a proper Center although communication was very sparse.

After considerable discussion Juul was not seated, and Moudoués was instructed to speak with her about the problems.

Venice Congress: Biotto presented the invitation for ASSITEJ to hold their next Congress in Venice, Italy from 1-6 October 1970. He indicated that the Biennale would assist in every way, and Venice will provide theatres and all that was necessary. He was optimistic of foundation support. The offer was accepted with thanks. Moudoués stated that a theme needed to be selected, and her office would accept recommendations with a deadline of March 1969. The membership would be solicited for suggestions.

Djokič spoke of hosting the next EXCOM meeting in Šibenik, Yugoslavia. It would coincide with the 10th Festival of the Arts in Šibenik, 25 June to 2 July 1969. With EXCOM approval he indicated that all the details would be sent to each Center.

Moudoués again proposed a discussion of play exchanges based on a proposal by Adamek. Also, she indicated that *The Review* would publish two plays a year. Finally she wished to ask each Center to send her a complete list of plays produced in the last two years by 1 January 1969. Shakh-Azizov commented that already the Soviet Union had produced some of the plays published in the USA's Anchorage Press book *Twenty Plays.*

Shakh-Azizov then requested the EXCOM consider encouraging more meetings with actors, including more actors and young people in their delegations to Congresses, more contacts with UNIMA, discussing possibilities for ASSITEJ Centers in Asia, Africa, and South America, creating a list of films on children's theatre, and lastly exploring a theme of "Dramatic Art for Children in TV and Radio."

Cojar announced that Romania had invited the EXCOM to meet in Bucharest in late March of 1970, which would coincide with a Festival of Plays for Children and Teenagers. Details would be given at Šibenik. The meeting was adjourned.

The 3ʳᵈ EXCOM Meeting-24 October

Present were Shakh-Azizov, Moudoués, Cojar, Biotto (arrived late), Snoek, Rodenberg, Djokič, Georgiev, and Corey. The majority, or 9 out of 15, constituted the quorum.

After a reading of letters of regret for non-attendance from Tyler and Enderson, Shakh-Azizov proposed sending letters of thanks to both of them. Moudoués then reported on her meeting with Juul. A center in Denmark may be swiftly established, and there is the possibility of a permanent theatre for Juul. However, she needed help to establish her credentials. Moudoués recommended that based on her past assistance to ASSITEJ, her work in professional theatre, and her personal qualities, she should be appointed as a Technical Advisor so she could attend the EXCOM meetings. The Committee voted unanimously to appoint Juul as Technical Advisor, an appointment that would assist her in seeking a new theatre.

Georgiev then presented the history of the Bulgarian Center, since it was only 18 months old.[72] Moudoués announced that Poland, Portugal, Hungary, and Egypt were in the process of organizing Centers. She gave a précis of Egypt's background in children's theatre, and then announced that a group from Guatemala, Venezuela, and Nicaragua wanted to form a single Center, but they were not ready yet. Shakh-Azizov also mentioned Japan was forming a Center soon.

ASSITEJ Exhibit: Moudoués mentioned a possible ASSITEJ exhibit in Paris at the International Center for Youth. After much discussion on materials, quality, and selection, they decided to have all materials sent to Paris by the end of March 1969. Yugoslavia hoped the exhibit could be sent to Šibenik for the June meeting. However, shipping costs would have to be borne by each Center. Shakh-Azizov said they had talked of an exhibition for three years. He asked Moudoués to send the details to all Centers and let them decide what to send, and if they wished to pay the costs. Materials to be included should be from the National Centers only. **Publications:** Moudoués stated that no *ASSITEJ Reviews* for 1968 had been published until now since she hadn't received enough material. She begged for more materials for *The Review* and the *Czech Bulletin.*

Financial Report: Cojar distributed the Financial Report. After a citing of special individual problems, he specifically asked Centers to make donations beyond paying their annual dues. Also, Corey was to ask Eek to seek more money from USA Foundations. Cojar listed those countries that had not paid their dues, with Brazil two years in arrears.

Shakh-Azizov said that ASSITEJ could exist without Brazil's fifty dollars.

Moudoués presented the draft of the letter to be sent to Great Britain re: their protest of the Czechoslovakian invasion, in which she merely quoted the "non-political" statute. The Committee approved the letter and its being sent. The meeting was adjourned.

The Final EXCOM Meeting—28 October

All delegates were present. Since this was a public meeting, visitors and guests were also present.

Performances: Shakh-Azizov opened the meeting welcoming all, and asked Moudoués to speak about the work of the Committee, which she proceeded to do citing all the decisions made. Shakh-Azizov then asked for comments on the productions seen so far by the delegates. These included: *The Adventures of the Brave Little Tailor* by the Bulgarian National Theatre; a musical version of *Twelfth Night* by the GDR Theater der Freundschaft; *The Adventures of Pacala* by the Ion Creanga Theatre of Bucharest; *Koko the Conjurer* by the National Youth Theatre of Bulgaria; A modern revue, created by the young people of the Gavenda Theatre of Warsaw, Poland; *The Tale of Four Caps* by the Kyustendil Drama Theatre of Bulgaria; and *Mummy's Wedding* by the Bulgarian National Youth Theatre. To be seen later that day were *Tales of Marshak and Tales of Pushkin* by the Central Children's Theatre of Moscow.

There were final speeches by several of the delegates which lasted about 75 minutes, Shakh-Azizov gave a speech of gratitude to all the participants and organizers who attended the Festival and the EXCOM under difficult conditions, and he pledged that ASSITEJ would work faithfully on their mutual problems. Georgiev expressed his thanks and gave to each delegate a mask of a primitive Bulgarian spirit, a spirit of Gaiety and Virtue, appropriate for this occasion. The meeting adjourned for an official dinner at the Mayor's invitation.[73]

"The Prince and the Pauper" after Mark Twain. Performance by the Youth Theatre of Sophia, Bulgaria. Courtesy of the Bulgarian ASSITEJ Center. 1968.

"The Adventures of the Brave Tailor", after the Brothers Grimm. Performance by the Youth Theatre of Sophia, Bulgaria. Courtesy of the Bulgarian ASSITEJ Center. 1968.

1969
EXECUTIVE COMMITTEE MEETING
Šibenik, Yugoslavia / 25 June-3 July 1969

The Executive Committee of ASSITEJ met in Šibenik, Yugoslavia 25 June–3 July 1969. Vladimir Adamek (Czechoslovakia) as 1st Vice-president presided, with Nat Eek (USA) as 2nd Vice President, Ilse Rodenberg (GDR) as 3rd Vice-President, and Rose-Marie Moudoués (France) as Secretary-General.

Other members of the EXCOM attending were: Joyce Doolittle (Canada), Hanswalter Gossmann (FGR), Gerald Tyler (Great Britain), Benito Biotto (Italy), Hans Snoek (Netherlands), Ian Cojar (Romania), and M. Kisilov for Konstantin Shakh-Azizov (USSR). Victor Georgiev (Bulgaria), Bjorn Endreson (Scandinavia), and Ljubiša Djokič (Yugoslavia) had been co-opted in The Hague meeting, Inga Juul (Denmark) was a Technical Advisor, M. Bergman (Sweden) was an observer. However in a spirit of peace, no one challenged anyone's presence at the meeting.

Members absent: Géal (Belgium), Shakh-Azizov (USSR) represented by M. Kisilov, Cojar (Romania) represented by Djokič.

The Bureau Meeting—Friday, 27 June

The Bureau (Adamek, Moudoués, Djokič for Cojar, Tyler as Honorary President, and Eek) met to set the Agenda.

Moudoués suggested a time table, and then started with the Agenda forwarded by Shakh-Azizov:

- the discussion of activities should continue from the last meeting
- a financial report dated 15 June 1968 would be presented
- the publication report discussing the ASSITEJ *Review* and the *Czech Bulletin*
- a request to appoint a sub-committee on publication

It was recommended that each National Center submit a four-page report of activities from its founding to June 1970 to be presented to the Secretary-General at the Bucharest meeting. They approved holding the next EXCOM Meeting in Romania with date to be settled in consultation with Cojar and Shakh-Azizov.

Venice Congress: Biotto was to present the plans for the 1970 Venice Congress at the first meeting time. Adamek suggested as a theme: "Psychological Change of Children and Its Relation in Theatre for Children from Ages 8 through 11". He also suggested that each Center could report on the theme and this change in its own country.

Moudoués reported only four countries had sent in the Statutes of their Centers. All countries should send these in. Tyler suggested that Adamek send a letter to all Centers to send their Statutes in by the Bucharest Meeting. Moudoués added that the Scandinavian Center must have created their separate centers by the Venice Congress. Then the meeting was adjourned.

The 1ˢᵗ EXCOM Meeting—Saturday, 28 June

The first official session was opened by Djokič welcoming the members on behalf of Yugoslavia. He commented on the previous successful meetings of ASSITEJ, and mentioned the upcoming Congress in Venice in 1970, and an EXCOM Meeting in Bucharest in 1971. The EXCOM was then welcomed by the Deputy Mayor of Šibenik, stating that:

> Šibenik, gives much to educational support of children. Not just because children are our future, but children are the best expression of love between people and nations. We hope that during your stay you will all see and feel this, and when you return to your countries, we hope you will carry this love with you.[74]

Eek responded on behalf of ASSITEJ, thanking those responsible for the Festival, and mentioned that each ASSITEJ meeting allows the Committee to see the work, see new creative plays, and learn to know the people in the countries. He said they were honored to be invited by Yugoslavia, and personally regretted that he had had to miss the Sophia meeting. He also noted with regret the absence of Shakh-Azizov, and wished him a speedy recovery in his health.

Adamek agreed with Eek and added:

We know Yugoslavia forms an important part in the theatres of the world. We of the Executive Committee have made many friends here. One of the most important things in the world today is developing friendship among peoples. In Šibenik, we will find time to make good friends. I thank your country, not just for ASSITEJ, but for all the peoples of the world.[75]

Moudoués said she had little to add but commented:

I started in Šibenik, by going to an island between the sky and the sea, and picked an olive branch (the symbol of peace among all peoples), and place it here on the table.[76]

She then read a telegram from Shakh-Azizov:

Dear Friends, I greet all members of ASSITEJ at the opening meeting at Šibenik. It is a great and important step on the way to friendship and creativity. Each festival helps us to know each other better. This is the fifth year of this organization. It is not a big number but much has been done during this time to make contacts with people so that we could know better the creativity of Children's Theatre throughout the world. Unfortunately, my health doesn't permit me to be present at this occasion, but I do believe that this meeting of Children's Theatres will be very fruitful.[77]

Cojar had also sent a telegram that excused him for professional reasons. Caryl Jenner (Great Britain) also sent a telegram indicating her absence because of illness in the family.

The EXCOM then set the times for the sessions, suggesting that Adamek preside over the first day, Eek the second day, and Tyler the third day if needed. With this settled the meeting was adjourned.

The 2nd EXCOM Meeting—Saturday, 28 June

On Saturday 28 June Adamek opened the meeting noting he would preside in Shakh-Azizov's absence, and suggested ASSITEJ send him a telegram with wishes for a speedy recovery. Everyone agreed. He then announced the fifteen members of the EXCOM were present with Géal and Cojar excused. Juul was an advisor. Accordingly with pride he announced that the meetings would proceed according to the Constitution! Then he announced the Agenda and time table approved by the Bureau on Friday.

The Complete Minutes of the Sophia meeting as recorded by Orlin Corey were presented and approved without comment.

Moudoués gave her Report Morale, commenting first on the exhibition. It opened one week late in Amiens. Then it would go to Paris and other parts of France. Many materials kept coming in late. Centers represented were Great Britain, Canada, Belgium, Spain, France, Norway, Yugoslavia, Russia, GDR, Italy, Netherlands, Czechoslovakia, Bulgaria, and Romania. It would tour France until the end of the year.

The Paris Bureau Meeting: Next she reported on the Bureau meeting in Paris in May. Present were Moudoués, Djokič, Adamek, and Cojar. They saw two productions, and met with M. Jean Daconte of ITI who explained that ASSITEJ could not expect any financial help from ITI. However, they could hope for more help from new forming centers. Djokič had proposed a meeting of writer's of children's plays, and in May Adamek and Moudoués met with the Presidium of UNIMA, and they hoped to collaborate with them more in the future.

The Bureau discussed the need for more financial help and Moudoués suggested: 1) each Center should push ITI to create a children's theatre section, and 2) each Center should encourage the creation of more Centers.

Discussion on the Conference of Writers: As to location Djokič proposed making that decision at the Bucharest conference in 1971. They also decided the Conference should include dramaturgs who created repertory as well as authors. In an extended discussion on the Exhibition, Moudoués said that materials could still be sent in to the Paris office by 1 October to be included.

Since the next EXCOM Meeting was scheduled for April in Romania, Shakh-Azizov had requested it not start until April 28. Adamek suggested May in Bucharest. Moudoués said there would be need of two EXCOM meetings between the Venice Congress and that in the USA in 1972, one in 1971, and one in 1972.

5 Year Reports: At the Venice Congress ASSITEJ would have been in existence for five years. Consequently it was time for an organizational and financial balance. It was asked that at the Bucharest EXCOM Meeting each Center should send in a four-page report on the growth and activities of their Center during the past five years. The reports would be printed in the *Review*. Each report should be in one of the official languages, and should have a ten-line précis so Moudoués could have it translated into the other two official languages. Also each Center must send in its Statutes or Constitution of its Center so it can be recorded in the Paris office.

Venice Congress: Biotto was pleased to announce that Italy would host the 1970 Congress. He hoped it would give new impulses and development to ASSITEJ, united in brotherhood between countries and peoples. The dates would be between 10-30 October 1970 in Venice, since there would be a Festival of Film and Theatre for Children at the same time. Orlin Corey's theatre group, the Everyman Players, would perform, and Biotto would welcome other groups from ASSITEJ members who wished to perform. There would be tours to cities other than Venice. Upon his return he would approach the Cini Foundation for financial support. He explained the possibility of Italian radio-TV stations transmitting Italian and foreign plays for children. For a beginning he suggested three foreign plays and four in Italian. He asked each center to send suitable scripts for transmission in English or in French. By the end of the year he would report the results.

Finally, Biotto said the dates must coincide with those of the Venice Biennale. Rodenberg asked if there would be interpreters. Biotto said yes. Moudoués said the ASSITEJ Exhibit could be sent to Italy and would require 500 square meters of space. Gossmann requested that the meeting only last five days, and Eek suggested weekend to weekend.

Moudoués introduced the theme title suggested by the Bureau: "The Change (revolution) in the Psychology of Children and How It Is Reflected in Theatre for Children in Ages 8-11." After much discussion it was left that there might be two themes with separate discussion sessions, and then as requested by the membership a session for free discussion. The meeting was adjourned.

The 3rd EXCOM Meeting—Sunday, 29 June

The EXCOM next met again on 29 June with Eek (USA) presiding, Doolittle, Adamek, Juul, Gossmann, Rodenberg, Tyler, Biotto, Snoek, Enderson, Keesilov, and Djokič were all present.

The first part of the session was a press conference with interviewer M. Marinkovro of Radio Šibenik, asking EXCOM members questions about the organization, its activities, and its concerns.

Financial Report: Moudoués presented the Financial Report. She stated that all but Brazil had paid their dues for 1968. Yet to pay in 1969 were Spain, Netherlands, Belgium, Great Britain, Canada, Israel, and Brazil. She said while checks arrived from the USA, she did not know whether they were for dues or payment for the *Review*. In the discussion on the need for more financial support Moudoués said the dues could only be raised in the business session of the Venice Congress.

Publications: Moudoués reported there were now two *Reviews* in print for 1969. One contained the report of The Hague Congress of 1968, and the second would contain a play by Pierre Gamarra. The third would contain texts from the USA, GDR, Czechoslovakia, and Yugoslavia. She still needed more articles from the Centers. Each Center must be responsible to send in at least one article a year. She also needed an assistant editor. Rodenberg suggested Christel Hoffmann (Theater der Freundschaft-GDR) and Eek suggested Jed Davis (University of Kansas-USA). Adamek asked for more information to be sent to the *Czech Bulletin* with three deadlines—30 June 1970, 31 October 1970, and 28 February 1971.

New Centers: The Bureau had felt that admission should be stricter. Each proposed Center should send in its Statutes first to the Paris Office for approval. Then the EXCOM could decide whether or not to admit the new Center. When asked if there were any new applications, Moudoués said: Portugal, Poland, Hungary, and Japan.

Exchange of Plays: Moudoués said that each Center should send a list of such plays to the Paris Center. That Center in turn would request a list of all foreign titles produced during one year in a particular country and will distribute that list. The entire EXCOM approved this concept. When asked if publishers should be included, the response was yes. Juul commented that Pugh had yet to distribute his bibliography of new plays. Djokič asked if the *Czech Bulletin* could list the bibliography, but was told that the list would be too long. Moudoués wanted the titles to be in two languages for comparison and understanding. Biotto suggested that each Center merely send their listing to all the other Centers.

Venice Congress: The dates 18-25 October 1970 were selected and approved. After considerable discussion two themes were selected with Biotto's approval: "The Psychological Development of the Child from 8 to 11" and "How Psychological Development is Reflected in the Plays of the Theatre".

New EXCOM meetings: Moudoués noted the need for meetings in 1971 and 1972. The Czech Center had extended an invitation to meet in Prague in May 1971, the GDR Center to meet in East Berlin in March 1972, and the British Center to meet in London in 1973. All three invitations were accepted.

1972 Congress: The US Center and the Canadian Center then presented their joint proposal for the International Congress to be held in North America in the spring of 1972. There would be two assemblies—one in Canada and one in the USA. Tyler moved that EXCOM accept the joint invitation and place it on the Agenda for approval by the entire Venice Congress. This was approved unanimously, and the meeting was adjourned. When not in meetings, there were plays and films that the delegates could attend.

(Left to right) Berislav Frkič, play director, and Zvjezdana Ladika, Director of Zagreb Children's Theatre, Member of the ASSITEJ EXCOM, and co-director of the Šibonek Festival. June 1984. Personal photo courtesy of John Tolch.

1970
EXECUTIVE COMMITTEE MEETING
Bucharest, Romania / 7-10 June 1970

The Executive Committee of ASSITEJ met in Bucharest, Romania on 7-10 June 1970. Konstantin Shakh-Azizov as President (USSR) presided, with Vladimir Adamek (Czechoslovakia) as 1ˢᵗ Vice-president, Ilse Rodenberg (GDR) as 3ʳᵈ Vice-President, Rose-Marie Moudoués (France) as Secretary-General, and Ian Cojar (Romania) as Treasurer.

Other members of the EXCOM attending were: José Géal (Belgium), Victor Georgiev (Bulgaria), Benito Biotto (Italy), Hans Snoek (Netherlands), and Lubiša Djokič (Yugoslavia).

Members absent: Joyce Doolittle (Canada), Hanswalter Gossmann (FGR), Gerald Tyler (Great Britain), Bjorn Endreson (Norway), and Nat Eek (USA).[78]

The 1ˢᵗ Executive Committee Meeting / 7 June

*M*Ion Brad, Deputy Minister of Culture of the Romanian Socialist Republic and other significant representatives of Romanian art and culture were present at the official inauguration.

Shakh-Azizov expressed his deep sympathy on behalf of the EXCOM to the Romanian representatives for the natural calamities their country had suffered. Romania had experienced disastrous floods that spring, which in turn had severely restricted travel to Romania. Then Moudoués made her Report, and Cojar gave the Treasurer's Report. [No copy was available in the Arizona Archives, nor was there any mention of it in the Minutes.]

The ensuing discussions covered the following points:

- The International Exhibition had toured many towns in France, and was installed at Šibenik, Yugoslavia for the month of June. In the autumn of 1970 it would be moved to Venice. Interested countries could apply to the Paris Office for the Exhibition.

- The Secretary-General asked all Centers to send on a regular basis as many documents as possible related to theatrical activities, particularly play texts, photographs, and programs of performances, plans for coming seasons, and dates when their various theatres were playing and when they were closed.
- The Secretary-General once again asked the Centers to continue their exchanges of information among each other.
- The latest issues of *The Review* had just been published, but as always more articles were needed from the National Centers along with reports of their national activities.
- *The Czech Bulletin* had continuing problems because Centers did not send their information and news items in on time.
- New Centers to be founded in the near future included: Argentina, Australia, Dahomey, Egypt, India, Ireland, Japan, Hungary, Poland, Portugal, Senegal, Switzerland, and Tunisia.
- An international colloquium of playwrights of children's plays would most probably take place in Bordeaux in the spring of 1971.

With M. Arcurio, the Italian attaché for culture in Romania present, the EXCOM took up the Report on the Venice Congress. The dates were 19-24 October 1970. The Bureau and the EXCOM will meet on 17-18 October. The introduction to the discussions would be given by Shakh-Azizov and Lucian.

Future meetings of the EXCOM were selected as follows: 1971—Czechoslovakia; 1972—GDR; 1973—Brussels; and 1974—Leningrad.

Reports: The EXCOM then received the following reports: from Georgiev—reported on their participation in a Festival that took place in Nuremberg, Germany; from Juul—renewed activities for children in Denmark and plans for an international documentation library on theatre art for children and young people; Ion Lucian—many activities taking place in Romania for children, as well as numerous other projects.

Performances: The delegates saw four performances at the Ion Creanga Theatre in Bucharest: *The Mill Wheel* by Gh. Scripca; *The Unfinished Story* by Alecu Popovici, directed by Ian Cojar; *At Full Sail!* by Dinu Bondi, directed by Ion Lucian; and *The Naughty Cockerel* written and directed by Ion Lucian. They also studied the activities of the national Centre for the Research of Youth Problems, visited the Palace of the Young Pioneers, saw a special program of Romanian films, and had a reception at the Theatre and Music Association.

Included in the Minutes were a variety of news items from various Centers. The Minutes concluded with a request for members to pay their dues on time, prepare their reports for the Paris Center, and signed off with the phrase *"Au revoir en Venice!* (Until we meet in Venice!)"[79]

ASSITEJ Treasurer Ian Cojar (Romania) at the Moscow, USSR EXCOM Meeting. March 1968. Courtesy of USSR ASSITEJ Center, Moscow, USSR, 1968.

1970
IIIrd INTERNATIONAL CONGRESS OF ASSITEJ
Venice, Italy / 19-24 October 1970

The IIIrd International Congress of ASSITEJ met in Venice, Italy on 19-24 October 1970. Konstantin Shakh-Azizov (USSR) presiding as President, Vladimir Adamek (Czechoslovakia) as 1st Vice-President, Nat Eek (USA) as 2nd Vice President, Ilse Rodenberg (GDR) as 3rd Vice-President, Rose-Marie Moudoués (France) as Secretary-General, Ian Cojar (Romania) as Treasurer, and Gerald Tyler (Great Britain) Honorary-President.

Other members of the EXCOM attending were: José Géal (Belgium), Victor Georgiev (Bulgaria), Joyce Doolittle (Canada), Hanswalter Gossmann (FGR), Caryl Jenner (Great Britain), Benito Biotto (Italy), and Hans Snoek (Netherlands). Co-opted Bjorn Endreson (Norway) and Ljubiša Djokič (Yugoslavia), and Inga Juul (Denmark) as Technical Advisor.

Members absent: none.

National Centers listed as present at that time were either (current): Belgium, Brazil, Bulgaria, Canada, Czechoslovakia, FGR, France, Great Britain, GDR, Israel, Italy, Netherlands, Norway, Romania, Spain, USA, USSR, and Yugoslavia or (*forming*) *Argentina*, *Austria*, *Australia*, *Dahomey*, *Egypt*, *Hungary*, *India*, *Ireland*, *Japan*, *Poland*, *Portugal*, *Switzerland*, *Tunisia*. This made a total of 18 active National Centers with 13 forming.[80] Twenty-three countries were listed as attending.

The Bureau Meeting-17 October
The Bureau met two days before the Congress officially started, and the EXCOM on 18 October, one day before.

The Bureau met at 4 pm in the Salla degli Specchio. The

following members were present: Shakh-Azizov presiding, Adamek, Eek, Moudoués, Lucian, Biotto, Tyler, and Lavagna. Lucian was present as Treasurer, and Biotto and Lavagna were present representing the host country.

The meeting primarily dealt with the details of the Congress. Biotto said there were many difficulties regarding materials arriving late for the Exposition. Program materials would be available as of Monday. Groups of the delegates would be arranged by language for the discussions. They decided to put the speeches of Shakh-Azizov and Lucian together on the Tuesday program, and then have two days of discussion. Moudoués raised the question of Spanish as a fourth language, and that it should be added to the Agenda.

Translation: Many of the Eastern delegates would have an "elbow" translator seated with them who would quietly provide immediate translation while the meeting went on. The delegate would reply in his or her own language, and then the translator would translate their reply into English. Other translators would then quietly translate the response into their language. However, many delegates were multilingual with English and French being the basic languages of choice. Simultaneous translation devices ultimately replaced this need, although some countries continued to bring their own translators, especially those with unusual languages.

Of all the translators Galina Kolosova (USSR) proved to be the most constant and reliable of the Russian to English translators. She functioned as secretary and translator for the Soviet Center of ASSITEJ from 1969, and attended many sessions of the EXCOM and Congresses from 1970 until 1996. In 1975 the Theatre Association of Russia (STD) designated her as the official Secretary of the Soviet ASSITEJ Center. (See Biography in Appendix B.)

Besides translating accurately and carefully, she was remarkably diplomatic in dealing with the various delegates, many times clarifying or smoothing over controversial discussions or political positions either at the time of the meeting or in private conversations later. However, she always properly deferred to the head of the Soviet delegation. Her background in and love of theatre were tremendous assets. No other translator stayed with the Association as long as she did.

The 1ˢᵗ EXCOM Meeting

The Executive Committee met at 10:30 am in the Salla degli Specchio, 3ʳᵈ Floor. Present were Shakh-Azizov, Adamek, Eek, Moudoués, Lucian, Rodenberg, Klaus Urban (GDR), Snoek, Juul, Géal, Biotto, Lavagna, Jenner, and Tyler. Absent were: Georgiev, Djokič, Enderson, Gossmann, and Doolittle.

The 1970 Venice Congress occurred two years after the Prague Spring of 1968, and the Soviet delegation and the Czechoslovakian delegation sat far apart and had little communication with each other. Ironically it was frequently announced in the General Assembly that ASSITEJ was a non-political association.

Shakh-Azizov welcomed the EXCOM to Venice after their two previous years of hard work. He expressed gratitude to Biotto and Lavagna for their preparation of the Congress.

Moudoués informed them of the decisions of the Bureau Meeting yesterday. There would only be 3 official delegates from each Center at the General Assembly. As to changes in the program: the first day would contain the Secretary-General's Report Morale, the President's Report, and a Report of the Future. The second day would feature speeches by both Shakh-Azizov and Lucian, followed by two separate groups for discussion. The third day would feature an open discussion. On Friday the groups would prepare a report to be delivered to the General Assembly at large. She then asked for a new program to be printed for the delegates showing the changes.

Financial Report: Cojar presented the Financial Report. Prior to this time dues were 75 USD. An increase was voted in with a dues range from 50 to 150 USD with the hope that the wealthier centers would pay the top amount. Cojar's Report listed the countries that had paid their dues and those that had not. Brazil had not paid for 3 years. Moudoués would discuss this with the delegate. She stated that the USA had paid all its dues on time, and had subscribed to 300 copies of *The Review*. But ASSITEJ still needed more money. Each year the French Center paid 13,400 French Francs in rent, 3,000 French Francs for a secretary, and 8,000 French Francs for *The Review*. There was a balance of 15,400 French Francs in the bank (3,150 USD) and after tomorrow it would be 23,889.32 French Francs (4,777.81 USD). The US Center asked Moudoués to send out an annual bill to each Center, to which she agreed.

It was decided at the previous EXCOM to publish a report for the Venice Congress on each Center's activities during these first five years of ASSITEJ. Moudoués stated she did not receive reports from all Centers; some sent them late; and some without the two language summaries. At the request of Biotto and Eek, it was decided to print what she had.

There followed a discussion of whether to print everything *in toto* in all three official languages. The costs were prohibitive. Maria Sunyer (Spain) requested in a letter that Spanish be added as a fourth language. The EXCOM voted against this.

The Elections: Moudoués opened the discussion on the upcoming elections: 13 countries could be elected to the EXCOM and two had been nominated, and the EXCOM could co-opt 2 more. All members could be re-elected, and candidates should have sent their nominations in three months in advance in written form. Only one nomination was received—Lucian of Romania. The current EXCOM must decide if they wished to nominate themselves; all others arrived too late.

After much discussion Tyler pointed out that only National Centers can be nominated. Lucian was then proposed as an Advisor along with the re-appointment of Juul. Also, it was understood that the current EXCOM was nominated. Enderson of Norway was excluded because of his lack of interest and attendance. The meeting was then adjourned.

1st General Assembly Session—19 October

On October 19 at 10:30 am the Mayor of Venice welcomed the delegates commenting that there were representatives from 24 countries and workers of the theatre of all types. Prof. Matrinke, Secretary-General of the Cini Foundation of Venice, stated that they were happy to support the ASSITEJ Congress, since they realized that children's theatre requires special techniques and understanding. He also remembered with pleasure their support of the meeting in Venice in 1964 which helped start the creation of ASSITEJ. Welcomes followed from Dr. Lopez (Institute General of Tourism), Prof. Agosina (Minister of Public Instruction), and Dr. Bianccini (Bureau of Tourism). Biotto responded with thanks.

The Congress was opened by President Shakh-Azizov by thanking those responsible for the Congress. He stated that the Italian Theatre historically was one of the most important in the world. Mr. Dorita brought greetings from the Biennale, which offered elements in theatre, and he felt such an exhibition continued to develop work for children by theatre and the arts.

Report Morale: Moudoués gave her Report Morale saying there were 19 National Centers and 12 correspondents. Progress seemed very slow. Reporting on the EXCOM Meetings, she said the Bureau met in Paris in the spring of 1969, but Shakh-Azizov was ill and could not attend. The EXCOM met in Šibenik, in June 1969, and in Romania in June 1970. During the past two years she had attended many artistic events, and had made many contacts. The Exhibition had not been a complete success. Some Centers did not send materials, some arrived in bad shape, some sent too much. She hoped to avoid such problems in the future. *The Review* needed more subscribers and more articles, and the *Czech Bulletin* requested more information on activities in the Centers. She also had not received all the 5-year Reports from the Centers. She gave a new deadline of November 15. Djokič added a welcome, said he had a book of their Children's Theatre activities for the delegates to see, and would be showing films of Šibenik. Then the meeting was adjourned.

2ⁿᵈ General Assembly Session—20 October

1ˢᵗ Vice-President Vladimir Adamek presided. After announcements Shakh-Azizov gave his opening speech. Its main points were: The modern child is ahead of the earlier child. He sees more of the contemporary world. Historic and biographical plays are of increased importance. Also, the child has great interest in science-fiction, but this is hard to portray in the theatre. Today's child is closer to his society. The growth of the musical and opera form of theatre for children is very significant.

Lucian gave the second speech on the actor's and director's role in children's theatre. He said: The actor cannot be forced to act for children. If he is, the child senses it and resents it. The role of the director is to win the actor over to the concepts of children's theatre. Contemporary theatre can use all types of techniques, but the actor must have direct contact with the child. He must go to the schools, talk with the children, etc. As the director has become more important, the group concept has lessened. The director has now become almost a co-author of the play.

The theatre must encourage the child to develop intellectually, and we must know that intellectual level so the theatre doesn't lose the child. Today's theatre requires active participation between the actor and the audience. When the child is required to use his imagination, he tends to participate actively. The actor receives new energy from this contact.

These two speeches were to be the springboards of the group discussions the next day. After they were concluded, Moudoués moved to the discussion of establishing a method for keeping the Association's documents. She said not only is the Paris Center receiving a great deal of material, but there is an increase in requests for materials from university students. She hoped that the Society of Author's Meeting in France in 1971 would consider the problem.

Financial Report: Cojar presented the Treasurer's Report. There was a balance of 3,500 French Francs, but there were no funds for new activities. The French Center continued to support ASSITEJ financially, so Cojar asked all Centers who have not paid to send in their dues as soon as possible.

In general discussion Tyler noted that Mme. Hans Snoek (Netherlands) had received the Award of Grand Dame of Society, a great honor, and that she was in charge of building a new theatre for children. Michael Pugh (Great Britain) announced that his 4th Bibliography of children's theatre plays was available, and asked for comments on its format. Adamek welcomed the delegates, calling the Congress a sentimental reunion because of the Preparatory Committee Meeting in Venuice in 1964. He also commented that while we have learned more of each other's activities, we must discuss how to develop more theatres for children, and get theatres in countries which have none. He also wished for more contact with young people, and recommended the conferences of actors.

3rd General Assembly—Discussion Session—21 October

This primarily dealt with the Reports of the discussion in the three study groups: No. 1 discussing Shakh-Azizov's paper; No. 2 discussing Lucian's paper; and No. 3 an open discussion.

Play Texts: Prior to these Reports M. Charpentier (France) spoke on behalf of the playwright. He said in the British Restoration the playwright appeared immediately after 18 years of suppression by the Cromwellians. There would always be playwrights, and chances now were very good for writers of children's plays, but they must be paid. A playwright can write under any conditions as long as he isn't restricted in his means of expression. His object is to conquer the heart and bring joy. The writer must be a poet and use magical language. The text must not be a secondary consideration. When characters talk without necessity, then we drive away the child audience. The writer is not a pedagogue. He must create a work of art that is on the level of the sensibility of the child. We have no reason or right to give children a nightmare view of the world.

In discussion Tyler commented that too many plays nowadays were computerized and mechanical. Doolittle urged that we go back and talk to the children some time after they have seen the play to see if their reactions are the same. Immediate impressions are usually surface. Sats stated that music is terribly important in theatre. There is a danger in mechanical reproduction; it should be live. Words and gesture are best when put on the wings of music. Tyler added that opera is the most expressive of all forms, and many children come to theatre through music. Biotto added that an author must write what children can understand and appreciate. Tyler closed the discussion by saying that there is no such thing as children's theatre, just theatre!

Discussion Session Reports: After a brief recess the Reports of the three discussion groups were presented. Sara Spencer (USA) reported on Group I [in synopsis] as follows:

> Children and adults live in the same world. Fairy tales show the hero achieving his goal without witchcraft but through courage and ability. Do we know children? They mature faster today. Is it possible to know their world? In England two TV shows which poked fun at parents were most popular with children, but they were condemned by Swedish critics as bad because they made parents appear ridiculous. However, it showed children how parents are human, and would help them grow up. We must show how a child can fight against evil. Teach him control. What children learn from each other is more important than anything else. Children's games can be an important source of dramatic inspiration.

> Theatre for children should be a field for critical research. A seminar should investigate these areas. We must write to express

ourselves, not just for children. As artists we will demand more of ourselves. Children's theatre must be entertainment; it must inspire them. Avoid mannerisms. Children today have a fast youth, but they are not communicative to adults. We must face this gap.

Artistic values of our modern plays do not live up to the classics. We must show the beauty of the world to children. We must show black and white, and must find ways to show the shades of grey. Some commonalities in plays for children were agreed upon: a central character, a single direct conflict. Children can identify with the villain. Let's not lose our sense of fun. The playwright must have a theatre to write for, but he must be paid for his labors. The writer is not a pedagogue, and must observe the rules of the stage; but he must be free to express himself his own way. The aim of the author is to create a work of art aimed at the sensibilities of children.

Ion Lucian (Romania) reported on Group II [in synopsis] as follows:

Fifteen countries participated. We discussed the role of the director in the theatre. Theatre must use all its techniques, and children should not perform in children's theatre. This leads to professional children [with the connotation of artificiality] in the theatre. If the director cannot find the proper actors, he should not do the play. Actors must communicate with their audience. Training must take place in the special techniques of acting for children. There is always the danger of a company becoming settled artistically, so it is desirable to bring in guest artists. Sometimes it is really the adults that come to the theatre, not the children.

We must find a common language and sense of procedure, so that children will accept this changed world. Besides it being a violent world, children should learn about their family problems through the theatre. There is no standard form in plays nowadays; there can only be artistry. We must give children meaningful images, which is also the mark of good literature.

The Report could not include everything in the discussion. They requested that the next Congress set up a group to discuss the language of the actor.

Hans Snoek (Netherlands) reported on Group III [in synopsis] as follows:

- We had a very active small group, and everyone took part. Nicholas Wandmacher (USA) and A. Koufoud (Netherlands) wrote the following recommendations: It is important to have major speeches in three languages immediately. Will the delegates bring their speeches in three languages with them for distribution?
- The EXCOM should compile a bibliography of books, theses, dissertations, etc. on Children's Theatre.
- ASSITEJ should create a large central archive. All National Centers should prepare and send their materials to it.
- All Centers should send bibliographic information to other Centers as well as the Paris Center.
- At the 1972 Congress we would like special information on special visual effects—sets, lighting, mime, etc. It would be desirable to have a workshop for participants in ASSITEJ, with them actively working in the creations.

The Bureau Meeting-21 October

At 1:30 pm the Bureau met to decide how to handle the election. Present were Shakh-Azizov, Tyler, Adamek, Eek, Moudoués, and Cojar. Moudoués proposed that the election move in the following stages:

1) The delegates of the Centers must elect the Executive Committee.
2) From that Committee they must elect the President and 3 Vice-Presidents.
3) There will be an interruption for the EXCOM to recommend a Secretary-General and a Treasurer to the delegates.
4) The EXCOM can give the names of co-opted persons and advisors (counselors).

The meeting was adjourned.

The EXCOM Meeting-22 October

On October 22 at 3:30 pm the EXCOM met to discuss the election process with recommendations from the Bureau.

Moudoués said "...after the EXCOM has nominated the Secretary-General and the Treasurer, their names will be presented to the delegates for their approval. We have 16 persons currently on the EXCOM—13 are elected and 2 are appointed (Secretary-General and the Treasurer). We have 19 Centers now, but only 17 are working. We can have all 17 on the EXCOM if we wish, since we can co-opt 2 members. We must decide two propositions: 1) the appointment of Lucian of Romania, and 2) the question of re-electing Juul as an advisor. Then the last thing we have to do is to elect the President and the two Vice-Presidents." The meeting was adjourned.

4th General Assembly Session-The Elections-23 October

With Shakh-Azizov presiding, the Bureau (Adamek, Eek, Moudoués, Cojar, and Tyler) sat on the rostrum.

Financial Report: Jenner (Great Britain) asked if there was a balance on hand? She said the Report was merely a statement of Income and Expenditure, not a Financial Report. The Constitution states there are to be two professional auditors appointed. Where is the statement of auditing? The Report is only in French. Shouldn't it be in the three official languages? Where are the Exhibition expenses?

Shakh-Azizov replied that these statements would be considered by the Secretary-General. Then he said if there are no objections, we will consider the Report accepted.

Bureau Election Recommendations: Shakh-Azizov continued by saying that yesterday the Bureau met and recommended continuing the appointment of Moudoués as Secretary-General and Cojar as Treasurer. He then appointed Natalia Sats (USSR), Sara Spencer (USA), and Flavio Bertello (Italy) as election tellers.

The Elections: Questions began coming thick and fast. Tyler asked since each Center can have three votes, must each Center vote the total number? Corey requested that there be answers to the Financial Report before the vote. Shakh-Azizov again said the Secretary-General will take it into consideration, and it should not be gone into at this time. Eek asked for the names of all centers that were eligible to vote. Moses Goldberg (USA) said there are a total of 47 votes which means that 24 are necessary to elect a Center. In explaining the voting process Moudoués stated that you could *vote* or *not vote* for any Center which led to considerable discussion. Eek commented that by *not voting*, only 6 Centers could end up with a majority vote!

The delegates then voted by paper ballot for *accepting* or *not accepting* Moudoués as Secretary-General and Cojar as Treasurer. Out of a possible 47 votes: Moudoués: For—35, Against—4. Cojar: For—39, Against—3. Both were re-elected, and the Centers of France and Romania took the first two places on the EXCOM.

Shakh-Azizov announced the voting for the EXCOM. Much discussion followed. Both Tyler and Moudoués read parts of the Constitution. The EXCOM could consist of up to 15 members, and there could be nominations from the floor. Spain and Israel were added to the ballot. Shakh-Azizov said that the delegates may vote for 13 Centers, since France and Romania were already elected. Paper ballots were cast and counted.

The result was announced by Sats with the top 13 being elected to the EXCOM as follows: USA—47; Italy—47; Canada—47; FGR—47; Great Britain—47; Netherlands—47; USSR—44; GDR—44; Yugoslavia—43; Czechoslovakia—43; Bulgaria—42 ½; Belgium—42; and Spain—26. Israel—19 and Lucien (Romania)—8 were not elected.

The Congress then recessed temporarily while the EXCOM met to consider the officers. Again much discussion in the EXCOM; then the Congress was re-convened. Moudoués explained the EXCOM decisions.

EXCOM recommended the same Bureau as last year-Shakh-Azizov, Adamek, Eek, and Rodenberg, with Moudoués and Cojar. Snoek nominated Eek for President; Eek nominated Adamek, Snoek, and Rodenberg as Vice-Presidents.

The results of the Presidential ballot: Shakh-Azizov—25; Eek—22.

The election was held for the Vice-Presidents. The Bureau had nominated Eek, Snoek, and Rodenberg. The US Center nominated Biotto, but he declined.

The results of the Vice-Presidential ballot: Eek—44; Adamek—41; Rodenberg—27; Snoek—20. The first three were elected, and became 1st, 2nd, and 3rd VP respectively.

1972 Congress: During the voting process Doolittle and Eek presented their proposals for the 1972 Congress to be held jointly in Canada and the USA. Following the presentations, the Congress voted to accept the joint Canada-USA invitation.

The Congress was adjourned, and there were no further meetings. The Italian program included an international festival of plays, which were presented concurrently with the Congress as part of their Bienale.

Island of San Giorgio Maggiore, Venice, Italy. Site of the IIIrd International Congress of ASSITEJ. October 1970. Personal photograph.

Cathedral of St. Mark, Venice Italy. October 1970. Personal photograph.

The Hare ensnared. "The Great Cross Country Race" by Alan Broadhurst. Everyman Players, directed by Orlin Corey, designed by Irene Corey. Photo courtesy of the US Center for ASSITEJ., 1977. Everyman Players performed "The Great Cross Country Race" and "The Book of Job" at the Venice Congress. [slide]

A SUMMARY OF 1968-1970

1968

*O*nly five months after The Hague Congress of 1968, the first meeting of the new EXCOM occurred in Sophia, Bulgaria in October. Tragically the world was a different place. Gone were the optimism and the concept of free exchange of information in ASSITEJ. The "Prague Spring" had shattered the sense of a world at peace. In addition, there was political turmoil in France along with bank scandals during the spring of 1968, and funds earmarked for the Treasury of ASSITEJ had disappeared.

Czechoslovakia Invasion: In August of 1968, two months before the EXCOM Meeting of ASSITEJ in Bulgaria, members of the Warsaw Pact Nations (USSR, GDR, Hungary, Poland, and Bulgaria) sent troops into Czechoslovakia to restore order in a situation and in a country that was becoming dangerously Westernized and liberal under the "Prague Spring" leadership of Alexander Dubcek. After securing the country, they deposed Dubcek in 1969. The new Czech leaders then agreed to restrain their liberal policies in return for gradual withdrawal of the occupational forces.

The Statutes of ASSITEJ state that the organization was non-political, but the events of the previous months, and the continued divisions between East and West completely affected the tenor of all discussions and decisions at the Sophia conference.

Sophia EXCOM: Those present for this EXCOM Meeting in Sophia were: Bulgaria (co-opted), Denmark (observer), France, GDR, Italy, Netherlands, Romania, USSR, Yugoslavia, a representative from Great Britain (an appointed representative), and the USA (an appointed representative), plus many guests. Absent were: Belgium, Canada, Czechoslovakia, FGR, and Scandinavia.

Eek, who could not attend, had appointed Orlin Corey to serve in his stead. Since the EXCOM had delegated the writing and the dissemination of the Minutes of the meetings to Eek, Corey as Eek's official representative took careful and concise Minutes. Corey wrote two sets of Minutes: one as they happened, and the other excluding the divisive and political discussions. Both were distributed to the Executive

Committee of the US Center for a decisive vote. The decision was to send the Minutes of events as they happened to the Centers, especially since all the delegates had personally experienced the divisiveness. It was the first time that such an open political dissension had been recorded in ASSITEJ.

At Sophia the first item of discussion was attendance. The East and West clearly sat themselves separately. Adamek had sent word that he could not attend "...because I am concerned night and day with events in Czechoslovakia." Tyler reported he could not attend, and had appointed Peter Mitchell in his stead. The British Drama League had sent a letter to ASSITEJ protesting the meeting in Bulgaria following the invasion of Czechoslovakia, and stated that they would not send a representative. A similar letter came from Norway, and Enderson was not in attendance. There was no mention of the FGR. Only eight out of the fifteen elected EXCOM members were in attendance.

President Shakh-Azizov stated that "...this association is free of every political restriction since its founding in 1965, and so I cannot understand these letters from London and Norway. The one matter of prime importance to us is our work with children, not such matters. We should write to know if they will still cooperate or will quit ASSITEJ." To which the Secretary-General replied "I do not believe it is the intention of the English to withdraw from ASSITEJ."

Corey proposed seating Juul as an "observer", but the Secretary-General protested saying that Denmark had no Center, and only Scandinavia (Norway) had a proper Center although communication was very sparse. After a later meeting with Juul, the Secretary-General reported that a center in Denmark could be easily established, and there was the possibility of a permanent theatre for Juul. The Committee voted unanimously to make Juul a Technical Advisor, an appointment that would assist her in seeking funding for a new theatre.

Venice Congress: The plans for the next Congress in Venice in 1970 were accepted with enthusiasm, and Šibenik, Yugoslavia in June 1969 was accepted as the location of the next EXCOM Meeting.

New Centers: Poland, Portugal, Hungary, and Egypt were in the process of organizing Centers. A group from Guatemala, Venezuela, and Nicaragua wanted to form a single Center, but they were not ready yet. Japan was also forming a Center soon.

ASSITEJ Exhibit: A possible ASSITEJ exhibit in Paris at the International Center for Youth was mentioned. Materials were to be sent to Paris by March 1969, Paris would pay the costs of the exhibit, but Centers would pay their own shipping costs. The creation and the ultimate fate of this exhibit were to be a major topic of conversation and concern in the following years. As a result of these many problems, never was another international exhibit contemplated.

Eight different productions, all from the Eastern countries, were seen by the delegates, and discussions followed many of them. The Secretary-General was instructed to send letters in response to the absences merely stating that ASSITEJ was a non-political association. There was a decided sense of relief when the meetings were over.

Despite the Soviet President's protests to the contrary, the events in Sophia were political. There was tension and disagreement, and while the world had condemned the Eastern bloc led by the Soviet Union in their occupation of Czechoslovakia, the world had done little about it. Fear of a major war was paramount in everyone's mind. While ASSITEJ came nowhere near to dissolving, its relationships were scarred, and the "peace and love" stance at the Šibenik conference to come in 1969 proved the need for a future healing process.

1969

Šibenik EXCOM: The EXCOM Meeting in Šibenik, Yugoslavia in June 1969 provided that necessary healing process. In his Report to his national constituency, Eek stated "While the Šibenik conference was not as theatrically exciting as previous ones, it was most successful politically. We had excellent representation from all countries, and deliberations were handled in a cordial manner. It helped reaffirm the faith that all of us have in ASSITEJ—that of an important organization working in a vital artistic area."

However in a spirit of peace, and perhaps cowardice, no one challenged anyone's presence at the meeting. The entire tone of this meeting was one of conciliation and friendship! One cynical delegate wondered if the Soviet President's personal absence was a result of his unwillingness to face Adamek, as well as other possible confrontations. The world had condemned the invasion of Czechoslovakia, but still had taken no physical action in retaliation. The great concern over a possible war still hovered!

All countries were represented. Adamek presided as 1ˢᵗ Vice-President, undoubtedly another olive branch. To solidify the peace-making process, the Secretary-General later commented "I started in Šibenik, by going to an island between the sky and the sea, and picked an olive branch (the symbol of peace among all peoples), and place it here on the table."

The EXCOM approved the holding of their next meeting in Romania with the date to be settled later, as well as changing the dates for the Venice Congress in 1970 to conform to the Biennale dates.

New Centers: Finally, Portugal, Poland, Hungary, and Japan had applied as new centers. They were all accepted. Over the years the Secretary-General had always presented the names of new potential Centers to the EXCOM for approval and forwarding to the General Assembly for final acceptance. To the best of Eek's knowledge during the time he was an officer, there was never a presentation or comparison of a new Center's Statutes by anyone other than the Secretary-General. The EXCOM and the General Assembly always accepted the recommendation of the Secretary-General, and she kept a careful balance of East and West in her recommendations.

"Ghost" Centers: Many times a Center was formed, or in process, and then formed again over a considerable period of time. Centers were announced that never appeared. This led to the concept of "ghost centers"—centers that had no existence except through a representative or two, who would periodically show up at the Congresses or EXCOM Meetings and would be welcomed with enthusiasm. In some cases the better corresponding and active "Ghost" Centers and their self-appointed representative would refuse to allow other active theatres in their country to belong. The representative's motivation seemed to be fear of a change in political loyalty or a personal loss of governmental financial support. This was the continuing problem in Denmark, Israel, Portugal, and much later in France. (See Appendix H.)

5-Year Reports: ASSITEJ had been in existence for five years, and with the up-coming Venice Congress in 1970, it was time for an organizational report. It was recommended that at the next meeting in Bucharest each Center should send in a four-page report on the growth and activities of their Center during the past five years. The reports would be printed in the *Review*. Each report should be in one of the official languages, and should have a ten-line précis so the Secretary-General could have it translated into the other two official languages.

Publications: Publications continued to be a thorn in the side of ASSITEJ. *The Review* was consistently behind on its publishing schedule, and did not always have information or plays of great importance, but it was the official publication of ASSITEJ and as such was properly honored. The *Czech Bulletin* thanks to Adamek's leadership was consistently on time, and contained all the information sent to him. Of course, he always asked for more reports as Moudoués asked for more articles.

There was the usual discussion about receiving new scripts. Michael Pugh (Great Britain) in 1964 had been the first to publish an international bibliography of plays for young audiences recommended by the various centers. However, its publication was irregular, and eventually it ceased to exist.

In 1984 ASSITEJ/USA decided to continue Pugh's work by publishing *Outstanding Plays for Young Audiences (An International Bibliography)*.[81] They asked each national Center to recommend 3 plays for young audiences which they thought would be of interest to producers in other countries. It was still in publication as of the 1990s.

Performance Rights: Most Centers wanted information and hopefully rights to produce new plays, especially foreign ones. However, translations and payment of royalties were hard to acquire. Even well-known authors had trouble collecting royalties from many countries, despite their belonging to the Stockholm convention. There was always the fear on the authors' and publishers' parts that once a script was made available, it could be pirated and produced with no acknowledgment and possibly under another name, much less a payment of royalties. The discussions over publications continued from Congress to Congress with very little progress. New plays were most successful when one theatre wrote another theatre, and together they negotiated the translation and the payment of royalties with each theatre being the negotiator between authors and publishers in their country.

In his written report on the Šibenik meeting for the *Children's Theatre Review*[82] Eek stated that:

> Djokič and [Zvjezdana] Ladika proved to be charming

and considerate hosts. It was a leisurely meeting set in a town placed on the side of a hill that spilled down into the turquoise blue Adriatic. The buildings were of native limestone and stucco, and   staggered along narrow winding streets. Life came to a halt at mid-day because of the heat, so boat rides and swimming became the recreation of choice.

The plays of the Festival in Šibenik were presented in an open air square bounded by a gothic cathedral, the city hall opposite, and four-storied apartments in between. The stage was a temporary wooden one, much like the ancient Roman stages, narrow in width and great in length. Lighting instruments were hung on battens attached to the façade of the cathedral. Wooden bleachers before the stage completed the theatre seating of about 600. During performances adults and many children lined the sides and spilled up the streets along the sides, while the apartment residents had first class seats from their windows.

This Festival was unique in comparison to others seen since it featured children as performers mixed in with adult actors. This made for an uneven quality in performance, and the outdoor stage eliminated any elaborate scenic techniques. Performances started at 9 pm with a blanket of stars for a roof. The programs included a TV-style variety show, a well-disciplined Zagreb children's choir, a *Tom Sawyer* true to the book, a puppet show, and a musical unfortunately rained-out. A midnight boat ride to a fishing village and a delicious fresh fish fry concluded the Festival and the EXCOM Meeting. Apparently the Secretary-General's olive branch was working, since the meetings had been leisurely and disagreements few.

While the Šibenik conference was not as theatrically exciting as previous ones, it was most successful politically. We had excellent representation from all countries, and deliberations were handled in a cordial manner. It helped reaffirm the faith that all of us have in ASSITEJ—that of an important organization working in a vital artistic area.[83]

In retrospect it is entirely possible that sharp questioning and more willingness to enter into controversy by the members of the EXCOM, including the author, would have moved the work of the Association forward faster.

1970

The EXCOM Meeting in Bucharest, Romania had to be postponed until June of 1970 because of the disastrous flooding that overtook much of the country.

General Discussion: The Secretary-General reported that the Exhibit had opened in Paris successfully, had toured many French cities, and was present in Šibenik for the month of June in 1969. New Centers to be founded in the near future included Argentina, Australia, Dahomey, Egypt, India, Ireland, Japan, Hungary, Poland, Portugal, Senegal, Switzerland, and Tunisia. This constant mention of new forming centers was an attempt by the Secretariat to satisfy the EXCOM's demand for new growth in the Association. Unfortunately these announcements were many times "smoke and mirrors".

Venice Congress: The Venice, Italy Congress came at a welcome time with marvelously warm late fall weather which made outdoor sitting for drinks, meals, and conversation a constant pleasure. St. Mark's Square provided an ever-present meeting ground both day and night. In many ways this Congress was a sentimental reunion since the Preparatory Committee had first met in Venice in September of 1964 to write their new constitution.

However, there was still a distinct coolness which led many of the most involved delegates to avoid anything other than polite conversation. The Soviet and Czechoslovakian delegations sat far apart and had little communication with each other. Ironically it was frequently announced in the General Assembly that ASSITEJ was a non-political association.

All the members of the EXCOM were present, and National Centers listed as being there for the Congress were Belgium, Brazil, Bulgaria, Canada, Czechoslovakia, FGR, France, Great Britain, GDR, Israel, Italy, Netherlands, Norway, Romania, Spain, USA, USSR, and Yugoslavia. Those countries present but still forming a center were listed as Argentina, Austria, Australia, Dahomey, Egypt, Hungary, India, Ireland, Japan, Poland, Portugal, Switzerland, and Tunisia. This made a total of 18 active National Centers with 13 forming.

The Elections: A major agenda item for discussion and resolution in the previous Bureau and EXCOM meetings had been the process of handling the elections. Assuming that the Eek Minutes are accurate, there were many contradictions in the directions, and the articles written by Ann Hill (USA)[84] bear up these contradictions. As the Association grew larger, things became more complicated, and the election details seemed to change with each Congress. Both the Bureau and the EXCOM failed to resolve the contradictions as expressed by the Secretary-General. Questions left unresolved were: Elect or approve the Secretary-General and the Treasurer *before* or *after* the EXCOM is elected? Are there to be two or three Vice-Presidents? How can an individual be nominated when only Centers can be elected? Where did the stated number of co-options and advisors come from? None of these questions were resolved by the EXCOM meetings. They had to be resolved on the floor of the Congress, which added to the tumult and confusion of the Venice elections.

In the elections the next day the delegates first voted approving Moudoués as Secretary-General and Cojar as Treasurer. These two countries were automatically seated, and the following 13 countries were elected to the EXCOM for the next two years: Belgium, Bulgaria, Canada, Czechoslovakia, FGR, GDR, Great Britain, Italy, Netherlands, Spain, USA, USSR, and Yugoslavia. The EXCOM recommended the same Bureau as previously-Shakh-Azizov, Adamek, Eek, and Rodenberg, with Moudoués and Cojar, and they were all elected by the General Assembly.

After the elections further dissatisfaction erupted over arbitrary decisions.[85] The President, probably in collaboration with the Secretary-General, had ruled that each Center would only have two or three official delegates, one for each vote of the Center. Also, only these few delegates could attend the official business meetings, and all other members of the national delegations were barred from attending. This was an arbitrary ruling, and is nowhere stated in the Constitution. Prior to this time entire delegations were seated for the Plenary Sessions. Later, the Congresses returned to seating all members of a national delegation together, but allowed only the two or three official delegates to receive the ballots and vote. This decision of having only three voting delegates was undoubtedly caused by the possible political concerns and fallout from the invasion of Czechoslovakia.

Performances: The Italian program included an international festival of plays which were presented concurrently with the Congress. A troupe from Nancy, France presented a play entitled *Harlequin Va-T'-En Guerre (Harlequin Goes to War)*. Pat Ruby of the Canadian delegation wrote:

> The play was a combination of bastardized commedia, Punch and Judy, and a 3 Stooges production. The sets were cutouts...colors of both scenery and costumes were primary. The plot line was that of two suitors for the same woman, a fat mama in commedia nose with a bratty kid with Shirley Temple curls. The actors shrieked their lines; there was no variety in vocal pitch or in pacing, which was continually frenetic....The children in the audience seemed to enjoy it, but they were extremely rambunctious, perhaps taking their cue from the performance itself. The first act lasted an hour and a half.[86]

After seeing the remarkable production of *Doqtor Faust* from Ostrava, Czechoslovakia, American delegate Moses Goldberg commented:

> ... [It] included numerous symbols of death: death masks, scythes, hanging ropes. Folk dances and songs were incorporated in the action, and the simplicity of the peasant folk was one of the most outstanding qualities of the production. Mephistopheles had an impish female servant who served as his liaison, and who slipped in and out of the action. During the death fight between Faust and Marguerite's ex-suitor, the servant moved between the combatants and took the blows of the fight. Death was indicated by draping black veils over the various dead. At the conclusion, small [actual] children dressed in white appeared, and the impact of hope and innocence was moving. The production was poetically conceived and carefully performed.[87]

Ruby wrote further that Biotto's company from Milan performed a play entitled *The Voyage of the Clowns*. Two stylized periaktoi revolved indicating scene changes. The play was episodic, including scenes in the jungle, on the seas, under the sea, Hawaii, Egypt, etc. The plot consisted of a search for stories, rather an elusive subject for a quest when one does not speak Italian, but it reinforced Italy's feeling about theatre for children. During the Assembly there were discussions about the relevance today of fairy tales, and the Italians favored this type of play.

Eek noted that The Everyman Players of Pineville, Kentucky, USA presented two plays: *The Great Cross-Country Race* by Alan Broadhurst, and *The Book of Job* adapted from the Bible by its director and producer Orlin Corey. Under deft direction the comic highlight of the tale of the tortoise and the hare occurred when the Grandmother appeared to hang her laundry, trapping the hare and hanging him by his ears on the clothesline. Unfortunately the child audience was very restless and bored during *The Book of Job* since the mosaic-appearing stylization of the production and the language were too sophisticated for a child audience.

Ruby[88] commented further that having an Italian child audience gave a healthy perspective to the Congress. The children were most attentive to performances in their own language. However, each foreign performance was preceded by a plot summary in Italian. The greatest challenge to companies invited to perform at ASSITEJ Congresses is the question of language, and a visiting theatre company would be wise to take its audience into consideration when selecting a play from its repertory. For example, at this Congress a Polish puppet theatre troupe wisely presented its play in Italian, specifically memorized for this performance.

1972 Congress: For several years according to Eek the US Center had sensed that ASSITEJ wanted to receive an invitation from the USA to have an international meeting there. With a growing sense of world peace and the growth in the prestige and power of the USA, there was an increased desire to visit this emerging political power. Also, there was a constant desire of the Eastern delegates to visit the Western countries officially, a visit that allowed them to escape the travel restraints in many of their homelands while being provided financial assistance from their governments.

At the Congress in The Hague in 1968 Joyce Doolittle (Canada) and Patricia Snyder (USA) met for the first time, and it was serendipity that both were enthusiastic about ASSITEJ. When Ann Hill (USA) suggested to Doolittle that Canada might co-host the 1972 Congress,

Doolittle agreed to investigate the possibility, and the three ended up working together in planning the joint Congress of 1972.[89]

The major impression held by all the USA delegates of the first three Congresses was of the high artistic quality of the productions from the various European countries, productions featuring well trained adult actors, imaginative directing and design, and which were totally professional in every aspect. At the same time the US Center felt that they would like to show ASSITEJ what the children's theatre in the USA was doing, since up to now everything had been centered on the European children's theatre.

At the meeting of the US Center for ASSITEJ in 1968 at Santa Barbara, California, during the discussion about the possibility of the USA hosting a World Congress, Patricia Snyder of the State University of New York at Albany presented a letter from Dr. Paul Pettit, Chair of their Department of Theatre, inviting the US Center to hold the 1972 International Congress on their campus.

The committee burst into laughter, and Snyder was quite upset that the US Center was treating this generous invitation in such a cavalier fashion. It was immediately explained to her that the laughter was a result of immense relief that the Center had a bona fide and generous sponsor. By a unanimous vote the remarkable invitation from the State University of New York at Albany was accepted.

One year later in Šibenik in 1969 the US Center and the Canadian Center presented for the first time their joint proposal for the International Congress to be held in North America in the spring of 1972. There would be two assemblies—one in Canada and one in the USA. The EXCOM accepted the joint invitation and placed it on the Agenda for approval by the next Congress. In 1970 at the Venice General Assembly the invitation was accepted officially.

But all was not sweetness and light! In a final speech at the Venice Congress Eek stated that the US Center was disturbed by the political overtones that ASSITEJ had taken on, especially since this was in violation of the Constitution. He also mentioned that the US Center was concerned about the lack of progress in setting up new Centers, and the lack of growth in membership.

Finally, he said that the US Center would retain the right to withdraw the 1972 invitation if the management of ASSITEJ did not improve. While these were valid concerns, neither the USA nor Canadian Centers were about to withdraw their invitations once the process of holding a Congress was started. However, ASSITEJ for a while seemed to be better organized, more open, and more responsive after this admonition.

Hotel Metropole, Moscow, USSR. March 1968. Where the USA and Congress delegations were housed. Personal Photograph.

1971
BUREAU MEETING
Paris, France / 3 May 1971

The Bureau of ASSITEJ met in Paris, France on 3 May 1971 according to copies of the correspondence from Moudoués.[90] There are no Minutes in the Arizona State University archives to indicate who attended and what business transpired. This meeting was held in conjunction with an International Colloquium of Writers in Bordeaux, France on 5-8 May 1971. Considering proximity and ease of transportation it is probable that Moudoués, Adamek, Rodenberg, and Lucien met at this time.

The Colloquium Program indicates that it was organized by the French Center (ATEJ) and its Theme was "The Playwright and the Theatre for Children and Young People." The discussions were divided into three parts: 1) the role of the playwright; 2) themes in the theatre for children and young people; and 3) methods of artistic expression of the playwright. The program flyer indicates that this was one of many projects of the French National Center in its role to further the promotion of theatre for children and young people.

On 19 May 1971 Moudoués replied to a letter sent to her by Eek listing some of the plans for the 1972 Congress. In his report to the US Center's EXCOM he translates her letter, gives a suggested reply, and comments that he is not sure if anyone attended the Bureau Meeting, especially considering Rodenberg's continuing visa problems in Western countries. Moudoués suggested that her response was that of the Bureau, and her questions were valid and deserved a response.

- Moudoués felt the SHOW AND TELL part of the program was too complicated and unrealizable, but the US Center had already received 6-7 acceptances. It was left in place.
- The theme sent to them was "Creativity with Children and Youth". Moudoués felt it was too ambiguous, but Eek remembering the wrangling over themes in the past recommended it stay as is, but the theme for individual sessions could be changed in the future Bratislava-Prague Meeting.

- Moudoués felt that the food and lodging expenses for the delegates should be provided, because of the high costs of the travel to North America. Eek said if the US Center wished to go this way, they would have to limit the number of officially supported delegates. At its meetings, the ITI in New York City always limited representation to two delegates per country. Eek continued that if all the delegates were to be supported much more money would have to be raised to support this request.
- Good translators and a simultaneous translation system should be provided, she was assured accordingly.
- The US Center would do everything possible to get visas for delegates with political problems such as those from the Eastern bloc, Rodenberg in particular.
- Eek confirmed the dates of the EXCOM in Bratislava-Prague 17-23 October 1971, and Berlin-Leipzig-Dresden 4-11 March 1972.
- Moudoués' suggestion of statute modification is unclear, but both Tyler and Eek felt that some changes were needed, and these would be proposed at the 1972 Congress.

Entrance to the State University of New York's Performing Arts Center. Photo by Edward Wozniak. Photo courtesy of SUNY Dept. of Theatre, Albany, New York. June 1972.

1971
EXECUTIVE COMMITTEE MEETING
Bratislava, Czechoslovakia / 17-18 October 1971
Prague, Czechoslovakia / 20-22 October 1971

The Executive Committee of ASSITEJ met in Bratislava and Prague, Czechoslovakia from 17-22 October 1971. Konstantin Shakh-Azizov as President (USSR) presided, with Nat Eek (USA) as 1st Vice President, Vladimir Adamek (Czechoslovakia) as 2nd Vice President, Ilse Rodenberg (GDR) as 3rd Vice President, Rose-Marie Moudoués (France) as Secretary-General, and Ion Lucian (Romania) acting as Treasurer for Cojar (Romania).[91]

Other members attending were: José Géal (Belgium), Victor Georgiev (Bulgaria), Joyce Doolittle (Canada), Hanswalter Gossmann (FGR), Benito Biotto (Italy), Hans Snoek (Netherlands), Maria Sunyer (Spain), and Ljubiša Djokič (Yugoslavia).

Members absent: Gerald Tyler and Caryl Jenner (Great Britain), and co-opted Orna Porat (Israel) all of whom sent their regrets.

The Bureau Meeting-Bratislava-Sunday, 17 October

The Bureau met at 9:30 am to set the EXCOM agenda. Present were Shakh-Azizov as President presiding, Eek, Adamek, Rodenberg, Moudoués, and Lucian.

The EXCOM then met with Shakh-Azizov as President presiding.

Shakh-Azizov opened the meeting thanking all for coming, and hoping they could resolve the questions about which Moudoués had written him. Moudoués then informed them that her Report Morale of the Venice Congress would be given at 3 pm Monday.

Meeting Dates: Lucian presented the Financial Report for Cojar which was approved. Géal sent an invitation for the next Congress to be held in Brussels, Belgium in 1974 around the Easter holidays in April. Shakh-Azizov said approval cannot be given until the 1972 Congress, but the EXCOM can approve since they consist of 15 out of 19 Centers. He continued that he had received a letter from Tyler inviting the EXCOM to meet in Great Britain in 1973. For the moment he listed the following meetings:

IVth Congress—14-25 June 1972—Canada and USA
EXCOM Meeting—4-11 March 1972—GDR
EXCOM Meeting—1st Part in 1973—London
EXCOM Meeting—2nd Part in 1973—Leningrad

Moudoués then announced that Bordeaux had decided to hold their playwriting colloquium on an annual basis, and recommended that the Bureau meet at that time in October 1972. Adamek announced their Actors Assembly would meet in Czechoslovakia in June of 1973 or 1974, hoping to invite people from 30 different countries. Shakh-Azizov asked for the status of the Irish Center, and Moudoués replied that there was nothing new. However, she said that Portugal was formed as well as Switzerland for the EXCOM to approve. Also, a Mme Tomascetti was here from Australia, and Shakh-Azizov said they would hear her. Moudoués was in contact with someone in Peru, and perhaps there will be a Center there to approve by the IVth Congress in North America.

Lucian explained an experimental study in Romania utilizing Shakespeare's *Romeo and Juliet,* where students would write it up using their contemporary classmates. He suggested that this might be an interesting ASSITEJ project. Eek asked if the Centers had received a billing for dues, and Moudoués replied that billings were mailed in March, and then a follow-up letter if the dues were not received. Shakh-Azizov asked Rodenberg about Hungary. She replied that she had been there twice but that they felt their ITI Center was sufficient. Shakh-Azizov commented that his Center had received word that Mrs. Margarite Duka had formed a Center in Budapest. Rodenberg added that they had pushed Egypt, but they have not joined. Shakh-Azizov stated that the organization must grow. ASSITEJ had been formed for five years, but still did not grow. Moudoués said a USA letter asked for names of playwrights for children, and she wanted to know to whom she should write. The request was tabled.

Snoek said EXCOM should discuss the avant-garde in children's theatre, and Moudoués responded that this could be a theme for a conference. Sunyer asked if it would be possible to have a Congress in Spain in 1974? Or perhaps an EXCOM Meeting in the fall of 1974? It was noted.

Auditors: Moudoués then read a letter from Caryl Jenner (Great Britain) again requesting an audit of the ASSITEJ finances. This was discussed in Venice, but no auditors were appointed. Moudoués replied that France now had two auditors, and they were serving without expense. They also handled the expenses of the Ministry. Cojar worked with the two of them to check expenses.

Keeping of Minutes: Eek was appointed as the keeper of the Minutes. He asked that the appointment be made official, and that he would distribute them to the individual Centers. This was approved.

The Agenda for the EXCOM Meeting was settled as follows:
1. Report Morale of the Secretary-General
2. Financial Report
3. Report of the IVth Congress – Doolittle and Eek
4. Reports of Projects – next meetings – Moudoués
5. Reports of the Spanish and French Centers
6. Approval of Portugal and Ireland as new Centers
7. Report of Lucian
8. Report of Australia
9. Report of Czechoslovakia
10. Question of Constitutional Statutes

Statute Changes: These changes should be sent to the Secretary-General, and would be accepted for discussion on the Berlin Agenda. Snoek's question on the avant-garde theatre was tabled until the Berlin meeting. Shakh-Azizov commented that he would ask for any other items for the Agenda at the beginning of the next meeting. This meeting was then adjourned.

The EXCOM Meeting—Bratislava—Monday, 18 October

The EXCOM met at 3:00 pm. Members of the EXCOM attending were: **Géal, Georgiev, Doolittle, Adamek, Gossmann, Moudoués, Biotto, Rodenberg, Snoek, Lucian, Sunyer, Eek, Shakh-Azizov, and Djokič. Shirley Harbin (USA) as an invited guest.**

Shakh-Azizov welcomed the delegates, announced the absences, and stated the Agenda:
1. Report Morale—Secretary-General
2. Financial Report—Lucian

3. Canadian presentation
4. USA presentation
5. Next sessions of EXCOM—Moudoués
6. Lucian proposal for experimental study
7. Short report on Spanish Center—Sunyer
8. Short report on French Center—Moudoués
9. Short report on Australia—Tomascetti
10. Discussion of new Centers—Portugal and Ireland—Moudoués
11. Activity of Czechoslovakia Center—Adamek
12. Other business

In her short Report Morale Moudoués mentioned the June Bureau Meeting.

International Relations: Moudoués noted that more people from other countries were visiting the Paris office for contacts and information. Most of them were from the USA. They are usually writers, people who wanted to know what was going on in European theatre, and students who wanted to get information directly from foreign theatre workers.

She announced there was a new venture in Bordeaux. As a result of the success of the Playwright's Seminar in June with attendance from many National Centers, their Committee had arranged to make it an annual event in order to codify the bases of theater and technology. A professor there would create a class on international children's theatre, and a center for international information on children's theatre, and the language area would help in multi-language publication.

New Centers: Moudoués reported that three new Centers were asking to be approved. Poland's application was complete and in order; Ireland had not sent in their statutes; and Hungary had no statutes yet to send in. They were accepted provisionally, with full approval once the omissions were corrected and dues were paid.

Publications: Moudoués said that the first issue of the *1971 Review* had been mailed and Nos. 3 and 4 were in publication. Next year they would need many articles on adolescence in the theatre. These could be published as a special issue, and she would need material for three issues. She would work with the Bordeaux Center, but she had no articles for the third and fourth issues. She could possibly publish 1 or 2 plays.

Statutes: Moudoués said the Bureau stated it was time after five years of existence to look at the Constitution. Nothing could be changed until the next Congress. Requests for amendments must be received by the Secretary-General three months ahead of time. Then the EXCOM can discuss them at their next meeting. If she sends the notice for the next Congress six months ahead of time, she can include any suggested amendments. She would also need the nominations for Centers and for the new officers. This concluded her Report Morale.

The Financial Report was given by Lucian, replacing Cojar. Everyone had received a hand-out of the Report. Lucian said Expenditures included costs of translation, office rental, postage and mailing, costs of travel of the Secretary-General, and shipping costs of the Exposition. Income was listed, and there was a current deficit of 622.02 French Francs. The Report was as of 30 September 1971. The list of payments was handed out. Lucian recommended that non-paying Centers should not vote. Shakh-Azizov said that the Secretary-General would notify those Centers accordingly, but they could wait a little longer.

Sunyer asked about Israel's non-payment of dues, and Moudoués replied that the current political situation made payment impossible at this time, but Porat had assured her that payment would be made in 1972. She then added that the French Government would pay the rent and the cost of publications for 1972, so ASSITEJ was assured of financial support for the next year. This ended the Report and its discussion.

1972 Canada Congress Report: Doolittle then made the Canadian Report on the IVth Congress of ASSITEJ. They planned to have performances from 8 companies. Of the four Canadian companies, two would be French Canadian and two English. The exact companies were to be chosen by two judges. Each day would be divided into six sessions, a mixture of meetings and performances. At noon there would be films from the Canadian National Film Board and lunch. From 2-5 pm there would be performances each day. From 4-6 pm would be special time for special things—workshops, video tapes, puppets, street theatre. This had been a suggestion from the Venice Congress. There would be a dinner hosted by the Mayor of Montreal on the first day. There would be performances on the other evenings.

On Sunday 18 June the delegates would take buses to Albany, New York. A Registration Fee of 65 USD would have to be paid which included registration, room and breakfast, and bus transportation. Everyone would have to make their own flight arrangements to Montreal. Canada hoped to invite companies to perform at the Ottawa National Center after the Kennedy Center in the USA.

1972 USA Congress Report: Eek presented the US Report on the IVth Congress of ASSITEJ. Session 2 will be on the campus of the State University of New York in Albany, New York on 18-25 June 1972. The program was outlined to include: 4 foreign productions, 5 USA productions, critiques of each production, discussions of children's theatre, creative drama demonstrations, and films. Shirley Harbin (USA) discussed international video and film presentations with the delegates. Eek concluded by mentioning a three-day meeting in New York City was being scheduled for the foreign delegates, which would feature sightseeing, plays, and tours.

The Bratislava meeting was closed by Mr. Stanislav on behalf of the Slovakian Theatre thanking the delegates for having their meeting there. The previous day had been the 50th Anniversary of the Slovakian Theatre and the 25th Anniversary of their children's theatre. Their socialist theatre had the responsibility of finding every means possible to make life easier. Shakh-Azizov then adjourned the meeting to reconvene in Prague.

The Bureau Meeting—Prague-20 October

The following special meeting of the Bureau was held in Prague on Wednesday 20 October at 10:00 am. Present were Shakh-Azizov, Eek, Adamek, and Moudoués.

Shakh-Azizov stated that since some of the delegates had to leave early, it was suggested that the final meeting be held that night, with the closing session the next day eliminating Saturday as a conference day. The Agenda would have to cover the Canadian and USA proposals on the 1972 Congress, Rodenberg's information on the Berlin EXCOM, and the admittance of 3 new Centers. Shakh-Azizov then read a telegram from the Hungarian National Center giving salutations and regrets for not attending the Prague meeting because of a heavy work load, but asking that they be admitted as a National Center. It was signed Suzanne Gal, Secretary.

1972 Congress: The Bureau then turned to a discussion of the IVth Congress. What was the theme? The discussion centered on the words "the creative process of children". Moudoués said it must not include child performers. Understandably Moudoués' prejudice was based on her aversion to the child performer companies in France which were apparently very poor in performance, and appropriately shunned by the professionals. Shakh-Azizov added that he did not disapprove of children playing for children, but they did not have professional standards. Lucian hated to see professional companies replaced by children's companies, so he recommended enlarging the program. The number and length of the plenary sessions was discussed, and the need for a Bureau meeting in advance. They recommended adding an extra plenary session.

Also, the elections would take two sessions: one to elect the EXCOM and one to elect the officers. Moudoués proposed for the Congress to elect the EXCOM, then a short meeting of the EXCOM to select a slate of officers, then the election of officers, then a meeting of the new EXCOM, and a "long" meeting of the new Bureau. Shakh-Azizov said he wished to have the greatest number of delegates speak as possible, so they agreed to talk only on international issues, and would ask each Center to submit their report of activities as a paper, not a verbal report. This led to a discussion about translations of the National Center Reports. Moudoués asked for a discussion about some financial help. Shakh-Azizov said his Center would help, and all agreed that extra money would need to be raised for the translation and printing of the 5-year reports of the Centers.

Exhibition: Tyler had written to Moudoués that the ASSITEJ Exhibition arrived in poor condition in Great Britain and could not be used. Moudoués said it was well packed in France. It was then sent to Šibenik, but arrived in Italy from Šibenik, in a poor state according to Biotto and Lavagna. Tyler proposed returning the Exhibition to France and letting the Secretary-General return the materials. Many problems were cited: costs of shipping, unknown addresses and materials, etc. Shakh-Azizov said if it had lost value, don't send it back but keep it in Great Britain. Lucian said he would write Tyler that in Šibenik there was only one photo and models were lost. Shakh-Azizov said to put it on the EXCOM Agenda, and Eek commented since the EXCOM approved it, it could also decide its fate.

Eek then returned to the 1972 Congress and asked if they wanted the theme changed? Shakh-Azizov suggested "Creative Activity with Children and Young People and the Role of the Children's Theatre in This Process." Rodenberg commented that the aim of ASSITEJ was to foster professional theatres throughout the world, so the theme should emphasize "professional". Moudoués said the new title is good, and everyone agreed. Over the years when there was consensus in the EXCOM meetings, the French word "D'accord" was used for agreement, so the EXCOM could move on to the next item.

Shakh-Azizov closed the discussion by saying that tomorrow they would discuss the admission of the three new centers, discuss the IVth Congress, and then hear the Rodenberg and Lucian proposals. Adamek said in as much as they had a written program of the IVth Congress, there was no need for further discussion. Lucian gave the times of the next day's program, and the meeting was adjourned.

The EXCOM Meeting—Prague-21 October

The EXCOM met the next day 21 October at 11 am in a small office, so Shakh-Azizov said the meeting must be "quick".

New Centers: Moudoués said there were three Centers to be approved. Portugal had sent in their statutes and they were in agreement with the Constitution. Ireland had had a change in secretary and they had not sent in their statutes, but they considered their dues paid and they might still attend. Hungary had no statutes yet, but she believed they were able to be accepted. Shakh-Azizov called for a vote. Eek moved to accept them provisionally. Shakh-Azizov said they could not vote, and then suggested asking these Centers to send in their statutes and dues, and the next day they would be full members.

The 1972 Elections: Moudoués returned to the IVth Congress saying she must send out the information. Because of the problems of delegates and voting privileges, all information about ASSITEJ business must come from the Paris office. She would send a nominating form to the Centers to nominate members of the future EXCOM. This meant that each Center must nominate itself. Article 9, No. 3 of the Constitution was not clear, but this would have to be clarified at the March meeting.

Eek said that his Center wished to be able to nominate other Centers as a courtesy to them, and Moudoués countered that nomination was a legal question, not a sentimental one. And then she added that in all elections one should receive the approval of the nominee before he is nominated. In the active discussion that followed Adamek pointed out two problems for ASSITEJ: who will be nominated and whom we would like to see nominated. Shakh-Azizov suggested a compromise—each Center could nominate itself, and then add names of other Centers at the bottom of the ballot. This ended the discussion.

Australian Center: Mme. Maria Tomasetti of Australia addressed the EXCOM, and gave her report on the possible establishment of an Australian Center. She and her husband Anthony Roberts represented the South Australian Theatre Company. She cited their professional company, the foreign tours, and a list of some of their productions as evidence of their satisfying the ASSITEJ statutes. She submitted their membership, and requested to be accepted as a Center. Moudoués thanked her for the report, but asked her to get in touch with Mme. Raynor in Australia in order to establish a Center. Shakh-Azizov said he hoped they would soon become a Center.

New EXCOM Meetings: They next turned to Rodenberg's proposed EXCOM meeting in Berlin-Leipzig-Dresden. The discussion indicated that the proposed time frame went on too long, and should be shortened to three days. Sunyer wanted another meeting added. By a show of hands all indicated that they planned to attend. The Berlin date was set at March 3; the IVth Congress in June; the Bordeaux EXCOM and Bureau Meetings in October. They also set the London EXCOM—1st half—in 1972, date and time to be set; and the Leningrad EXCOM—2nd half—in 1972, date and time to be set following the London meeting. They also agreed to have the Vth Congress in Brussels, Belgium based on an invitation from José Géal indicating that it was the 20th Anniversary of the Belgian Children's Theatre. They also approved having an EXCOM meeting in Spain in the fall of 1974.

Karel Richter (Czechoslovakia) spoke of an Actor's Conference being scheduled in Czechoslovakia in June of 1973, and asked for advice and names and addresses of possible delegates. More information was to followSunyer commented that originally they wanted the EXCOM in Spain in 1973, but would reschedule hoping that at that time she would not be told that there were other invitations. The Paris office was obviously picking and choosing on its own, but Moudoués replied that the other invitations came in before that of Spain, and Šibenik had priority. Sunyer asked then if 1974 was a firm commitment, and Shakh-Azizov replied that the new EXCOM would vote on her proposal, and that the Congress would vote on the dates and places approved by the EXCOM. When Biotto asked if the dates of the London EXCOM could be in the summer, a good time to get away, Shakh-Azizov said they had already approved that date.

Lucian then proposed an opinion poll to find out the imaginative qualities of young people, their degree of perception of their environment, and their ability to express their aspirations through the theatre. Using Shakespeare's *Romeo and Juliet,* he would ask young people to write a play using that theme but with complete freedom to imagine the elements. The aim would be to create a play that would represent the viewpoint of young people at Shakespeare's time. The work would then be analyzed by experts. Utilizing the same concept with children, he would have them write shorter pieces. He promised to share the results.

Doolitle asked if they were to meet tomorrow, and Shakh-Azizov said there are three points on the Agenda—reports of the French, Spanish, and Czechoslovakian Centers, followed by miscellaneous discussion. This will be the last meeting. Before Biotto left Shakh-Azizov thanked him for the Venice Congress and gave best wishes for a safe return.

The EXCOM Meeting / Prague / 22 October
The final meeting of the EXCOM was held on 22 October at 11:30 am. There were complete presentations and discussions of the French Center (Moudoués), the Spanish Center (Sunyer), and the Czechoslovakian Center (Adamek).[92]

A critique of some of the plays seen while in Bratislava and Prague ensued. Shakh-Azizov commented that he liked the USA idea of having critiques after each play seen. Moudoués then returned to the question of what to do with the Exhibition. After much discussion Eek moved to disband it. Again more discussion, and it was decided to send Moudoués to London to evaluate the problem.

The session concluded with reports of various national publications, and then Shakh-Azizov thanked all concerned for the conference and Eek for recording the minutes. He stated that at the next

Berlin EXCOM meeting the Centers of GDR, Netherlands, and Yugoslavia would give their reports. Wishing all Centers great success in the future, Shakh-Azizov adjourned the meeting.

EXCOM Meeting, Bratislava, Czechoslovakia. October 1971. Identified delegates attending (left to right, top row): Milka Natcheva (Bulgaria), Konstantin Shakh-Azizov (USSR), Joyce Doolittle (Canada), Victor Georgiev, partially hidden (Bulgaria), Ljubiša Djokič (Yugoslavia), Ion Lucien (Romania), Inga Juul (Denmark), Nat Eek (USA), Klaus Urban, with bottle in hand (GDR), Vladimir Adamek, right of waitress in white apron (Czechoslovakia); (bottom row): Rose-Marie Moudoués (France), Hans Snoek (Netherlands), Galina Kolosova (USSR), Maria Sunyer (Spain), and Ilse Rodenberg (GDR); Hans Dieter-Schmidt, lying down (GDR). Personal photograph courtesy of Karol Richter, Czechoslovakian Center for ASSITEJ, 1972

EXECUTIVE COMMITTEE MEETING
Berlin and Leipzig,GDR / 4-8 March 1972

The Executive Committee of ASSITEJ met in Berlin, Leipzig, and Dresden, GDR from 4-11 March 1972. Konstantin Shakh-Azizov as President (USSR) presided, with Nat Eek (USA) as 1st Vice President, Vladimir Adamek (Czechoslovakia) as 2nd Vice President, Ilse Rodenberg (GDR) as 3rd Vice President, Rose-Marie Moudoués (France) as Secretary-General, and Ian Cojar (Romania) as Treasurer.

Other members of the EXCOM attending were: Victor Georgiev (Bulgaria), Joyce Doolittle (Canada), Hanswalter Gossmann (FGR), Gerald Tyler, Caryl Jenner (Great Britain), Benito Biotto (Italy), Hans Snoek (Netherlands), Ion Lucian (Romania), Maria Sunyer (Spain), and Ljubiša Djokič (Yugoslavia). Inga Juul (Denmark) and Orna Porat were present as Advisors.[93]

Members absent: José Géal (Belgium).

The EXCOM Meeting / Berlin / 4 March

The meeting began at 4:00 pm on Saturday 4 March. Shakh-Azizov welcomed the members and expressed appreciation to Rodenberg for her hospitality. Because Doolittle and Eek had to leave the GDR early, they requested two sessions on Monday to clear up any questions about the IVth Congress.

Moudoués listed the following items for the Agenda:

1. The General Meeting
2. Membership Fees and Financial Report
3. Publication of *The Review* and *The Czech Bulletin*
4. Report from the Netherlands
5. Report from Yugoslavia
6. Report from GDR
7. Miscellaneous questions
   a. The forming of new Centers
   b. The creation of the Bordeaux Center for Creative Arts
   c. The creation of a children's theatre among the nations

Publications: The objectives of *The Review*. Moudoués suggested that *The Review* should present theories and opinions, as well as providing information. At least two articles could come from the North American Congress. Tyler said that *The Czech Bulletin* was for information and *The Review* for more philosophic material.

Tyler listed several questions that had been raised through correspondence that should be considered at the EXCOM Meeting:

- Question from the British Center about the Exhibition
- Question from Spain about discussing Spanish as an official language
- Question from the British Center about a separate Center to concentrate on publications for ASSITEJ

Financial Report: Cojar requested that the presentation of the Financial Report be delayed until Sunday, since most countries will have paid their dues by then. Sunyer invited ASSITEJ to Madrid in March, 1973 for a meeting concurrent with a children's theatre festival. Rodenberg reported that due to illness, Professor Schumacher would be unable to present his thesis at this Meeting. but he would be invited later. The GDR's Report in three languages would be distributed to shorten procedure. Tyler stressed the need for official minutes and procedures. Eek distributed Minutes from the last meeting, and asked that discussion of the IVth Congress wait until the arrival of Doolittle.

Publications: On*The Review* Moudoués had only been able to print two issues, the second issue dealing with the Spanish Center. She still needed manuscripts from the other Centers in order to print the next two issues. At least one play and ten articles are needed. Eek suggested that the 5-Year Reports from each Center might be assimilated in *The Review*. Juul noted that articles would be preferable to statistics, and inquired if the British Center's Bulletin could be circulated, though it was only in English.

Lucian urged that the EXCOM become a specialized group, and consider new themes and new working methods to inspire the children's theatre movement. Rodenberg illustrated Lucian's suggestion with statements of two themes: 1) How can the difference between children's theatre for children and adult theatre for children be eliminated? and 2) How can children be portrayed more realistically on stage?

Lucian then proposed that these two themes be included in *The*

Review so that members might exchange theories and viewpoints. Shakh-Azizov suggested that ASSITEJ adopt the Soviet Center's policy of holding semi-annual committee meetings, with one devoted to a discussion of artistic problems, the other devoted to business.

At the Leningrad conference in February 1972, a theme had been discussed on classic tales for children, and some of it might be suitable for publication. Moudoués said *The Review* could be ready if articles would be contributed by June,

Rodenberg ventured other possible themes: What influence does the performance of children's theatre have on the performance of adult theatre productions? How can the standard be raised? She also said she had invited wives of ambassadors to meet for an introduction to ASSITEJ, and just last week the International Theatre Institute (ITI) of UNESCO met in the GDR for the first time.

Miscellaneous Discussion: Moudoués distributed information on the Bordeaux Festival of 16-21 October 1972 that would occur during the scheduled EXCOM Meeting. The Festival would be in two parts: 1) a visiting to the theatres, meeting with authors, actors, etc.; and 2) abstract discussions of point, questions, and solutions submitted in advance. The Bordeaux format was designed to keep discussions in hand and to the point. Shakh-Azizov commended the French Center.

Moudoués recommended that a letter be sent to Jean-Louis Barrault, Director of the Theatre of Nations, inviting him to the Festival and assuring him of the support of ASSITEJ. Then the meeting was adjourned.

The EXCOM Meeting / Leipzig / 6 March

The EXCOM next met at 9:30 am on Monday, 6 March with Shakh-Azizov presiding. Doolittle had just arrived. Shakh-Azizov announced the remaining items on the Agenda:

1. The 1972 Congress
2. Membership Fees and the Financial Report
3. Report from the Netherlands
4. Report from Yugoslavia
5. Report of the FGR
6. Miscellaneous discussions

Registration: Eek reported that 250 brochures for the Congress were mailed 1 January to all the Centers. Members should register immediately, and notify the US Center if more registration forms are needed. The Registration Fees of 10 USD must be returned with the forms immediately. Room and Board can be paid for later. Doolittle noted that if members arrived on 11 June, they could stay in the dormitory for 8.50 Canadian Dollars. That cost would include breakfast and dinner. Lunch would be the only personal expense. Sunyer asked for 20 more registration forms.

Visas: Members should ask for Multiple Entry Visas, and send their names to Doolittle and Eek as soon as possible.

Exhibits: They should be sent to Don Moshon (USA) by 15 March. Eek said they would do everything possible to return them.

Program: The First Session would have 4 Canadian productions; the Second Session will have 5 USA productions. Eek and Doolittle then presented an outline of both programs to the EXCOM.

At Montréal the EXCOM Agenda would include a discussion of membership, elections, and the possibility of raising dues. Moudoués noted that statute changes must be submitted by 14 March, and that she had yet to receive any. Eek presented the schedule for the General Assembly sessions and the EXCOM Meetings. In the USA Monday 19 June would be a general Business session; Friday 23 June would be for the elections. Moudoués reminded members that any Center can send in proposals for the EXCOM. She had received nominations from Spain, GDR, Italy, Great Britain, Netherlands, France, and Yugoslavia. This concluded the discussion of the upcoming Congress.

Cojar presented the Financial Statement written in three languages. Centers were divided into four categories: 1) Active Centers which have paid dues; 2) Active Centers which had delayed payment; 3) Non-replying Centers; and 4) Forming Centers.

Centers: The status of the Centers in Austria, Brazil, and Belgium was discussed, since they had not paid their dues. Snoek suggested that Géal be approached personally about his representation and that of the Flemish Theatre for Children. Tyler asserted that ASSITEJ should not continue carrying anyone who was no longer interested in the organization. Cojar agreed with Tyler, but added that ASSITEJ must broaden its base. He mentioned that the three new Centers admitted in

Prague in October—Ireland, Portugal, and Hungary—would pay later.

Of the countries in arrears—Norway, Austria, and Brazil-Doolittle proposed that they be dropped, and give them a chance to renew. Eek noted that they had been given from three to six years already, and dues of 800 USD had been lost. Moudoués and Rodenberg agreed with Doolittle and Eek.

Tyler proposed the creation of four lists: 1) those full member Centers who had paid and were eligible to vote and to be elected; 2) those Centers who had not paid and who would lose membership in two years; 3) those corresponding Centers who would fall into Category Number Two after two years; and 4) those countries with whom negotiations were in progress.

Moudoués noted that if those countries were expelled, they would have to be notified in writing. Adamek reported that Centers could be expelled by a two-thirds vote majority, and in reference to Tyler's proposal, he said that corresponding Centers are required to pay dues. Tyler withdrew his proposal.

The Doolittle proposal that Norway, Austria, and Brazil be dropped was approved by a vote of 11 for, 1 against. The Secretary-General was instructed to write a letter to those countries notifying them of their expulsion, and that they may be reinstated by application and payment of dues, and then resume their regular representation at meetings.

The question of Israel's non-payment for the past three years was taken up. Porat stated that she would decide about payment by June, suggesting that since she had only recently established the Israeli Center, she could not be responsible for past dues. Eek reminded Moudoués that Israel had voted by proxy for three years without paying, and that was a dangerous precedent. Cojar said he could inform the Congress at the beginning of the session which members could vote.

Financial Report: Jenner pointed out that the accounts must be audited and signed off on. Moudoués noted that only the Congress could name the auditors, and ASSITEJ had financial experts whose abilities could be useful. Gossmann reported that Munich had one such person, and there was a fault on the blue-sheet related to Brazil's non-payment of dues. It was decided that a resolution about the audit of accounts would brought up at the Congress' General Assembly session in Montreal.

Snoek presented The Netherlands Center Report as follows:

The Center is experiencing enormous activity as well as some confusion. There is a movement against authoritarianism, a protest of the young against established systems. These changes are reflected in their theatre. More creative work is now allowed in the schools, but too frequently opportunists have taken advantage of the funding. The child and creative instincts are in the foreground, but production development has been subjugated. (Both Gossmann and Juul agreed with her evaluation.)

In the Netherlands five companies exclusively for children are being financed. As the economic situation worsens, each group regards the others as competitors for money. Consequently there is a lack of mutual support.

Snoek is a government artistic advisor, and she felt opinions are split, with one faction declaring that there should be no proscenium theatre for children. Instead they should substitute improvisation, creative play, and pieces dealing with social issues.

The Netherlands Center is changing so that individual members can belong, and Snoek urged a change in the ASSITEJ statutes accordingly. She was no longer associated with the Scapino Dance Company, since it is negotiating for a new theatre building for children.

Gossmann presented the FDR Center's Report as follows:

Gossmann spoke of their Center's activities and the growth of anti-authoritarianism. One very successful such group performs in a small theatre called Reichskabarett in Berlin, and calls itself Grips. They use and change the art of theatre through agitation and agi-prop styles, although they have little formal theatre training.

However, there are still conventional plays being done. Other non-professional groups also work either in the form of creative drama, or with "proletarian children's theater". Many in the theatre are engaged in new content and forms of children's theatre, and amateur groups primarily exist in the education departments of universities.

He also expressed concern that pseudo-socialists suddenly believe they understand how to produce plays for children through the destruction of the old methods. This discredit established children's theatres without suggesting solutions or utilizing trained theatre workers. He asked that ASSITEJ fight this destructive trend, and encourage production of high quality performances.

There are 146 professional theatres in the FGR which produce some plays for children. All are members of the FGR Center, and in closing he asked everyone to join in celebrating the 25th Anniversary of the Nuremberg Theatre. (The above narrative incorporates Gossmann's written concerns over misinterpretations from the original minutes.)

Djokič presented the Report on the Yugoslavia Center as follows:

There are four professional children's theatres in Yugoslavia. One presents adult theatre in the evening, and children's theatre in the morning and afternoon. Adult theatres in Zagreb, Sarajevo, and Split occasionally play for children. Zagreb has an experimental group with children under the direction of Zvjezdana Ladika. All these theatres are members of the Center except the theatre in Belgrade. Yugoslavia also tends to adapt radio plays for the theatre.

Miscellaneous Discussion: Tyler urged that ASSITEJ consider the place of creative drama in the world of children's theatre, since the matter is now of world interest. Rodenberg agreed with Tyler, noting that each Center has three voices: two for professional and one for amateur, which may be educational and can include creative drama. Doolittle asserted that the use of drama for human understanding had more to do with education than amateur plays. Eek said this new direction must be considered. Tyler said that Great Britain would present a resolution on this subject at the next Congress.

Jenner spoke of theatre education programs in Great Britain, and others mentioned similar programs in their countries. Georgiev said that sometimes actors and directors were invited by schools to speak, and Rodenberg reported a permanent program of actors helping teachers give their lessons in history, music, etc. in Berlin (GDR). It was agreed that further discussion was needed.

The meeting was adjourned.

"The Rulers of the Beach" (Die Herren des Strandes) by Friedrich Gerlach and Georg Katzer, from the novel by Jorge Amado. Photo: Hans-Joachim Kuka and courtesy of the Theater der Freundschaft, Berlin, GDR. 1972.

The Executive Committee of ASSITEJ met in Dresden, GDR on 10 March 1972. Konstantin Shakh-Azizov as President (USSR) presided , Vladimir Adamek (Czechoslovakia) as 2nd Vice President, Ilse Rodenberg (GDR) as 3rd Vice President, Rose-Marie Moudoués (France) as Secretary-General, and Ian Cojar (Romania) as Treasurer.

Other members attending were: José Géal (Belgium), Georgiev, Gossmann, Jenner, Tyler, Biotto, Snoek, and Djokič. Juul, Ian Lucian (Romania), and Porat served as Advisors.[94]

Members absent: Joyce Doolittle (Canada), Maria Sunyer (Spain), and Nat Eek (USA).

The EXCOM Meeting / Dresden / 10 March

The EXCOM meeting began at 5:15 pm on Friday with President Shakh-Azizov presiding. This was a continuation of the meeting which started in Berlin on 4 May 1972. The US, Canadian, and Spanish delegates had already left for home, so it is unclear who took the Minutes of this meeting, probably the British delegate.

The Secretary-General presented the Agenda, and the first item was the admittance of new National Centers. Moudoués announced that Hungary, Peru, Portugal, and Ireland had all met the requirements for membership, and the EXCOM accepted them. She then indicated that negotiations were continuing with Australia, Switzerland, and Argentina, and that Jenner should continue her contact with Iran.

Before leaving, the Spanish Center had requested that Spanish be added as a fourth language, since next to English, Spanish was the most spoken language in ASSITEJ. Moudoués immediately mentioned the many difficulties in administration and finance that this would create. Jenner moved that the Spanish request be refused on the grounds that it would be impossible to handle another "official" language. After this denial, the Spanish Center with the knowledge and approval of ASSITEJ began publishing an ASSITEJ Journal at their own expense in Spanish listing activities, festivals, and general information, and distributed it to all Spanish-speaking Centers as well as other Spanish-speaking countries in ITI and UNESCO.

The ASSITEJ Exhibit: It had arrived in Great Britain without a Bill of Lading, and in a broken, ragged condition, making its display impossible. It had been returned to the Paris office with a request for reimbursement of £34 for the transportation costs. Shakh-Azizov proposed that 1) since there was no way of controlling a traveling exhibit, in the future such an exhibit should only contain non-returnable materials; 2) the amount of £34 should be paid to the British Center by the Paris Office as well as any additional costs; 3) that if the contributing countries wanted their materials returned, they should pay those costs to the Paris Center; and 4) that at the closing of any future exhibitions, the contributing Centers should expect to pay for the return of their materials. These proposals were accepted without comment.

Adamek raised his concerns about the inaccuracies and errors in format written in the reports of the previous meetings of the EXCOM. The Secretary-General stated that Minutes of the current meeting would be taken and distributed to all Centers. A suggestion was made that two people working in two different languages should take the Minutes, but no action was taken. Gossmann and Georgiev proposed that all meetings be tape recorded which was accepted, but a proposal that a group of two or three persons check the facts was not accepted. It was agreed that the names of all those present at any meeting should always be listed in the Minutes. Tyler proposed that the Minutes should always reflect the resolutions made, and Adamek seconded this. Tyler also stated it was not necessary to write up in detail all the discussions. Eek was not present for this discussion.

Jenner noted that at the 1970 Venice Conference a few Centers had distributed a list of all children's theatre companies in their country who belonged to their Center, and these lists gave considerable detailed information. This was an excellent source of information on that country's activity, as well as a contact source for foreign visitors coming to that country. She asked that Centers produce similar lists, and have them available at the upcoming Congress. Shakh-Azizov asked that all Centers do this, and there was general agreement on its value and need.

Publications: The possible publication of a book on children's theatre throughout the world was discussed. Rodenberg responded that she had approached a publishing firm in the GDR. It was quite possible, but it would take several years to be done.

Porat proposed that all Centers try to raise funds to finance a working party that would write a history of theatre programs that could be easily understood by children. It should take the form of a television series that could be narrated in various languages. Everyone commended the proposal, and the President requested that all Centers explore the possibilities of implementing the proposal.

Creative Dramatics: Tyler presented a proposal from the British Center that the next Congress set up a working party to study the relationships between children's theatre and creative dramatics, and to make a report to the EXCOM for possible action. Shakh-Azizov stated that this would create a sharp and serious discussion in the General Assembly, but that the British Center should prepare a clear statement of what Creative Dramatics was with appropriate examples, and that this statement be made available to all members. With this document the Centers would be able to have a more meaningful discussion in the General Assembly. The proposal was accepted.

Proposals were then made for EXCOM meetings to be held in Bulgaria in 1974 and Romania in 1975. Juul commented that commitments so far in advance did not allow for new Centers to be hosts. Shakh-Azizov said these proposals could be considered later. The Secretary-General said they would be noted but not considered at the present time.

Adamek spoke of the greater importance of the International Congress in 1974. Géal said that his Center had presented a proposal in 1970 that Belgium could host the Congress in 1974, and it was urgent that a firm commitment be made as soon as possible.

Here the Minutes ended.

"How the Devils Got Married" written and directed by Vaclay Tomsovsky.
Produced by the Jiri Volker Theatre, Prague, Czechoslovakia. June 1978.
Photograph courtesy of William H. Gleason, US Cenyer for ASSITEJ.

1972
IVth INTERNATIONAL CONGRESS OF ASSITEJ
Part I / Canada
Montreal, Quebec, Canada / 14-17 June 1972

The IVth International Congress of ASSITEJ met in Montreal, Quebec, Canada on 14-17 June 1972.

Konstantin Shakh-Azizov(USSR) presided as President, with Nat Eek (USA) as 1st Vice President, Vladimir Adamek (Czechoslovakia) as 2nd Vice President, Ilse Rodenberg (GDR) as 3rd Vice President, Rose-Marie Moudoués (France) as Secretary-General, and Ian Cojar (Romania) acting as Treasurer for Ion Lucian.

Other members attending were: José Géal (Belgium), Victor Georgiev (Bulgaria), Joyce Doolittle (Canada), Hanswalter Gossmann (FGR), Caryl Jenner (Great Britain), Benito Biotto (Italy), Hans Snoek (Netherlands), Maria Sunyer (Spain), Ljubiša Djokič (Yugoslavia), and Gerald Tyler, Honorary President (Great Britain). Inga Juul (Denmark), Orna Porat (Israel), and Ion Lucian (Romania) served as advisors.

Members absent: none.

Countries attending were: Austria, Belgium, Bulgaria, Canada, Czechoslovakia, Denmark, FGR, France, Great Britain, GDR, Ireland, Israel, Italy, Japan, Netherlands, Norway, Poland, Portugal, Romania, Spain, Sweden, Switzerland, USA, USSR, and Yugoslavia; a total of 25.[95]

In 1972 the International Congress of ASSITEJ was jointly sponsored by the Centers of Canada and the USA. The first part took place in Montreal, Canada, and then the delegates were driven by bus to the campus of the State University of New York in Albany, New York, USA for the second part.

The Bureau Meeting—Montreal—Tuesday, 13 June
The Bureau met at 11am in Room 350 of the Arts Building at

McGill University in Montreal, Canada. Present were Shakh-Azizov, Eek, Adamek, Rodenberg, Tyler, Moudoués, and Cojar acting for Lucian.[96]

President Shakh-Azizov presided, and welcomed the Bureau by commenting on the present atmosphere of success, and indicated that the business at hand was the development of an Agenda for the General Assembly.

Moudoués announced that there would be an EXCOM Meeting that afternoon, and that the Bureau needed to set that Agenda first. In her Report Morale she stated there were a number of items, but the Report was in French. Eek asked for a translation, and asked if the Canadian Center could do it. Since Ion Lucian as Treasurer was absent, Moudoués presented the Financial Report. She indicated that her bank had advised her that with the devaluation of the dollar, the costs next year would be greater, which must be considered.

Looking at the Program, she stated that there would be no business sessions in Canada, but that the EXCOM needed to prepare the Agenda for the General Assembly in Albany that afternoon. The election procedure needed to be very carefully prepared. Also, she had received a joint request from the Centers of Great Britain and the USA for changes in the statutes, and they needed to be presented to the Assembly.

Tyler asked if the Statute changes had been presented to the Centers so they would have time to study them. Moudoués replied that she had not been able to do so, but they were simple, and could be handled easily once each Center had the text. Shakh-Azizov said it could be discussed at the EXCOM meeting, and Tyler responded that no one could vote intelligently if they had not received the text. Moudoués agreed and apologized for her neglect, and indicated that family problems had prevented her doing so.

Moudoués continued stating that a sub-committee needed to be established to discuss student and theatre game involvement in ASSITEJ, and that the General Assembly needed to discuss the Spanish request for Spanish as the fourth official language. Shakh-Azizov stated that this had been discussed at the Berlin EXCOM, that it was defeated in vote, and asked why she brought it up again. Moudoués said Spain wished to bring the question to the General Assembly. Tyler commented that a Center always had that right.

Other items for the Agenda included:
- A presentation by the Treasurer of those Centers that had paid their dues, and were therefore entitled to vote in 1972
- A presentation of the Statute Amendments in translation and in Xeroxed form
- A presentation of the Reports
- The Elections

According to the Eek Minutes on the Bureau Meeting, they also received the following Report on the Voting Procedure prepared by Adamek. He presented the voting procedure and listed the following items:

1) Each group would claim and then return their ballots to the ballot box
2) A list of the names of the eligible Centers
3) A list of the voting procedures must be prepared in the three official languages
4) The list of all eligible Centers would receive ballots
5) There would be a list of the proposed changes in the statutes
6) There would be copies of the Creative Dramatics Proposal

Also according to Eek's Minutes:

1) Centers must nominate themselves to be on the EXCOM three months before the next General Assembly
2) Officers must indicate their willingness to serve three months before the next General Assembly
3) Officer nominations could be made from the floor of the meeting

Adamek then stated that the following items would be needed for the Election:

1) A list of the voting rules, with 5 copies in Russian
2) 51 copies of the ballot for the Secretary-General vote
3) 51 copies of the ballot for the Treasurer vote
4) 51 copies of the list of eligible Centers, including France and Romania to be used as a ballot
5) A ballot box for the deposit of the ballots
6) Ballots to be marked for or against the Proposals: Creative Dramatics, the Spanish Language, the changes in the Statutes

Eek's Minutes also stated the following clarification:

1) The Secretary-General is nominated by the General Assembly on the recommendation of the EXCOM (Statutes: Chapter 4, Article 9, Paragraph 13)

2) The Centers receive the number of ballots corresponding to the votes to which they are entitled

3) The name of the Secretary-General recommended by the EXCOM is placed on the ballot; "only the EXCOM is empowered to recommend another person".

The meeting closed with Shakh-Azizov stating that the Statute changes would be discussed in the Bureau meeting on Friday 16 June.

The EXCOM Meeting on Tuesday 13 June at 2:15 pm in Montreal, Canada

Members of the EXCOM attending were: Adamek, Moudoués, Rodenberg, Klaus Urban (GDR), Tyler, Jenner, Biotto, Snoek, Cojar, Lucian, Sunyer, Eek, Shakh-Azizov, and Djokič.

Members absent: Géal, Georgiev, and Doolittle.

Shakh-Azizov presided, welcomed the Committee, announced that Bulgaria would be late, and then turned the meeting over to the Secretary-General. Moudoués stated that the EXCOM needed to set the Agenda for the Albany General Assembly session, and that this would be the business meeting and election session. The General Assembly session in Montreal would be for general discussions. She stated that the Bureau had discussed and had agreed upon an Agenda. Tyler called Point of Order that Minutes of the last meeting needed to be approved first. Shakh-Azizov stated that no one had had a chance to read them yet, and recommended approval at a later date. Tyler responded that "we need to follow normal procedures in the future!" Moudoués said that the Minutes would be approved at the next meeting.

Moudoués then proposed the following Agenda for the General Assembly on Monday 19 June in Albany:

- The Report Morale on the ASSITEJ activities since the Venice Meeting in 1970

- The amendments to the Constitution (which were primarily in terminology), would be read and then distributed in writing to be voted upon at the next General Assembly session
- Adamek's report on the election procedure
- The eligibility of the voters would be checked and announced
- The election and the announcement of the results
- Future Reports

For Friday 24 June Moudoués proposed the following Agenda for the 2nd General Assembly session:

- The election of the new Bureau
- A vote on the statute changes
- A decision on the location of the next international meeting
- A consideration of raising the amount of dues because of the devaluation of the dollar

There was then considerable general discussion: indicated by seven (7) pages of notes, and the meeting lasting almost four (4) hours! The highlights are summarized as follows:

Eek notified the EXCOM that all sessions would be on television. They agreed that the televising of the General Assembly was all right, but not that of the EXCOM or the Bureau.

This discussion pinpointed the differences between East and West. The Eastern delegates were concerned that their votes would be revealed, and in turn there could be repercussions upon their return to their countries. The West was more inclined to "let it happen" with little recrimination.

Shakh-Azizov asked what Centers are eligible to vote. Cojar replied that most Centers were paid up. He assumed the Centers with dues outstanding would pay them at the Congress in order to vote, as had been done in the past. Ireland, Peru, and Portugal were the only three left unpaid.

MOUDOUÉS: Peru was only admitted at Berlin in 1972. It is a poor center and must put on a performance to raise money for its dues.

COJAR: We have no proof that Yugoslavia has paid. Djokič will pay here in order to vote, and we will credit his 1973 account.

SUNYER: The delegate from Portugal is here, but she was never advised of admittance. She will be asked if she can pay here, and be allowed to vote.

MOUDOUÉS: There is always a problem of lost mail between France and Portugal.

SHAKH-AZIZOV: I'm confused about Israel?

COJAR: Israel paid for this year, but not the two previous years.

SHAKH-AZIZOV: Why credit her for 1973 when she is unpaid for '70, '71, and '72?

COJAR: They reorganized this year, and will try to pay up.

SHAKH-AZIZOV: I am not satisfied with this explanation. We should say to Israel that "you are welcome to attend but not to vote!"

JENNER: It's very difficult since we've allowed voting in the past and *not* now!

SUNYER: In Israel the same person has represented both centers.

RODENBERG: It's a question of principle. We should help new centers, but if the same person represents, then it is complicated.

EEK: This is the history of the Israel Center: It was present at Paris in 1965, The Hague in 1968, and Venice in 1970, and was allowed to vote each time. We have not voted it out of ASSITEJ. It is not a *new* center, but an accepted center in arrears on dues. She should not vote until dues are paid up.

The Israel Center was a continuing problem. From the very beginning the Center had been represented by Orna Porat, a talented leading Israeli actress with her own theatre company. However, she was the only one in the Center, and its status was always in question. Moudoués was extremely protective of the Israeli Center. However, it was decided to let Israel vote, as had been done in the past.

Moudoués then said she had Statutes from the Swiss Center, and they should be ready to form. They requested consideration for admittance and would pay their dues immediately. The Swiss Center was unanimously approved as a new Member.

A Center's vote usually reflected the orientation of a particular

National Center in terms of East-West sympathies in approval or disapproval, and the following EXCOM discussion as recorded was assessing the vote and lining up the delegates of each Center for the election.

MOUDOUÉS: There is the problem of Australia. There has been much correspondence between Mme. Tomascetti and ITI. Tomascetti explained the situation of her Center to us in Bratislava. Then ITI said they had appointed a person to form a center. I sent copies to both groups. At an all-Australian meeting of directors, another center was formed. At the next EXCOM meeting we shall ask both representatives to appear and present their ideas. At Berlin we discussed a center in Iran, and Don Lafoon is here to present this. Also, there is a possible center in Jordan represented by Abdul-Rahm Omar.

Adamek's Voting Procedure proposals were discussed:

Proposal Part 1—Before the General Session. Three months before the General Assembly, there will be an agreement on the centers to be nominated. The Secretariat will send out a list of all centers eligible to vote and their number of votes each—2 for professional theatres and 1 for non-professional theatres.

Proposal Part 2 – During the General Assembly. Discussion followed about nominations, and the importance of their being accepted by the National Center first. The following Centers were eligible to vote: Belgium, Bulgaria, Canada, Czechoslovakia, FGR, France, GDR, Great Britain, Netherlands, Romania, Spain, USA, USSR, and Yugoslavia. Israel was not eligible. All the other Centers have sent in their willingness to serve in writing. There were 14 candidates since Israel was ineligible.

Proposal Part 3 – The election of the Bureau. Within the EXCOM the following officers must be nominated: the President, the 3 Vice-Presidents, the Secretary-General, and the Treasurer. 2 members may then be co-opted who may vote. Considerable discussion followed.

MOUDOUÉS: We must elect the EXCOM, then the President and the Vice-Presidents. Then appoint the Secretary-General and the Treasurer.

This statement is in conflict with the statutes and later practice: The Secretary-General and the Treasurer and their respective National Centers had to be elected or accepted first, since their national Centers had to be seated on the EXCOM according to the Statutes.

MOUDOUÉS: If you wish the Secretary-General to remain in France, then France will withdraw its candidacy for election to the EXCOM. Because of expenses the Secretary-General and the Treasurer never represent their countries. They represent general international interests. This is the way it is handled in the UN.

DJOKIČ: If we have double representation by one country, other countries must be excluded. I request that the General Assembly elect the Bureau first, then appoint the Secretary-General and the Treasurer.

TYLER: We've operated for eight years without problems. Let's continue as done in the past, and then change the text.

DJOKIČ: It is most desirable to have as many countries represented as possible. [This statement was probably prompted by Yugoslavia usually being the last Center at the time to be elected to the EXCOM, or even excluded by vote, and then just co-opted.]

Tyler then moved a proposal to leave the election as is, and then to change the statutes in the next two years. [Later even with the hiatus of 3 years between Congresses caused by the Brussels cancellation, the delegates still thought in terms of a two-year interval.]

The meeting was adjourned at 6:20 pm.

The 2ⁿᵈ Old EXCOM Meeting—16 June at 4:00 pm in Montreal, Canada

Konstantin Shakh-Azizov(USSR) presided as President, with Eek, Adamek, Rodenberg, Moudoués, Cojar, Géal, Doolittle, Gossmann, Urban, Tyler, Jenner, Biotto, Snoek, Sunyer, and Djokič. Juul and Porat as Advisors.

President Shakh-Azizov presided, and opened the discussion on the election procedure and the election of the Bureau. He proposed that Nat Eek be elected as the next President, and expressed the hope that the EXCOM would approve his proposal. The EXCOM approved the proposal unanimously, and asked that it be sent forward. Tyler noted appropriately that there could be nominations from the floor.

Shakh-Azizov then asked Cojar to read the names of those countries eligible to vote. Cojar said there are 21 Centers at the moment. At this moment 17 can vote, but 3 have not paid—Ireland, Peru, and Portugal. Switzerland is too recently formed to vote, making the total of 21. Therefore the eligible voting Centers are: Belgium, Bulgaria, Canada, Czechoslovakia, FGR, France, GDR, Great Britain, Hungary, Israel, Italy, Netherlands, Romania, Spain, USA, USSR, and Yugoslavia making a total of 17.

Thus, 17 Centers could vote, each with 3 votes, making a total of 51 legal votes, and a majority of 26 would be required for election. Shakh-Azizov asked if there were nominations of Centers for the EXCOM. She said all have arrived in time: Belgium (represented by José Géal); Bulgaria (Victor Georgiev); Canada (Joyce Doolittle); Czechoslovakia (Vladimir Adamek); FGR (Hanswalter Gossmann); GDR (Ilse Rodenberg); Great Britain (Caryl Jenner); Israel (Orna Porat); Italy (Benito Biotto); Netherlands (Hans Snoek); Romania (Ion Lucian); Spain (Maria Sunyer), USA (Nat Eek); USSR (Ivan Voronov); and Yugoslavia (Ljubiša Djokič). [plus France]

Shakh-Azizov recommended that the current Vice-Presidents—Adamek and Rodenber—should be retained for further work. Adamek recommended Doolittle for the 3rd Vice-President, and Sunyer recommended Snoek.

Shakh-Azizov then said the new EXCOM would be able to co-opt 2 centers and appoint 2 advisors. He then recommended that Moudoués be reppointed as Secretary-General, and that the Secretariat be kept in Paris. Cojar stated that he wished to resign as Treasurer in favor of Ion Lucian. He also announced that they now had two Romanian Auditors. Their credentials were never checked, and they eventually disappeared. The vote for approval for all the recommendations was unanimous.

Dues: Moudoués announced next that they must discuss the raising of dues, stating that the Paris bank advises us that we should. After much discussion they approved recommending to the General Assembly that the dues should be raised to 75 USD as a minimum, with 150 USD as a maximum.

Eek proposed that ASSITEJ create the title of President Emeritus to honor those past presidents who have served well.

Recognizing that there was more on the Agenda, a rump session later was proposed, and the meeting was adjourned at 6:15 pm.

Performances and Events / Montreal / 14-18 June: The Montreal portion of the Congress included 8 companies performing a total of 22 times in 4 theatres in 6 days. 500 delegates from 25 nations attended the events in Montreal.

There was a pre-Congress arrival day with time allotted for Bureau and EXCOM ASSITEJ meetings and a non-festival bonus—an evening performance of *Bobby Boom*, a prize-winning play for young people about a hockey star, performed by La Nouvelle Compagnie Theatrale.

On Wednesday 14 June, delegates were welcomed by representatives of the federal, provincial, and municipal governments at the official opening ceremonies. Ilse Rodenberg (GDR), 3rd Vice-President of ASSITEJ, and Director of the Theater der Freundschaft in Berlin, delivered a speech on "Creativity in Children and Young People and the Role of Theatre for Children in the Process". This was followed by detailed Reports of Activities from ASSITEJ Centers, moderated by Adamek.

After lunch Les Jeunes Comédiens du Théâtre Nouveau Monde (Montreal) presented *Les Fouberies de Scapin* of Moliere. The vitality, imagination, and charm of the company were remarked upon both in Montreal and in Albany, where the company performed as Canada's contribution to the USA sessions. At the afternoon Plenary Session, Professor Richard Courtney, President of CCYDA spoke on "Creativity and Theatre for Children".

Courtney cited Canada's contributions to theatre for children, both in quality and diversity:

As befits a bilingual nation, we have performances in both English and French—and some companies perform equally well in both. As you travel across the four-and-a-half thousand miles of this country you can see large, expensive companies financially well supported by their provinces, and you can witness a performance by four players who have traveled to a cold barn on the northern prairies in an old Jeep. You can visit a large playhouse and be warmed by a full-scale musical, or you can wander into a school gymnasium and see children sitting in a circle around a company of players encouraging the children to participate.

Canada is not standing still. Our diversity is increasing. And the flexibility and originality of our companies continue to grow. In such a way, I feel, Canada is making her unique contribution toward the relationship between creativity and Theatre for Children.[97]

This was followed by statements on the theme of the Congress and a discussion period.

Other performances: Productions from Canada included: *Shakespeare's Women* (The Globe Theatre, Regina, Saskatchewan), *Where Are You When We Need You, Simon Fraser?* (Playhouse Holiday, Vancouver, British Columbia), *The Clam Made a Face* (Young People's Theatre, Toronto, Ontario), and *Operation-Theatre* (La Nouvelle Compagnie Théâtrale, Montreal, Quebec). The three English speaking companies showed delegates the kind of theatre most common in Canada in the past decade—five young actors with minimal scenery and costumes who tour elementary schools with a play (usually including audience participation) or a collective creation (usually in presentational style) for junior or senior high schools. Delegates were interested, but not very impressed. "Why," asked one European, "did English Canada choose to show such slight pieces?" The reason was perhaps because that was what English Canada had to offer at that time. One was pleased that the companies chosen by the adjudicator represented three of the longest-lived and most committed theatres for children in the country and that two of the three had featured Canadian scripts. At the same time one wished that at least one of the three works might have been more compelling.

Two companies from Eastern Europe, where government support for theatre for young audiences is immense, provided an enormous contrast in style, intent, and audience response. *The Fairy Tales of Pushkin* presented by the Moscow Central Children's Theatre in the two thousand seat Expo theatre was a two hour spectacle requiring six tons of scenery and a company of forty. That same evening, at the Gesu, a theatre seating seven hundred persons, the Ion Creanga Theatre of Bucharest, Romania performed *Tales with Masks* with its actor-director-creator Ion Lucian, playing the seven deadly sins with the help of seven marvelous out-sized masks.

The other invited foreign company was the Minneapolis

Children's Theatre of Minnesota, USA. This company comprised of adult professional actors and child and adolescent student actors presented the most controversial show in the Congress. *Hang on to Your Head* was presented by a company of 50. There were two truckloads of scenery. Although Director John Donahue devised an entertainment of great skill and artistry, the reactions of delegates in Montréal (and later in Albany) were almost entirely negative regarding the theme of the play.

There were three parties for delegates. On the opening day there was a buffet in the lobby of the Place des Arts, sponsored by the City of Montréal and hosted by Jean Louis Rioux, an outstanding Canadian actor and director. On Friday evening there was a sit-down dinner and dance in the ballroom of the Sheraton-Mount Royal Hotel, hosted by the Province of Alberta, and there was an open bar, a dance orchestra, and a multi-coursed meal provided.

The Montréal sessions were exciting. The only complaint was that there was not enough time for general discussion about the plays and speeches. Four days was not really long enough for the program as presented. However, most delegates boarded the buses to Albany in good spirits and with a sense of anticipation for the USA segment of the Congress. For Canada, the Congress called attention to an often neglected part of the arts and led, eventually, to the network of Annual International Festivals for Children which began in the late 1970s and which continue to thrive to this day.

Operation Theatre", a performance by La Nouvelle Companie Theatrale of Montreal, Canada, at the IVth International ASSITEJ Congress in Montreal, Quebec, Canada. Photo courtesy of SUNY Dept. of Theatre, Albany, New York.

IVth INTERNATIONAL CONGRESS OF ASSITEJ
Part II / USA
Albany, New York, USA / 18-25 June 1972

For the Albany part of the program of the Congress, the US Center had determined:

- to feature USA productions chosen from across the country by three theatre experts—Dan Sullivan, drama critic for *The Los Angeles Times*, Clara Hieronymus, critic for *The Nashville Tennessean*, and Orlin Corey, publisher of The Anchorage Press;
- to present professional critiques of each production followed by open discussion;
- to showcase a day long presentation on creative drama (a form of theatre that had been deliberately excluded from the statutes of ASSITEJ in 1964);
- to offer a three-day excursion to New York City for the international delegates following the Congress.

*T*he delegates arrived in Albany, New York, USA by chartered buses on a Sunday afternoon, with a stop enroute at Ausible Chasm. They arrived at the State University of New York (SUNY) campus where they were hosted by the Department of Theatre. After they registered, they were shown a one-hour live stage presentation utilizing television and music titled *Children's Theatre, USA, A Visual Report* created by William Snyder. This was followed by formal speeches of welcoming by: Ruth Mayleas of the U.S. ITI representing President Richard Nixon, Arthur Kerr representing New York State Governor Nelson Rockefeller, and USA Representative to the United Nations Shirley Temple Black. Never in the previously recorded history of ASSITEJ had a head of state issued an official greeting at the start of a Congress.[98]

President Konstantin Shakh-Azizov representing ASSITEJ gave welcome to the Association. An additional welcome came from Sara Spencer representing the US Center for ASSITEJ, Jarka Burian representing the SUNY Department of Theatre, President Louis Benezet of SUNY, and Chancellor Ernest Boyer of SUNY. Nat Eek, Chairman of the US Center, presided giving special notice and acclaim to Joyce

Doolittle of the Canadian Center, Patricia B. Snyder of SUNY, and the US Center for their work on local arrangements. President Nixon and Governor Rockefeller declared June Official Children's Theatre Month in New York State. A champagne reception and a formal dinner, followed. There were a total of 500 delegates from 25 nations with the US Center limiting the number of USA delegates to 300 because of financial and space restrictions.

General Assembly / Monday 19 June / Albany

The Second General Assembly was held in Albany from 9 am to noon with President Shakh-Azizov presiding.

Shakh-Azizov welcomed the delegates, and then announced that he regretted that he had to leave for a radio interview, and turned the meeting over to 1st Vice-President Eek. The Agenda covered the following items:

- Reading and approval of the Minutes of the IIIrd International Conference in Venice in 1970, and presentation of the Financial Report
- Certification of the voting Centers and those ineligible to vote
- The need to increase the amount of the dues
- Announcement of the new Centers
- New proposals: word changes in the Constitution for clarification; the inclusion of Creative Dramatics within the formal organization forwarded by Gerald Tyler from the British delegation; and a request from Maria Sunyer on behalf of the Spanish delegation to have Spanish included in the organization as an Official Language
- Open discussion and critiques of the plays and demonstrations seen

Moudoués began the Assembly by presenting the Minutes of the last General Assembly meeting in Venice, Italy in 1970. They were approved.

Financial Report: Cojar presented the Financial Report, and it was approved by the Assembly. As part of the Report he announced that at this election there were now 21 National Centers of ASSITEJ, 17 centers who were up to date on their dues were eligible to vote, and 4 in arrears who could not vote. 3 of those Centers—Austria, Brazil, and

Norway—were stricken from the official list for failure to pay their dues. Switzerland was too recent in forming to vote.

Report Morale: Moudoués then presented her Report, and announced future meetings: the 1972 fall Bureau meeting in Bordeaux, the next EXCOM Meeting in London in June 1973, the next EXCOM Meeting in Spain in the fall of 1973, and the next International Congress in Brussels, Belgium in June 1974. These were approved. Also, Moudoués in her Report stated that there were 5 new countries that were joining ASSITEJ: Hungary, Ireland, Peru, Portugal, and Switzerland.

Creative Drama: Tyler presented the British Proposal on Creative Dramatics: that ASSITEJ appoint a Working Party to investigate the relationship between Creative Dramatics and Children's Theatre, and to show its aims, principles, and practices and that these be incorporated into ASSITEJ. The Working Party was to report to ASSITEJ on its progress from time to time.

Spanish Language Report: Sunyer presented the Spanish Center's Proposal regarding Spanish as a 4th Official Language: ASSITEJ recognizes three official languages: French, English, and Russian. Since at least 25 different countries speak Spanish, her Center requested that Spanish be added as a fourth official language.

Porat requested that ASSITEJ recognize and state that in creativity in the theatre, the play itself was the most important thing. In today's theatre the Director was manipulating the text too much. "We must consider the audience, and strive for honesty without destroying the author's original concept."

General discussion: M. Meyer (FGR) said there was no time for discussion during the Montreal meetings. Rodenberg (GDR) said she hoped for more discussions. She continued that while many theories could be correct, we need a greater ability to recognize our theatrical problems. Delegates from France, FGR, USA, Venezuela, Israel, and Yugoslavia all presented papers. Following this general discussion, the meeting was adjourned.

The afternoon's activities centered on an extensive display of international children's theatre trends, highlighted by performances of members of the Soviet delegation.

Monday, 19 June

The Monday afternoon meetings featured films and slides from various countries, a performance by Vera Singaeuskaya from the Latvian Republic, a presentation of excerpts from the Moscow State Theatre for Children under the direction of Natalia Sats, a reception for the delegates by Mayor Corning at the Albany Institute of History and Art, and a production of *Tales with Masks* by the Ion Creanga Theatre from Bucharest, Romania.

Tuesday, 20 June

The first thing Tuesday morning was a critique by two US theatre critics—Louis Chapin of *The Christian Science Monitor* and Terry Kay of *The Atlanta Journal*—of the previous evening's performance of *Tales with Masks*. Orlin Corey (USA) moderated. This was followed during the day by demonstrations and panel discussions, all with simultaneous audio translations in English, French, and Russian. That evening the Children's Theatre Company of Minneapolis, Minnesota performed *Hang on to your Head* directed by John Donahue, which had already proved to be controversial in Montréal. The performance was followed by a reception hosted by the Albany Junior League at the Art Gallery.

Wednesday, 21 June

The next morning's critique session on Wednesday featured Norman Nadel of *Scripts Howard Publications* and Clara Hieronymus of *The Nashville Tennessean* discussing the Moscow Central Children's Theatre production of *The Tales of Pushkin*. The discussion centered on simplicity versus complexity, but with total agreement on its high quality and charm.

The discussion of *Hang on to Your Head* centered on it being totally inappropriate for children with its surreally distorted view of death. The original play depicted the adventures of a run-away girl in a series of surrealistic episodes before she becomes "Queen of the World". The play's director and author John Donahue stated the following, echoing the philosophy of Erik Vos at the Hague Congress of 1968:

The young people I know are not fools. They must decide for themselves what is good and true—and that may not be what is good and true for you and me—but they must make the decision.

And in order to do that at all, you must know who you are, and this play is dedicated to that quest.[99]

After the critique of this play, Natalia Sats, a formidable leader of the children's theatre movement in the USSR, strode to the front of the room and in her inimitable deep voice which required no amplification denounced this highly controversial production for failing to see the good in mankind and for the sexual overtones that she felt were evident. She urged the company "to learn how to love—and then let youth know that there is such a thing as love, real love."

Patricia Snyder (USA) responded to Sats and felt the ensuing discussions were remarkable. The play's title really should be *Open Up Your Head!*[100]

Not all delegates agreed with Sats's "official" opinion, and M. Chaikovsky of the Soviet delegation commented in a later open discussion that he had found the critiques wonderful and remarkable in their freedom of artistic opinion. However, several of the British and French Canadian delegates as well as some American ones were upset by the subject matter of the play, and felt that it was totally inappropriate for children.[101] After this formal critique and these comments, the election of the new Executive Committee was held.

General Assembly: The Elections./.Wednesday, 21 June / 10:50 am
President Shakh-Azizov and Vice-President Adamek presided.

The Secretary-General read the list of voting members and how many votes each Center had. Shakh-Azizov continued that the EXCOM then would recommend: the voting tellers, the nomination of the Secretary-General, the Treasurer, and the Auditors. The voting procedure in 3 languages was distributed and read by the Secretary-General in French while being simultaneously translated into English and Russian.

TYLER: The Constitution says that the election is to represent as many nations as possible. The Constitution says there will be 13 Centers to be elected to the EXCOM, but we can vote for less than this number. This might lead to a small EXCOM. Blocking voting could eliminate small votes. We should vote for all thirteen!

MOUDOUÉS: This is desirable, but a Center must get a simple majority to be elected.

ADAMEK: This should be clarified in coming assemblies. Let us proceed. The Bureau proposes as tellers: Ann Hill (USA), M. Kisilov (USSR), and M. Meyer (FGR).

A vote was taken and the majority approved these three. The vote for Moudoués as Secretary-General was: Yes—40; No—11. In response to her election Moudoués said "I shall work hard for ASSITEJ, but I ask you to work hard for me."

While waiting Shakh-Azizov stated that they would vote for the Treasurer, and the EXCOM recommended Ion Lucian. The votes for Lucian were: Yes—46; No—5.

Lucian then read the names of two Romanian Auditors—Cornel Popa and Elena Vladuti from Bucharest. The voting results for the Auditors were: Yes—44; No—7.

The EXCOM Vote: Adamek announced the voting for the new Executive Committee. The eligible names on the ballot were: Belgium (José Géal), Bulgaria (Victor Georgiev), Canada (Joyce Doolittle), Czechoslovakia (Vladimir Adamek), FGR (Hanswalter Gossmann), GDR (Ilse Rodenberg), Great Britain (Caryl Jenner), Israel (Orna Porat), Italy (Benito Biotto), Netherlands (Hans Snoek), Spain (Maria Sunyer), USA (Nat Eek), Ivan Voronov (USSR), and Yugoslavia (Ljubiša Djokič).

Adamek read again the rules for voting. At the end of the voting Shakh-Azizov announced the results of the election of the new EXCOM: USA (51), Czechoslovakia (50), GDR (49), FGR (49), Yugoslavia (48), Italy (48), USSR (47), Bulgaria (43), Canada (41), Great Britain (40), Belgium (39), Spain (34), Israel (31), and Netherlands (29). Since only 13 Centers could be elected. The Netherlands was not, so Hans Snoek was ineligible to run for Vice-President.

Then Eek requested that the title of President Emeritus of ASSITEJ be created to honor those that had served the Association well. This was passed unanimously. The title later became Honorary President.

Adamek congratulated all those elected and adjourned the meeting. While the elections went on The Little Theatre of the Deaf from New York City performed in SUNY's Studio Theatre.

Members of the EXCOM attending were: Géal, Doolittle, Adamek, Gossmann, Moudoués, Rodenberg, Jenner, Porat, Biotto, Lucian, Sunyer, Eek, Shakh-Azizov , and Djokič.
Members absent: Georgiev.
President Shakh-Azizov presided.

He congratulated those elected, stating they had been working long and hard for ASSITEJ. He then called on the Secretary-General to prepare Friday's meeting, and discuss the co-option of new members and counselors if desired. There would also be another meeting of the Bureau after the elections.

Shakh-Azizov stated that the EXCOM had recommended Nat Eek for President, and as Vice-Presidents: Rodenberg, Adamek, Doolittle, and Snoek. Snoek was no longer eligible since she was not elected to the EXCOM.

Biotto proposed that José Géal be considered for Vice- President since he would be hosting the next Congress. After further discussion they decided this was neither necessary nor desireable as a precedent.

The vote for the President and the 3 Vice-Presidents was: For—10; Against—4.

Doolittle proposed co-opting Snoek, and the vote was: For—11; Against—3.

The EXCOM then proposed the following three Advisors. The vote was as follows: Ian Cojar: For—11; Against—3. Sara Spencer: For—14; Against—0. Michael Pugh: For—9; Against—5.

With the election of 3 Advisors, the EXCOM proceeded to set dates of meetings. The next EXCOM Meeting would be in England on 9-17 June 1973. An EXCOM Meeting in Spain was approved for the last week in October or the first week in November in 1973. [This was later changed to April of 1974]. Further, they decided to put off the selection of a theme for the Brussels Congress until the Bordeaux Meeting in October 1972. The Meeting concluded as follows:

TYLER: Since Mr. Shakh-Azizov is retiring as President, I would like to say that the Moscow Children's Theatre has helped carry us to the heights. I thank him for carrying on so well despite his illness. And also for his great friendliness and his personal friendship.

SHAKH-AZIZOV: I thank you. And I hope I can help in the future to go on with our work. Thanks to Mr. Tyler for his kind words. We are adjourned.

Thursday, 23 June—Creative Drama Day

Thursday was designated as Creative Drama Day with multiple lectures and demonstrations that involved both the demonstrators and the audience.

The creative drama presentations included: an opening address by Dr. Jed Davis of the University of Kansas and President of the American Theatre Association; a media production "Dimensions of Creative Drama" by Ann M. Shaw of Queens College (NYC) and Ann Thurman of Northwestern University; a panel discussion on the "Simplifications of Creative Drama for the Development of the Child", moderated by Barbara Salisbury [Wills] of the University of Oregon with Geraldine Siks of the University of Washington, Deborah Wolfe of Queens College, and Brian Sutton-Smith of Teachers College, Columbia University as panelist, and a demonstration in Child Drama by Dorothy Heathcote of the University of Newcastle-Upon-Tyne, Great Britain.

Discussions continued in the afternoon with Stanley S. Madeja and Bernard S. Rosenblatt of the Central Midwest Regional Educational Laboratory in St. Ann, Missouri, speaking on the topic of "Aesthetic Education, A Social and Individual Need". Following this, each delegate choose the creative drama demonstration he or she wished to attend. The groups then reconvened to observe another group demonstration given by Jeanine Wagner.[102]

Despite the excellent programming, in the General Assembly the next day the Creative Drama Proposal was voted down: 24—Yes and 30—No. Ultimately in 1973 at the London EXCOM Meeting the creative dramatics proposal was again rejected decisively, and creative drama has never become part of ASSITEJ.

The day concluded with a panel discussion of professional theatre in the USA, a performance of *Johnny Moonbeam and The Silver Arrow* by Joseph Golden by the Atlanta, Georgia Children's Theatre, and a reception.

However, the performance was considered "too slick" by the guest critics, the company immediately left town, and in anger did not honor their commitments to further performances at the Congress and in town.[103]

Friday, 24 June

Friday featured presentations on research in Theatre with and for Children, followed by a performance of *Operation Theatre* by La Nouvelle Companie of Montreal, Canada and a critique of the play.

General Assembly-Elections continued / Friday, 24 June / 10:30 am

Rose-Marie Moudoués, the newly re-elected Secretary-General, presided.

Moudoués stated that the rules for election would continue as outlined at the last meeting. She announced that there were 17 official voting nations, each with 3 votes making a total of 51. 26 would be the required majority for the election of the officers.

Election of the Bureau: She announced the names of the New EXCOM members. She also announced that the New EXCOM had met in separate session, and brought forth the following slate of officers to be elected by the General Session: Nat Eek (USA) as President; Vladimir Adamek (Czechoslovakia), Ilse Rodenberg (GDR), and Joyce Doolittle (Canada) as Vice-Presidents. There were no nominations from the floor. She then turned the meeting over to President Shakh-Azizov.

The vote for Eek as President was: Yes—45; No—3; Abstain—3.

On the vote for the Vice-Presidents the French Center nominated José Géal, and the FGR nominated Hanswalter Gossmann. The results of the election were: Adamek—43; Rodenberg—35; Doolittle—28; Géal—17; Gossmann—3. Adamek, Rodenberg, and Doolittle were elected. Géal and Gossmann were not elected. This made the new Bureau as follows: Eek, Adamek, Rodenberg, Doolittle, Moudoués, and Lucian.

While the votes for the Vice-Presidents were being counted, the business of the Congress continued. Eek announced the following decisions of the EXCOM: they had co-opted the Netherlands Center

(Hans Snoek), and appointed 3 counselors (advisors)—Michael Pugh (Great Britain), Ian Cojar (Romania), and Sara Spencer (USA).

Michael Pugh presented information on his Play Bibliography, and asked for Centers to send their scripts to the British Center. Eek announced that the EXCOM had recommended accepting the invitation of the Belgian Center to have the next International Congress in Brussels in 1974. Géal was called upon to present the Belgian proposition. This was accepted by the Congress unanimously.

Statute Changes: The Assembly then considered 4 proposed constitutional changes, each requiring a 2/3 vote of 34 votes or more. Resolutions 2, 3, and 4, all of which were word and phrase changes, were approved. Resolution 1 which would have added Spanish as a fourth official language was then discussed. A motion was made and seconded to table the Proposal. It was tabled. Then Eek proposed his appointing an investigative committee that would study the proposal.

Creative Drama Proposal: Proposal Number 5 called for a committee to study Creative Drama techniques and present an appropriate resolution to the EXCOM for action. After much discussion the vote on the Proposal on Creative Dramatics was: For—20; Against—31. The Proposal failed.

Rodenberg presented information relating to the proposed GDR book on *International Children's Theatre since 1900*. There will be 20-30 pictures with a third of them in color, as well as a history of children's theatre in each country. While it will be published in German, materials can be submitted in any language, and she requested all Centers to send appropriate materials for inclusion to her Center by 31 December 1972.

Raoul Carrat (France) asked that the theme for the next Congress be chosen as soon as possible, so that others can work on it ahead of time.

Lucian asked that all official ASSITEJ correspondence for Romania should be sent to the Romanian Center for ASSITEJ whose office was PTTR 221 in Bucharest.

Karel Richter (Czechoslovakia) announced that the First International Meeting of Professional Actors for Children and Youth would be held in Prague 22-25 June 1973. It would consist of working sessions, and he asked that each Center send the younger generation actors only.

Moudoués announced the First International Annual Meeting for the study of the repertory of children's theatre plays in Bordeaux, France in October 1972.

Doolittle asked the Secretary-General for a letter listing: all the Statutes, whether a Center was in conformity with them; the Center's address; the name of a contact person; and the official language used by the Center for correspondence. Also, at the appropriate time, she asked if the Secretariat could send a dues notice to each Center as well as a request for nominations. The session ended.

Performances: Following the General Assembly and its elections, there were stagecraft and scenery demonstrations. Two productions were featured that day: *Georgia Tour Play* of the Academy Theatre of Atlanta, Georgia, and *The Tales of Pushkin* performed by the Central Children's Theatre of Moscow, USSR.

Saturday 25 June

Saturday featured a meeting of the new EXCOM followed by a meeting of the Bureau. While the EXCOM was meeting, the balance of the program was completed: a demonstration of stage makeup by Irene Corey and a performance of *The Capture of Sarah Quincy* by the Hopkins, Minnesota Eisenhower High School Theatre.

The New EXCOM Meeting-Saturday, 25 June

The New Executive Committee Meeting of ASSITEJ was held in Albany.

Nat Eek (USA) as President presided with Vladimir Adamek (Czechoslovakia) as 1st Vice President, Ilse Rodenberg (GDR) as 2nd Vice President, Joyce Doolittle (Canada) as 3rd Vice President, Rose-Marie Moudoués (France) as Secretary-General, and Ion Lucian (Romania) as Treasurer.

Other members attending were: Géal, Adamek, Gossmann, Tyler, Jenner, Porat, Biotto, Cojar, Sunyer, Shakh-Azizov, and Djokič.

Co-opted: Hans Snoek (Netherlands). Advisors: Michael Pugh (Great Britain) Ian Cojar (Romania), and Sara Spencer (USA).[104]

Members absent: Bulgaria.

Dues: President Eek presided who stated that they first had to vote upon a change of dues, which was not part of the original agenda. It was proposed to raise the dues to 75 USD minimum per annum per center. This was approved by a show of hands with 14 votes for, 1 against, and 3 abstentions. Co-opted members had a vote; Advisors did not have a vote. Eek commented that this special vote must not serve as a precedent. This was an action normally *recommended* by the EXCOM for approval by the General Assembly as part of its regular agenda.

Spanish Language Committee: Eek then returned to the EXCOM Agenda. He proposed a committee to study Spanish as a fourth official language, and appointed Sunyer, Adamek, and Doolittle to the Committee with instructions to report their findings at the London EXCOM meeting in 1973. and to send a report three months before the EXCOM Meeting to the Centers to give them time enough for study.

Future Meetings: The EXCOM approved holding the next Bureau Meeting in Bordeaux, France on 16-18 October 1972. 18 October 1972 was set aside for a discussion of the Spanish language question. They confirmed the London EXCOM Meeting dates as 9-17 June 1973 with the Bureau meeting on 11-12 June 1973. There would be events occurring out of town during the nine day meeting, but it would start and finish in London.

Future meeting invitations came thick and fast. Spain asked for the next EXCOM meeting to be held in their country, date to be established later. Other invitations came from Israel, Romania, Bulgaria, and USSR. Nuremberg requested a possible meeting which would coincide with their celebration of 25 years of theatre for children. Spain also issued an invitation for the General Assembly to be held there in 1976, and the USSR asked to hold the EXCOM that same year. The GDR put in a bid for the 1978 General Assembly to be held there. All the proposed invitations came from European countries.

GDR Book on Children's Theatre: There was further discussion on the proposed book on children's theatre to be published in the GDR. Rodenberg asked all official Centers to submit materials by 31 December 1972. She further said that materials should only cover the years from 1900 on. Educational theatre would be included, but nothing about puppet theatre. EXCOM accepted the GDR proposal unanimously.

Creative Drama: Snoek raised questions about the defeat in the General Assembly of the motion to investigate the area of "creative dramatics". She was surprised at the overwhelming negative response. Considerable discussion followed. Eek closed the discussion by advising everyone to bring their comments on creative drama in their countries to the London EXCOM meeting.

Miscellaneous items: The theme for the 1974 General Assembly was discussed. Adamek suggested "The Professional Theatre Artist and the Schools." Moudoués asked Canada and the USA to send articles on creative drama to the Paris office to be printed in the ASSITEJ Review.

Snoek said that there was a possibility of a television series on the history of children's theatre for children in her country. Porat asked for each Center to indicate such similar series in their countries and report them by 1972. Géal said he appreciated the use of professional critics at the Albany Conference, and he would try to do the same at the Brussels Conference in 1974.

Shakh-Azizov made a strong point that since the Constitution was adopted in 1965, there have been difficulties in interpretation and translation. The USSR Center suggested establishing a committee to clarify the Constitution, and submit a progress report. Eek proposed a Committee of Shakh-Azizov, Moudoués, and Tyler and for them to submit a report in London with copies in each language. Shakh-Azizov asked that Adamek be included in the Committee, and Eek appointed him accordingly. Moudoués proposed that the Committee meet in Bordeaux, and the EXCOM members should send their ideas to the Committee by a deadline of 1 October 1972. The meeting was then adjourned.

The Congress concluded Saturday night with a picnic for all the delegates and fireworks. Before breaking up Saturday night, delegates wandered about to wish everyone goodbye, and to cement new found friendships.

On Sunday morning one hundred foreign delegates departed for NYC for a three day program, which included a Broadway musical *Follies* by Stephen Sondheim, a three language tour of the new Metropoleitan Opera House, a boat tour around Manhattan Island, and a cocktail reception given by ITI and Rosamund Gilder with many Broadway luminaries invited to meet the delegates.[105]

An Evaluation: The Canadian and USA Committees in charge had never sponsored a meeting of this size, cost, and complexity before. Both Doolittle and Eek were delighted, feeling that their collaboration had lasting results beyond the Congress.

From the standpoint of the US Center, their part of the Congress was an unqualified success. Eek particularly praised Patricia Snyder's influence and expertise; Orlin Corey's Play Committee for assembling five USA plays of high quality; the excellent presentations by major practitioners in the field; Ann Shaw's assembling of the creative dramatics programs; and Ann Hill's scrupulous financial accountability.

This joint Canada/USA Congress had provided innumerable productions showing the tremendous range in approaches to children's theatre, along with a variety of programs and discussion sessions as a means to explore the theme of the Congress. While previous Congresses had concentrated on "theatre", this one concentrated on "the child." As one delegate put it, this Assembly:

> ...focused precise and unprecedented attention on the quality and diversity of theater experiences for children and youth and provoked an international reassessment of goals centering significantly in the needs and capabilities of the child, rather than the convenience and predisposition of those who write, produce,and schedule plays for children.[106]

A delegate from India added:

> Let those of us who come from older cultures not be complacent about our classical traditions and our conventions ...For me this has been a very memorable, exciting, rewarding week. We have not only seen and experienced much, but we have met colleagues from other countries, known their struggles, problems, and achievements.[107]

At the same time, delegates from the USA, who had never been to an international Congress for children's theatres, were impressed by the high quality and imagination of all the productions, and returned to their theatres resolving to upgrade their programs and bring them closer to the international models seen. This Congress would influence their theatres for years to come.

Formal dinner speakers (flanked by interpreters) at the IVth International Congress of ASSITEJ, SUNY, Albany, New York, USA, June 1072. Photo by Edward Wozniak. Courtesy of SUNY Dept. of Theatre, Albany, New York. (Left, top to bottom) Patricia B. Snyder (USA); Joyce Doolittle (Canada), Rosamund Gilder (USA), Barbara Good (USA); (Right, top to bottom) Konstantin Shakh-Azizov (USSR), Ruth Mayleas (USA), Nat Eek (USA), and Sara Spencer (USA).

President Konstantin Shakh-Azizov (USSR) addresses the General Assembly at the IVth International ASSITEJ Congress, State University of New York, Albany, New York, USA. June 1972. Galina Kolosova (USSR Interpreter) on the left. Photo courtesy of SUNY Dept. of Theatre, Albany, New York.

"Hang on to Your Head" created and directed by John Clark Donahue, Minneapolis Children's Theatre, June 1972.
Photo courtesy of Mrs. Donald F.Phillips.

"Hang on to Your Head" created and directed by John Clark Donahue,
Minneapolis Children's Theatre, June 1972.
Photo courtesy of Mrs. Donald F.Phillips.

"Tales with Masks" created, directed, and performed by Ion Lucien, Ion Creanga
Theatre, Bucharest, Romania, June 1972. Presented at the IVth International
ASSITEJ Congress. Ion Lucien in the center. Photo courtesy of SUNY Dept. of
Theatre, Albany, New York.

"Tales with Masks" created, directed, and performed by Ion Lucien, Ion Creanga Theatre, Bucharest, Romania, June 1972. Presented at the IVth International ASSITEJ Congress. Photo courtesy of SUNY Dept. of Theatre, Albany, New York.

"Tales with Masks" created, directed, and performed by Ion Lucien, Ion Creanga Theatre, Bucharest, Romania, June 1972. Presented at the IVth International ASSITEJ Congress. Photo courtesy of SUNY Dept. of Theatre, Albany, New York.

A SUMMARY OF 1970-1972

1970

*A*fter the Venice Congress in October of 1970, a Bureau Meeting was held in Paris, France in May of 1971. This meeting occurred in conjunction with an International Colloquium of Writers in Bordeaux, France on 5-8 May 1971. According to the author's research, there were no Minutes to indicate who attended and what business exactly transpired.

However, correspondence between Moudoués and Eek indicated that the discussion primarily covered concerns and suggestions related to the up-coming 1972 Congress in Canada and the USA. Moudoués felt the food and lodging expenses for the delegates should be provided because of the high costs of the travel to North America. Eek replied that they would have to limit the number of officially supported delegates. For example, the ITI in New York City always limited representation to two delegates per country. Eek continued that if all the delegates were to be supported, much more money would have to be raised to satisfy this request. This concern was not raised again, although both North American centers were able to provide food and lodging at minimal cost to the delegates. In addition, both Centers said they would provide simultaneous translation, and both would do everything possible to get visas for delegates with political problems.

1971

Four months later the EXCOM met for the first time after the Venice Congress in Bratislava, Czechoslovakia in October of 1971. All members were in attendance except Great Britain, Israel, and Romania.

Publications: The first issue of the 1971 *ASSITEJ Review* had been mailed, and Nos. 3 and 4 were in production. If no materials were forthcoming, they could publish one or two plays instead. The question of unpaid dues as a necessary source of income was raised again. However, the French Center would pay the cost of the publications as well as the rent for 1972. Doolittle and Eek both gave complete reports on the details of the 1972 Congress. Because of inclement weather the meeting dispersed quickly once its business was completed.

The Bureau reconvened in Prague for a discussion of particular points of protocol related to the elections and the use of creative dramatics in demonstration. Members still expressed concern that children were not professional, and they should not be performing in theatre for children.

The ASSITEJ exhibit had finally arrived in Great Britain, but was in such bad shape that it could not be used. The question of what to do with it was not resolved until the next meeting. The final solution was for ASSITEJ to pay for its return to France, and then to junk it. There was no disagreement.

Centers: Three new Centers were asking to be approved. For several years Poland had tried to be accepted as a Center. Perhaps it was only a one person center. However, Moudoués announced that its application was finally complete and in order. Ireland had not sent in their statutes; and Hungary had no statutes yet to send in. The three were accepted provisionally, with full approval once the omissions were corrected and dues were paid.

Because of the Secretary-General's personal involvement in the Spanish Civil War, she was initially quite hostile to the formation of a Spanish Center, since Spain was still ruled by General Francisco Franco. The Spanish Center was established due to the persistence of Maria Sunyer. Also, Japan had tried to join as a Center, and they were finally accepted in 1969 after three years of trying, despite their reported conforming to all the requirements. Because of Spain's fascistic involvement in WWII, that is probably why the Secretary-General opposed Spain's confirmation and blocked it informally. Her ignoring of Japan can probably be placed at the feet of Euro-centric attitudes, as well as Japan's involvement in WW II.

Australia: Mme. Maria Tomasetti of Australia addressed the EXCOM, giving her report on the possible establishment of an Australian Center. She and her husband Anthony Roberts represented the South Australian Theatre Company, and she cited their professional company, the foreign tours, and a list of some of their productions as evidence of their satisfying the ASSITEJ statutes. She submitted their membership, and requested to be accepted as a Center. The Secretary-General thanked her for the report, but in order to establish a Center she needed to get in touch with Mme. Raynor in Australia who supposedly was their representative, but who had not appeared in ASSITEJ since 1965.

Auditors: Caryl Jenner (Great Britain) again requested an audit of the ASSITEJ finances. This had been discussed in Venice, but still no auditors had been appointed. The Secretary-General now stated that France had two auditors, and they were serving without expense. The Treasurer had been working with the two of them to check expenses. From the comments on the Financial Report it can be seen that Jenner's demand for an audit and Eek's threat of canceling the 1972 Congress had a salutary effect on the Paris office's efficiency, although much of it still seemed to be smoke and mirrors.

Eek was appointed to keep the official Minutes, but he asked that the appointment be made official, and then he would distribute them to the individual Centers. After most of the delegates had left, two days later the Bureau met to discuss the details of the election at the upcoming IVth Congress.

Rodenberg proposed that the next EXCOM meeting be in Berlin-Leipzig-Dresden, and the Berlin date was set for March 3. The IVth Congress was scheduled for June; the Bordeaux EXCOM and Bureau Meetings set for October; and the London EXCOM for 1973. They also recommended having the Vth Congress in Brussels, Belgium based on an invitation from José Géal indicating that it was the 20th Anniversary of the Belgian Children's Theatre. Lastly, they approved an EXCOM meeting in Spain in the fall of 1974.

1972

The EXCOM next met in Germany in March of 1972. It was a moveable feast, since the GDR Center wished to show off Berlin, Leipzig, and Dresden to the Committee. These cities were still recovering from the damages of WWII, and the GDR had been sealed off by the building of the Wall. Dresden with great determination was re-building the beautiful Frauenkirche, symbol of the city, from the original rubble, and with great ceremony it was finally completed and re-opened in 2005!

All EXCOM Members were present except Belgium. The status of the Centers in Austria, Brazil, and Belgium was questioned since they had not paid their dues. Tyler asserted that ASSITEJ should not continue carrying anyone who was no longer interested in the organization. Cojar agreed adding that the three new Centers admitted in Prague in October 1971—Ireland, Portugal, and Hungary—were supposed to pay later.

Of the countries in arrears—Norway, Austria, and Brazil—Doolittle proposed that they be dropped, and then given a chance to renew. The Secretary-General was instructed to write a letter to those countries notifying them of their expulsion, and that they may be reinstated by application and payment of dues, and then resume their regular representation at meetings.

The question of Israel's non-payment for the past three years was taken up. Porat stated that she would decide about payment by June, suggesting that since she had only recently established the Israeli Center, she could not be responsible for past dues. Eek reminded the Secretary-General that Israel had voted by proxy for three years without paying, a dangerous precedent. Cojar would inform the Congress at the beginning of the session which members could vote.

Noting that the accounts still had to be audited, the EXCOM recognized that only the Congress could name the auditors. It was decided that a resolution for the audit of accounts and the names of the two auditors would be presented for approval by the General Assembly in Montreal.

New Centers: At the EXCOM meeting in Dresden the Secretary-General announced that Hungary, Peru, Portugal, and Ireland had all met the requirements for membership, and the EXCOM accepted them. Negotiations were continuing with Australia, Switzerland, and Argentina, and Jenner was asked to continue her contact with Iran.

Spanish as a 4th Language: The Spanish Center requested that Spanish be added as a fourth language, since next to English, Spanish was the most spoken language in ASSITEJ. The many difficulties in administration and finance that this fourth official language would create were cited, and the request was refused. After this refusal, the Spanish Center with the knowledge and approval of ASSITEJ began publishing an ASSITEJ Review in Spanish at their own expense listing activities, festivals, and general information, and distributed it to all Spanish-speaking Centers as well as other Spanish-speaking countries in ITI and UNESCO.

Minutes: At no time in these early years did the Secretary-General or the Paris Office send out any official Minutes following the international meetings of the General Assembly sessions, the EXCOM, or the Bureau. The only unofficial records of these meetings were personal notes taken by Eek, Doolittle, Tyler, Adamek, Corey, and other representatives. When notes are taken by a presiding officer or by a participant in the discussions, inaccuracies were bound to creep in.

At the Dresden EXCOM Meeting Adamek raised his concerns about the inaccuracies and errors in format written in the reports of the previous meetings of the EXCOM. Historically, in 1965 after the Constitutional Conference in Paris, Eek prepared an Informational Report of that meeting for distribution to the members of the US Center. As an informational courtesy he sent copies to various other Centers who requested it. He continued to do this as the USA Representative.

In 1971 he was asked by the EXCOM to make these notes the official Minutes of the Meetings and to distribute them to the members of the EXCOM. Eek did as requested, and eventually sent copies to all the official ASSITEJ Centers. It was these unintentional inaccuracies about which Adamek was concerned, but Eek was not present for the discussion, and was never told what these "inaccuracies" were.

With the election of Michael Ramløse (Denmark) in 1990 the Secretariat began distributing official Minutes recorded by a staff member of the International Center in Denmark of the meetings following each gathering.

The British Center asked the General Assembly to set up a working party to study the relationships between children's theatre and creative dramatics, and to make a report to the EXCOM for possible action. The President stated that the British Center should prepare a clear statement of what Creative Dramatics was and that this statement be made available to all members. With this statement along with appropriate examples in hand, the Centers would be able to have a more meaningful discussion in the General Assembly. The proposal was left at this.

1972 Congress-Montreal: When the IVth Congress was held in North America, it was the first time that ASSITEJ had met outside Europe, and 7 years after the Association's founding in Paris in 1965. Of the four previous International Congresses, 3 were held in the West, and 1 in the East. Of the previous 9 EXCOM Meetings, one 1 was held in the West and 8 in the East. This could have happened because it was easier and less expensive for the Eastern delegates to travel in Europe, or because they were better prepared to set up conferences quickly, and it was a mark of prestige to have Western delegates come. Also, things were much more expensive in the West, and government funding was harder to obtain to support international meetings.

All EXCOM Members were present at the IVth Congress except Bulgaria. The Congress was held in two (2) parts, and the first part met in Montreal, Quebec, Canada. Joyce Doolittle was the Program Director and organizer. By agreement, the Assembly's discussion meetings were to be held in Canada, and the business sessions and elections were to be held in the USA. Adamek had prepared a logical and well researched Voting Procedure for approval by the membership. Besides the elections, the USA and Great Britain had jointly presented changes in the Statutes to be approved by the General Assembly. Most importantly these dealt with the approval of the Secretary-General and the Treasurer before the election of the EXCOM. Thus the countries of those two individuals would automatically be seated on the EXCOM. Later in the 1990s this Statute would be changed to have these two positions filled in addition to a full EXCOM of fifteen members. This would make an EXCOM of seventeen, exclusive of co-options or advisors.

Centers: In their discussion about new centers in Israel and Switzerland the EXCOM focused on the Israel Center as a continuing problem, which many considered a "ghost" Center. From the very beginning the Center had been represented by Orna Porat, a leading Israeli actress with her own theatre company. However, she was the only one in the Center, and its status was always in question. The Secretary-General (apparently for personal reasons) was extremely protective of the Israel Center's status, even with Porat's history of emotional instability, which became publicly evident at the Lyons Congress in 1981. However, in 2002 at the Korean Congress Porat was named a Member of Honor. After further discussion the National Center from Switzerland was admitted to membership and full status, but full status for Israel required the paying of its dues.

A discussion of a Center's eligibility to vote always occurred in the EXCOM meetings just before an election, since the Secretary-General had to announce which centers were eligible to vote at the General Assembly before a ballot could be taken. The number of eligible votes determined the majority vote, and this was important politically to all the Centers, as they maintained the East-West balance. In addition, only the Secretary-General really knew which Centers had conformed to the statutes, paid their dues, and were active members. Those who were pro-East usually found themselves admitted and voting members, even when their statutes had not arrived, their dues had not been paid, and they may have had only a single representative with no Center or constituency.

At a Congress, sometimes a Center in arrears would pay their dues with check or cash to the Secretary-General from the floor of the General Assembly session just before elections were held. Some delegates suspected that another Center had just paid those dues for them in return for their vote. The Secretary-General would then announce their payment waving the check or cash, and their reinstatement, usually to tumultuous applause and a delighted smile on the face of the representative. It also meant that a non-paying representative could usually attend all the meetings, enjoy the benefits, and only have to pay up once every three years. As long as the Secretary-General and the EXCOM were lenient, this practice was continued. In later years, a Center was suspended after their first year of non-payment of dues.

Also, at a Congress some Centers voted proxies for other eligible Centers without a delegate present. Sometimes a Center, notably the French Center, would hold up to 4 official proxies. Many years later the Statutes were changed to allow only 1 proxy per National Center.

According to the Secretary-General, who was East in her sympathies, there were always problems with the mails and the transmission of funds for dues. This was the official explanation for the long delay in admitting Spain, Japan, and Australia who leaned toward the West, while Peru and Portugal, who were primarily East in their orientation, were always in and out depending on their payment of dues. However, many times the politics of a center reflected that of the representative, not necessarily that of the country represented. Sometimes membership was delayed by the Paris office until the representatives with the correct political persuasion were found to head the Center.

Pre-Election Discussions: Assessing the vote prior to the election always affected the EXCOM discussions and the decisions. At the North American Congress in 1972 there were 21 National Centers present. 1 Center was too new to vote, 17 could vote, but 3 had not paid their dues—Ireland, Peru, and Portugal. The eligible voting Centers according to the Treasurer were: Belgium, Bulgaria, Canada, Czechoslovakia, FGR, France, GDR, Great Britain, Hungary, Israel, Italy, Netherlands,

Romania, Spain, USA, USSR, and Yugoslavia making a total of 17.

In the early years the Secretary-General would personally select the Treasurer, and the EXCOM would approve her recommendation. All the Treasurers had been close personal friends of Moudoués–Géal, Cojar, and Lucian with Lucian serving longest. It was not until Paul Harman (Great Britain) was re-elected as Treasurer in 1990 and Michael Ramløse elected as Secretary-General at the 1990 meetings that the ASSITEJ finances were moved from the French Center and put on a sound basis. However, France in part supported ASSITEJ financially for twenty-five years, and without that support ASSITEJ could not have survived. Moudoués and her Center deserve to be honored greatly for that tremendous contribution. In addition, the fact that the Secretariat had been located in Paris at the same address for twenty-five years gave ASSITEJ stability in communications that was both admirable and well recognized.

In the general EXCOM discussion in Montreal President Shakh-Azizov proposed Eek as the next President. It was approved unanimously. However, this proposal might have been two-edged. First, it had the advantage of thanking the USA for co-hosting the Congress. When the USA first projected their invitation in 1968, it was quite obvious from the enthusiasm of the Centers that many very much wanted to visit the USA, and an official invitation allowed them to do so with the complete approval and financial support of their governments.

Secondly, by ignoring Adamek as 2nd Vice-President and proposing Eek who was 1st Vice-President after the Venice election, Shakh-Azizov showed how the USSR would vote while at the same time putting down Czechoslovakia, whom they had invaded in 1968. Logically by right of earlier succession and involvement Adamek should have been President before Eek. However, the Shakh-Azizov proposal seemed logical at the time. The Vice-Presidents were usually placed in numerical order depending on the number of votes they received.

Performances: The Montreal portion of the Congress included 8 companies performing a total of 22 times in 4 theatres in 6 days. 500 delegates from 25 nations attended these events in Montreal.

Scholar Richard Courtney cited Canada's contributions to theatre for children, both in quality and diversity:

As befits a bilingual nation, we have performances in both

English and French—and some companies perform equally well in both. As you travel across the four-and-a-half thousand miles of this country you can see large, expensive companies financially well supported by their provinces, and you can witness a performance by four players who have traveled to a cold barn on the northern prairies in an old Jeep. You can visit a large playhouse and be warmed by a full-scale musical, or you can wander into a school gymnasium and see children sitting in a circle around a company of players encouraging the children to participate.

Other performances from Canada included: *Shakespeare's Women* (The Globe Theatre, Regina, Saskatchewan), *Where Are You When We Need You, Simon Fraser?* (Playhouse Holiday, Vancouver, British Columbia), *The Clam Made a Face* (Young People's Theatre, Toronto, Ontario), and *Operation-Theatre* (La Nouvelle Compagnie Théâtrale, Montreal, Quebec). The three English speaking companies showed delegates the kind of theatre most common in Canada in the past decade—five young actors with minimal scenery and costumes who tour elementary schools with a play (usually including audience participation) or a collective creation (usually in presentational style) for junior or senior high schools.

Two companies from Eastern Europe, where government support for theatre for young audiences is immense, provided an enormous contrast in style, intent, and audience response. *The Fairy Tales of Pushkin* presented by the Moscow Central Children's Theatre in the two thousand seat Expo theatre was a two hour spectacle requiring six tons of scenery and a company of forty. On the afternoon of 15 July, the theatre was full of Montréal children and ASSITEJ delegates. That same evening, at the Gesu, an old, uncomfortable, but intimate theatre, seating seven hundred persons, the Ion Creanga Theatre of Bucharest performed *Tales with Masks* and its actor-director-creator Ion Lucian, played the seven deadly sins with the help of seven marvelous out-sized masks, charming the capacity crowd.

Reaction from the delegates was almost unanimous. The play from the USSR was considered heavy and old-fashioned, but brilliantly performed; the play from Romania was thought charming and imaginative. Since the delegates outnumbered the children six to one in the evening and children outnumbered the delegates three to one in the afternoon, a comparison of children's reactions is difficult. Besides the fine comic performance by Lucian, another element of the Romanian performance universally admired was the design. While the USSR production brought six tons of scenery, the Romanian "set" fit into fourteen canvas bags and weighed about six hundred pounds. It was, in part, to solve the problems of the cost of airfreight that the Ion Creanga devised scenery made of woven hemp and burlap, thereby converting a problem and political liability into an asset.

The other invited foreign company was the Minneapolis Children's Theatre of Minnesota, USA. This company comprised of adult professional actors and child and adolescent student actors presented the most controversial show in the Congress. *Hang on to Your Head* was presented by a company of 50. There were two truckloads of scenery. Although Director John Donahue had devised an entertainment of great skill and artistry, the reactions of delegates in Montréal (and later in Albany) were almost entirely negative. The technical aspects, impressive skill, and ensemble playing of the company were admired, but the script was considered by most to be inappropriate for children—too sophisticated on the whole and psychologically dangerous in part.

Montreal Crises: Anyone who has ever hosted an international event is familiar with unexpected events and crises. The Montreal Congress was no exception. The most dramatic problems were connected with union problems. There was a month long garbage strike in Montréal which ended only days before the Congress. The civic reception was moved from the Chalet on Mount Royal to the lobby of the Place des Arts—an elegant venue and completely appropriate for a theatre party.

The strike by dock workers was still in progress when the scenery and costumes for the USSR production of *The Fairy Tales of Pushkin* arrived. It was only through the last minute offer of Gigi Transport, a small moving company and the good graces of union bosses and members who ignored the dozens of trips by the small open bed truck back and forth from the docks to the Expo Theatre. Thus a bare stage, modern dress version of the Soviet play was avoided.

The first half of the Conference went very well, and the delegates were ready for a party. It was a good orchestra, they played during the meal, and couples took to the large ballroom dance floor with ease. After opening with the national anthems of Canada and the USA, they played a variety of dances. They were asked to play a rumba, and soon other delegates asked for favorites, and there followed a slow waltz, a Viennese waltz, a polka, a fox trot, a conga line, and even a bunny-hop. The evening had ended on a high festive note as delegates headed to their rooms.

Eek went over to the orchestra leader to thank him for their excellent playing, and the band leader replied: "Mister, we've had such a great time playing that if your group would fly us to your next convention, we will play free!" Unfortunately, ASSITEJ wasn't able to get the band's travel expenses into the next budget!

The Montréal sessions were exciting. The complaint that there was not enough time for general discussion about the plays and speeches was valid. Four days was not really long enough for the program as presented. However, most delegates boarded the buses to Albany in good spirits and with a sense of anticipation for the USA segment of the Congress. For Canada, the Congress called attention to an often neglected part of the arts and led, eventually, to the network of Canadian Annual International Festivals for Children which began in the late 1970s and which continue to thrive to this day.

1972 Congress./.Albany: For the Albany part of the program of the Congress, the US Center had determined:

1) to feature USA productions chosen from across the country by three theatre experts;

2) to present professional critiques of each production followed by open discussion;

3) to showcase a day long presentation on creative drama (a form of theatre that had been deliberately excluded from the statutes of ASSITEJ in 1964); and

4) to offer a three-day excursion to New York City for the international delegates following the Congress.

To lead the discussions on the plays seen in the USA, the American Committee had appointed panels of 3 professional critics, each to present a spoken review on the plays seen the day before. Their reviews were then followed by questions and open discussion which were candid and lively. This approach succeeded in de-fusing any standard and predictable responses to the plays, and took the delegates off the hook of having to make any politically correct statements.

The Elections: The new EXCOM comprised the following countries: Belgium, Bulgaria, Canada, Czechoslovakia, FGR, GDR, Great Britain, Israel, Italy, Spain, USSR, USA, and Yugoslavia, plus France and Romania ex officio. The new officers elected were: Nat Eek (USA) as President, Vladimir Adamek (Czechoslovakia) as 1st Vice-President, Ilse Rodenberg (GDR) as 2nd Vice-President, Joyce Doolittle (Canada) as 3rd Vice-President, Rose-Marie Moudoués (France) as Secretary-General, and Ion Lucian (Romania) as Treasurer. Han Snoek (Netherlands) was co-opted, and three Advisors were appointed: Ian Cojar (Romania), Sara Spencer (USA), and Michael Pugh (Great Britain).

The election of 3 Advisors or Counselors conformed to the Statutes (1965—Article X, Section 3), which does not indicate a number. Moreover, many times a country or an individual was selected not so much for their advice, but as thanks for services rendered or as a means to get government support for their travels and have the opportunity to get away officially from their countries. This was especially true of the Eastern bloc, and in this case Cojar.

In general discussion all the Statute changes passed, except the acceptance of Spanish as the fourth Official Language of ASSITEJ. This proposal was defeated. Lastly, the General Assembly accepted the Belgian invitation to hold the Vth ASSITEJ Congress in that country in 1974.

Creative Drama: Thursday had been designated as Creative Drama Day, co-chaired by Ann Thurman of Northwestern University and Ann Shaw of Queens College (City University of New York) with multiple lectures and demonstrations that involved both the demonstrators and the audience. The creative drama presentations included an opening address by Jed Davis of the University of Kansas and President of the American Theatre Association; the first multi-media production at an ASSITEJ Congress entitled "Dimensions of Creative Drama" narrated by Shaw; a panel discussion on the "Simplifications of Creative Drama for the Development of the Child", moderated by Barbara Salisbury of the University of Oregon with Geraldine Siks of the University of Washington, Deborah Wolfe of Queens College, and Brian Sutton-Smith of Teachers College, Columbia University as panelist; and a demonstration in Child Drama by Dorothy Heathcote of the University of Newcastle-Upon-Tyne, Great Britain.

Unfortunately, the Creative Drama Day was not attended by a number of delegates from the European countries who were only interested in professional theatre *for* children. One of the major purposes of this day of demonstrations by the US Center was to showcase Creative Drama, in the hope that ASSITEJ would favorably consider its inclusion in the international Association's agenda. However, creative drama was regarded by many of the European delegates as basically "Western", primarily educational, and not "adult professional"[108], despite the fact that Great Britain, the Netherlands, the Scandinavian countries, Spain, and Yugoslavia had active creative drama programs in their countries. In the General Assembly the next day the Proposal was voted down: 20—Yes and 31—No. Ultimately in 1973 at the London EXCOM Meeting the creative drama proposal was rejected, and creative drama never become part of ASSITEJ.

Performances: A performance of *Johnny Moonbeam and the Silver Arrow* by Joseph Golden performed by the Atlanta, Georgia Children's Theatre was performed for the delegates, followed by a reception. The choice of this play was deliberately made, hopefully to show the 1972 delegates that this was an excellent and appropriate USA play, despite its controversial reception in 1964 in London. However, the performance was considered "too slick", so its reappearance did not have the desired effect. The company immediately left town in anger, and did not honor their commitments to further performances at the Congress and in town.

In the final meeting of the New EXCOM the following decisions were made: 1) that the Creative Dramatics proposal be presented at the EXCOM Meeting in London in 1973 for a final decision; 2) that the Spanish Language proposal be presented as a committee report for a final decision; and 3) that a Committee be established to clarify and codify the language of the Constitution to avoid any further ambiguity in meaning.

Following the last General Assembly the delegates were able to see *The Tales of Pushkin* and *Georgia Tour* Play. Of the five USA productions the *Georgia Tour Play* was the favorite of the foreign delegates and the USA delegation, primarily because of its "...tackling of a contemporary problem in American society, the excellent ensemble acting, and the careful characterizations ...."[109] The core of the drama was the multi-racial casting of *Romeo and Juliet* in a southern USA town, and the personal and bigoted conflicts it caused.

While the EXCOM was meeting, the balance of the program was completed: a demonstration of stage makeup by Irene Corey, and performances of *The Capture of Sarah Quincy* by the Hopkins, Minnesota Eisenhower High School Theatre. The three professional critics referred to this play respectively as "not believable", "bursting with life", and "terrific". They also regarded the Canadian production of *The Follies of Scapin* as "an extraordinary theatrical performance."[110]

The Congress concluded Saturday night with a picnic for all the delegates and fireworks. Before breaking up Saturday night, delegates wandered about to wish everyone goodbye, and to cement new found friendships. The members of the USSR performing company were found gathered around the television screen in the lounge viewing the film *The Russians Are Coming! The Russians Are Coming!*[111]

NYC Excursion: On Sunday morning one hundred foreign delegates departed for New York City for a three day program, which included a Broadway musical *Follies* by Stephen Sondheim, a three language tour of the new Metropolitan Opera House, a boat tour around Manhattan Island, and a cocktail reception given by ITI and Rosamund Gilder with many Broadway luminaries invited to meet the delegates.

The Canadian and USA Committees had never sponsored a meeting of this size, cost, and complexity before. Both Doolittle and Eek felt that their successful collaboration had results that would last well beyond the Congress.

From the standpoint of the US Center, their part of the Congress was an unqualified success. Eek particularly praised Patricia Snyder's influence, support, and expertise; Orlin Corey's Play Committee for assembling 5 USA plays of high quality with their attendant and unique critiques; Ann Thurman's and Ann Shaw's organization of the creative drama programs and the excellent presentations by major practitioners in the field; and Ann Hill's scrupulous financial accountability.

Delegates from the USA, who had never been to an international congress for children's theatres, were impressed by the high quality and imagination of all the productions. Many returned to their theatres resolving to upgrade their programs and bring them closer to the international models seen. This Congress would influence children's theatre in the USA for years to come.

Most important from the perspective of ASSITEJ and North America, this fifth Congress was the largest one ever attended so far, over 500 delegates from 25 nations with 21 official National Centers present.

Performance by The Little Theatre of the Deaf, from The O'Neill Center, at the IVth International ASSITEJ Congress. Photo courtesy of SUNY Dept. of Theatre, Albany, New York.

PART II:

THE PERIOD OF DISILLUSIONMENT
(1972-1975)

1972
BUREAU MEETING
Bordeaux, France / 16-21 October 1972

The Bureau of ASSITEJ met in Bordeaux, France from 16-21 of October 1972. Nat Eek (USA) as President presided, with Vladimir Adamek (Czechoslovakia) as 1st Vice President, Ilse Rodenberg (GDR) as 2nd Vice President, Joyce Doolittle (Canada) as 3rd Vice-President, Rose-Marie Moudoués (France) as Secretary-General, and Ion Lucian (Romania) as Treasurer. Gerald Tyler (Great Britain) attended as Honorary President and Maria Sunyer (Spain) attended on invitation.[112]

Members absent: none.

The Bureau Meeting / Monday, 16 October
The first meeting was held at 4:45 pm with Nat Eek as President presiding.

*M*aria Sunyer had been invited to come and present her proposal for Spanish as a fourth language, since it was tabled at the IVth International Congress in the USA General Assembly session.

The following items on the Agenda were discussed: Moudoués recommended that a meeting of the Statutes Committee be held before the Bureau and EXCOM in London in 1973. Adamek pointed out that only the General Assembly could make Statute changes. The EXCOM can make recommendations, and send them to the Centers for discussion and eventual approval. Eek suggested the Committee meet the next day, pass their recommendations on to the Bureau, which in turn could pass them to the EXCOM by mail. Comments could then be sent to the Committee for their final report at London. Moudoués then stated that there had been no request from anyone to change the Statutes, but that the Committee would only be concerned with regularizing the text.

Eek pointed out that constant communication was absolutely necessary, and that some members of the EXCOM had complained that the Bureau was making too many independent decisions instead of the EXCOM. He felt it important that the EXCOM be kept informed of all decisions, and constantly be provided with information which should be sent out promptly. Doolittle asked who would send the Minutes of the Statute Committee to Eek, and Moudoués agreed to do so.

New Centers: On a point of information Moudoués said that the legality of the Portugal Center had been questioned, but the possibility of two national centers there would have to be solved internally. She had also written to Australia, but as yet had received no reply. Rodenberg reported that Egypt, Mongolia, and Ceylon had all expressed interest in ASSITEJ and in forming a center.

Publications: The GDR book on the *History of Children's Theatre Since 1900* was discussed. Adamek asked how many pages were in the book. Rodenberg replied that the publisher said it depends on how much material is sent in. A representative will be at the London conference to talk about the book. Moudoués suggested a limit of 100 pages.

The Minutes of the Old EXCOM and the New EXCOM Meeting in Albany were distributed. They were accepted with minor corrections by Rodenberg and given to Moudoués. Eek reported that the USA planned to distribute the Report of the 1972 General Assembly to each Center in February 1973. Doolittle reported that a national magazine published by the Canadian Center would be devoted to theatre for children, and would include a summary of most of the Canadian events as well as pictures and a report of the International Meeting in 1972. A copy would be sent to each Center, probably by December. Tyler requested that a copy each of the Canadian and the US Report be sent to each officer in ASSITEJ too.

Eek asked that Doolittle be appointed Recording Secretary for the Minutes of the Bureau and the EXCOM. This was agreed upon.

Financial Statement: Lucian distributed copies of the Financial Statement, and mentioned that the budget had been discussed in Paris preceding this Bureau meeting, and the two Auditors could now write official documents.

Lucian had several questions about dues. Ireland was admitted in 1972, but had only paid in 1971. Should this fee be credited to 1972? The EXCOM decided that Ireland should pay for 1972. Peru and Switzerland who were admitted in 1972 also must pay for 1972. Finally every Center was supposed to have written the Secretariat that they had accepted the increase in dues. None had done so. Moudoués would now write to each Center, inform them of the increase, and if any Center wished to protest, they could do so at that time.

The New ITI Committee on Youth: Moudoués reported that the ITI had created a new committee for youth and young adults, and each country had been asked to form a commission on this subject. Those representatives would meet in Budapest, Hungary in December 1972. The Secretary-General of ITI visited Moudoués to explain that no duplication of ASSITEJ was intended, and had invited her to attend that meeting as ASSITEJ's representative. Moudoués asked if we should collaborate.

Rodenberg pointed out that the ITI Representative from the USSR had asked her if she would like to attend. She had replied that all of ASSITEJ should be invited, not just a single member. Tyler asked if this was the same as the ITI committee that preceded the forming of ASSITEJ. The EXCOM generally felt it was not. Lucian said that ASSITEJ should be represented. Tyler mentioned that at the recent London Meeting of ITI, all children's theatre organizations were excluded! Lucian pointed out that ITI must be made to know that ASSITEJ does exist, and then "we can collaborate." Tyler asked Moudoués to write to the Committee to inquire as to what the Committee was charged to do. Moudoués replied that they had already done so, and reported that ITI intended to investigate the place of theatre in the lives of adults, but that they were concerned with a new young age group of 18-25 years. Eek asked how many would attend the ITI Meeting in Budapest. Moudoués replied that there were 50 active members, and they all expected to attend.

Lucian continued with concerns: In many countries ITI activities would conflict with ASSITEJ. While we cannot prevent them from forming such a committee, we can counter-balance it with developing our own activities with artistic content. ASSITEJ has done many things: it has helped form new National Centers; it has a Committee on Statutes; it has had excellent Congresses in the GDR, the FGR, in North America; and an important book on children's theatre is soon to be published. ITI is better at the exchange of new artistic modes, new ways of doing things, new bibliography. We run the risk of being an appendage to ITI. There should not be two centers for youth in each country.

Rodenberg suggested that ASSITEJ spend more time discussing artistic problems. Moudoués said there is always the danger of administrative problems overpowering the artistic questions. Lucian said that everyone should be encouraged to write theoretical articles. Moudoués replied that no one sends anything to her for *The ASSITEJ Review*.

Tyler asked if ASSITEJ had been close enough to ITI to communicate our work to them. Moudoués replied that she is in Paris and she is frequently contacted by ITI representatives. Eek commented that he feels that ITI has finally noticed ASSITEJ and the vast job it does with young people. Moudoués agreed, and said that ITI is trying to find a way to get young adults to come to the theatre. It was agreed to send Moudoués as the representative from ASSITEJ to the ITI Committee Meeting.

The dates of the next meetings were discussed. Moudoués pointed out that the EXCOM meeting in Spain would be better if held in the spring of 1974. If held in October, it would be too far from the last General Assembly and too near the summer holidays. Sunyer should be asked if a change is possible.

The meeting adjourned for dinner, and to meet again the next day.

The Bureau Meeting / Tuesday, 17 October

The second meeting was held on October 17 in Bordeaux with Nat Eek as President presiding. All members were present. Géal, Chairman of the 1974 Brussels Conference, joined the Bureau for the discussion of the upcoming international conference.

The Brussells Congress: Géal advised the Bureau that he felt ten days was long enough for the conference, and suggested that it begin around July 1. After discussion it was decided that the Bureau would meet before on Friday, June 29, the EXCOM would meet on Saturday, 30 June, and the Vth General Assembly of ASSITEJ would start on Monday, 1 July.

Géal suggested further modifications. With three official languages Géal felt he would have to add Flemish as a fourth for the Belgians, and that there would be one day of the festival dedicated to activities of that language. German would be a fifth language, with each of those two having their language for discussion and performance. When Doolittle asked who would choose the performances, Géal was not sure, but he suggested two performances a day would be sufficient, and everyone agreed. He also indicated that finances were much easier now than in the past, but there was concern about everyone participating. He would do his best. Doolittle also suggested that since Peter Brooke, the well-known British Director, had an institute for the study of theatre in Paris, he might be persuaded to undertake a performance for young people or perhaps speak to the Assembly about his work.

As to financing, discussion turned to the possibility of UNESCO support with suggestions, such as: The creation of children's theatre with scholarships offered to students from nations in Africa to study in Europe or America, or a tour followed by a teaching team. Since there was an UNESCO meeting in Paris the next month, Moudoués said she knew the Director, and would speak with him about the possibility of creating this innovative funding. It was also suggested that ASSITEJ draw up a brief of what it would like to do as an innovative project. This brief could then go to each National Center for approval, and then in 1973 the EXCOM could recommend it, sending it forth to UNESCO in 1974. If it could go to UNESCO with written reports from each National Center, it would be much stronger.

After considerable discussion of an invitation to Peter Brooke and the possibility of tapping into UNESCO's economic fund, the meeting was adjourned.

The 3rd Meeting of the Bureau / Wednesday, 18 October

Eek presided with all Members attending, plus Sunyer on invitation. This was a meeting of the official Sub-Committee concerning the use of Spanish as a fourth official language.

Sunyer presented the case for the inclusion of Spanish as a fourth official language by reading from a brief that provided the following information:

- 25 nations, particularly in Central and South America speak Spanish as their primary language.
- 240,000,000 people speak Spanish.
- Spanish is the second most used language in the world after English.
- If Spanish is not included as a fourth language, the Spanish-speaking nations will create their own ASSITEJ. This possibility had already been raised by Venezuela and Costa Rica. She would rather see them participate in the current ASSITEJ.
- When these Spanish-speaking people asked for an ASSITEJ bulletin, she was put in an impossible position, since she could provide none in Spanish.
- She recommended the possibility of only having Spanish as an official language at the International Assemblies.

Once Spanish as a fourth language was introduced for discussion, Rodenberg had requested that German also be considered as an official language. This was an obvious political move, and when the Spanish request was refused, Germany withdrew its request.

Eek outlined 5 possible solutions:

1) Spanish would become the fourth official language
2) Spanish and German would both become official languages
3) ASSITEJ might have only 2 official languages—English and French
4) English and French might become the standing Official Languages, with a third rotating official language, perhaps in a 5-year rotation
5) To keep the official languages as they are, but to publish

Minutes and Reports in Spanish and to distribute through the Spanish Center

Sunyer pointed out that the Spanish government had agreed to pay for translation into Spanish, and that she was already contacting all the Spanish-speaking countries through the Spanish section of ASSITEJ.

Eek pointed out that expenses for the General Assemblies are greatly increased due to the costs of simultaneous translation equipment and interpreters. In Albany these costs were 10,000 USD. In Montreal the simultaneous translation for 1 day cost 3,000 Canadian Dollars.

Adamek asked if South America has children's theatre. Sunyer replied that the Montreal and Albany Congresses had the following Spanish-speaking countries in attendance: Puerto Rico, Venezuela, Brazil, Portugal, Costa Rica, and Spain. She knew that there is a great deal of children's theatre in Argentina.

Doolittle asked if the Sub-Committee on the inclusion of Spanish as a fourth language might be able to change its charge in order to investigate how best to include the Spanish-speaking countries in ASSITEJ with Sunyer the main person to contact for research and information?

While reiterating their concern over increased costs to the Association, the Sub-Committee decided that Spain and Sunyer should be officially in charge of gathering information. Adamek suggested that the Spanish Center could edit all the materials and distribute a résumé to the EXCOM. Sunyer asked if she could add an editorial in Spanish to say what she was doing in *The Review*. She also proposed to make a Spanish edition of *The Review*, and was preparing a Report in Spanish on the Albany meeting, having given a copy to Eek. Eek said then we all agree in principle.

Sunyer requested that President Eek appoint her officially as the liaison between ASSITEJ and the Spanish-speaking countries, and send copies of this letter to Brazil, Venezuela, Peru, and Puerto Rico. Adamek reminded the Committee that all these countries could establish Centers by applying to the Secretariat in Paris.

The following became the *modus operandi* from this meeting:
- The Sub-Committee would make their recommendation to the EXCOM to be voted upon in June 1973 in London
- Moudoués would inform the Spanish-speaking countries of

this resolution appointing the Spanish Center as liaison to all Spanish-speaking countries

- Doolittle, as official recording secretary, would circulate the Minutes of this meeting, and would formulate a resolution to be circulated for corrections, additions, and changes. This in turn with any corrections would be passed on to the Secretary-General, and then on to the EXCOM for approval at the 1973 London Meeting. Sunyer would be responsible for dissemination of this resolution to all the Spanish-speaking countries
- The Secretary-General would be advised of all these deliberations
- Sunyer would keep the Sub-Committee advised and would pass on any information she received from South America
- Sunyer was charged to make a Report of her work at the 1973 London EXCOM Meeting

Adamek suggested that Rodenberg had the address of a children's theatre in Cuba. This finished the discussion of Spanish as a fourth Official Language, and the meeting of the Sub-Committee was adjourned.

(Left to right) Ilse Rodenberg (Vice-President, GDR), Rose-Marie Moudoués (Secretary-General, France), and Vladimir Adamek (Vice-President, Czechoslovakia). IVth International Congress of ASSITEJ, SUNY, Albany, New York. June 1972. Photo courtesy of SUNY Dept. of Theatre, Albany, New York, USA.

1973
EXECUTIVE COMMITTEE MEETING
London, England / 11-17 June 1973

The Executive Committee of ASSITEJ met in London, England on 11-17 June 1973. Nat Eek (USA) as President presided, with Vladimir Adamek (Czechoslovakia) as 1ˢᵗ Vice-President, Ilse Rodenberg (GDR) as 2ⁿᵈ Vice-President, and Joyce Doolittle (Canada) as 3ʳᵈ Vice-President, Rose-Marie Moudoués (France) as Secretary-General, and Ion Lucian (Romania) as Treasurer.

Other members attending were: José Géal (Belgium), Hanswalter Gossmann (FGR), Gerald Tyler (Great Britain), Orna Porat (Israel), Benito Biotto (Italy), Maria Sunyer (Spain), Ivan Voronov (USSR), and Zvjezdana Ladika (Yugoslavia). Co-opted member was Hans Snoek (Netherlands). Advisor members were Ian Cojar (Romania), Michael Pugh (Great Britain), and Sara Spencer (USA).[113] Don LaFoon (Iran) and M. Gridonis (a Netherlands playwright) were present as invited guests, and Inga Juul (Denmark) as an observer.

Members absent: none.

The Executive Committee Meeting / 11 June
President Nat Eek presided at the meeting.

The EXCOM reviewed the Minutes of the EXCOM Meetings in Montreal and Albany, and considered them approved unless Moudoués received any additions or corrections by 1 September 1973. Additional copies of the Minutes of the Bureau Meeting in Bordeaux taken by Doolittle were requested sent to the Paris office. Spain had not received them, and Italy requested a French translation.

A tentative EXCOM Agenda was agreed upon:
- Monday AM: Brussels Conference of ASSITEJ
- Monday PM: Reports on the ITI Committee on Youth meetings in Hungary and Moscow
- Tuesday AM: A tribute to Caryl Jenner of Great Britain, whose death left the British representation vacant. Discussion of the proposal for Spanish as the fourth official language. Reports

on Statutes, Publications, and Finances

- Wednesday AM: Discussion of the Sri Lanka (Ceylon) Center, the Iranian Center, the Portugal Center, activities in South America, and future meetings
- Wednesday PM: Open discussion on future projects of ASSITEJ, and any further business

1974 Brussels Congress: Géal opened the discussion on the Brussels General Assembly of ASSITEJ, which had been set for 16-22 June 1974, saying that he had written the USA and Canada about their funding of the IVth Congress in 1972. He pointed out that Belgium had had three changes of government in one year, and he had had to present his proposals to three separate governments. On June 22 there would be an important meeting in Belgium at which the funding for the Brussels conference would be considered.

Géal explained the proposed program. Each day would be devoted to the theatre of a particular language, and the theme would be "The Professional Theatre *and* the School". He said that the 3 official ASSITEJ languages would be available, plus 3 other languages—Flemish, German, and Spanish.

Géal suggested a tentative schedule for the Bureau and EXCOM meetings as follows:

- Sunday, 16 June, evening: the Bureau
- Monday, 17 June, 3:00 pm: the *old* EXCOM
- Wednesday, 19 June, 9:30 am: General Assembly to approve the Secretary-General and to receive reports
- Thursday, 20 June, 9:30 am: General Assembly for elections
- Friday, 21 June, 9:30 am: the *new* EXCOM
- Saturday, 11:00 am: the Bureau

Géal suggested that the Centers should choose the official plays for each day, and that the Belgian conference would pay hotel, food, and pocket money for each chosen company. The country of origin would pay the travel expenses of the company, and, in some cases, they might have to supplement the actors' *per diem* in order to bring it up to Equity standards, which would be based on Belgian Equity rules.

While desirable for companies coming from outside Belgium to tour further after performing for ASSITEJ, he said that this time of year was vacation time for the schools and scheduling would be very difficult.

Based on the IVth Congress in America, the Belgian Congress was planning on 500 delegates. For official ASSITEJ business each Center would have 3 official delegates. An invitation was to be issued from the Belgian Center for suggestions for speeches to be made at the General Assembly.

Meetings between Moudoués and Géal may be necessary, and EXCOM approved a budget for such trips if necessary. Géal asked that Centers send nominations and information about troupes to him, and information about speeches to Moudoués. This concluded the discussion of the Brussels Congress.

ITI Meeting on Youth in Moscow: The USSR representative to the EXCOM, Ivan Voronov, gave the report by first stating the theme as "The Progress of the Theatre in Modern Society." 52 countries were represented by 572 delegates, one-half of them from the USSR. Other organizations that had been invited were: UNIMA, ASSITEJ, and AICT, and the Student Theatres International Organization. Third world countries were well represented for the first time at an ITI Congress.

Mme. Furtseva, the Soviet Minister of Culture, opened the Congress, and 5 permanent committees were created: music, studies, youth, the Third World, and ITI problems. Performances in Moscow were made available to the delegates, and the USSR expressed pleasure over the progress of the Congress.

Doolittle said her complete Report on Youth was to be found in her separate paper on the ITI Congress. She felt cooperation, not competition, was to be encouraged with the ITI Youth Committee. Rodenberg said there was considerable confusion in the Committee, and when President of ASSITEJ Nat Eek stood and explained the intention of ASSITEJ, she felt it was the only concrete and helpful statement made during the ITI Committee's work. She continued that ITI is bigger and more powerful than ASSITEJ, so we should keep track of their activities, and invite them to Brussels.

Tyler said that the British ITI was not communicating effectively with the British ASSITEJ Center. All the British ASSITEJ communications were ignored, and Jenner was invited to meetings only at the very last minute.

Moudoués said she had continual conversations with the Secretary-General of ITI, and that, in discussions after the Moscow meeting, they had agreed that only problems common to both organizations should be discussed together.

Lucian felt that the prestige of ASSITEJ was a problem, and urged that they attack contemporary problems of the theatre with more courage than evidenced so far. He hoped that proposals for future actions would come from this meeting. A more general discussion followed which led to the quality of the troupes to perform at the Brussels Congress. Lucian felt it would be important to have only large troupes with a good reputation. Ladika urged ASSITEJ not to exclude other theatres which might have valuable artistic ideas. Rodenberg reminded the EXCOM that amateur and student theatre had their own organizations, and that the main task of ASSITEJ was to support professional theatre for children. Snoek urged that ASSITEJ should not limit its viewpoint, that the reaction of the child audience is important, and we should see all forms of theatre.

Eek pointed out that the theme for the Brussels Congress "The Professional Theatre and the School" had established that limit urged by Rodenberg, and that the selection of the performing companies would determine quality. ASSITEJ included representation from both professional and educational theatres.

Doolittle proposed that an official invitation be issued to the ITI Committee on Theatre and Youth to attend the Brussels Congress. EXCOM agreed unanimously. Tyler proposed that ASSITEJ offer the Committee a meeting place in which to conduct its own business, but this was rejected since it might constitute interference.

Tributes to Jenner and Sats: Eek proposed the following resolution about Caryl Jenner's death (Great Britain), and it was accepted and sent.

That the EXCOM of ASSITEJ express officially its sorrow at Miss Jenner's death and an expression of gratitude for the enormous work which her lifetime in theatre for children represented in furthering the cause of quality entertainment for the young.

The EXCOM proposed that recognition be made of Natalia Sats' (USSR) 70th birthday in August, and they recommended that a birthday letter formulated by the President be sent to her from the EXCOM. Both resolutions were approved.

The question of a replacement for the British representative was raised, and Tyler said consideration of a replacement was already underway.

Publications: Moudoués reported on publications. Adamek asked for news for the *Czech Bulletin* immediately. He also asked that Centers indicate what items they wanted published when they sent a large publication.

Moudoués said members would soon receive copies of the *1973 Quarterly Review*, and one of which featured a play entitled *Un Jour*. Another issue would feature the Bordeaux Meeting, and she asked for materials for the next issue. She pointed out that Spain always sent items, while other countries did not. Perhaps she said we should legislate contributions, and this led to a discussion and the following plan:

1. Each issue in the future would be shared by two or more nations. The articles will be in the language of the Center, with a précis submitted to the *Review* in the same language, which in turn the French Center will have translated into the other two official languages.
2. The first issue under these new rules will be shared by Canada and the USA in a North American edition with a deadline for materials of 1 October 1973.
3. The Romania and West Germany issue with a deadline of 1 January 1974.
4. Then Yugoslavia and the GDR with a deadline of 1 April 1974.
5. Then USSR and Bulgaria with a deadline of 1 July 1974.
6. Then Italy and Great Britain with a deadline of October 1974.
7. Then Netherlands and Israel with a deadline of January 1975.

Extra issues could be made available to the Centers involved. Since distribution is difficult and expensive, help from individual Centers would be necessary. Moudoués made a plea for each Center to try to sell more subscriptions.

The Financial Report: Lucian presented his Report as appended to the Minutes. Currently, there was a surplus in the bank, and Moudoués asked permission to invest 5% of the surplus in a fund which would draw interest. It was approved. Then Lucian suggested that each Center organize benefits whose proceeds would go to ASSITEJ. This was taken under advisement with several Centers expressing concern over the problems this would create.

Report of the Statutes Committee: Adamek as Chairman was ill, so Tyler made the Report. The Committee had begun working with the French and English translations of the Statutes to bring them in agreement while incorporating the suggestions made at the Albany Congress. Moudoués said that after Bordeaux, she compared the two translations and stated that the Committee was merely checking the translations, not making any fundamental changes in the rules. Changes in the Constitution could only be made by notifying the Secretary-General three months in advance of the General Assembly which had to vote on those changes. The EXCOM decided that any amendments or changes to be presented in Brussels must reach the Paris office by 1 March 1974. Moudoués said she would bring the proposals on the Statutes, especially those on the translations, to the EXCOM Meeting in Spain in April 1974.

New Centers: Moudoués presented the application of the Sri Lanka (Ceylon) Center. They had sent their Statutes and everything was in order. Eek asked if they had both professional and educational groups. Moudoués said only professional at the moment. In response to other questions Moudoués stated that they would name a representative and pay their dues after admission.

The discussion of the Iranian Center was postponed until Don LaFoon could be present. Moudoués continued that Sr. Garcia would probably form a Brazilian Center, and come to discuss its creation in Spain in 1974. Poland had not yet created a Center, although the country had many activities for youth, particularly puppet theatre. Apparently both Moudoués and Rodenberg consistently blocked the acceptance of a Polish Center as "...not being serious about the professional theatre." However, it had been accepted provisionally in Albany. Moudoués also said that Mr. Jurkowski of the Polish Ministry of Culture told her that there were only 2 professional children's theatre troupes in Poland, so why should they bother to create a Center. Finally Moudoués said she would try to engender more enthusiasm there for such a project.

Report of the Proposed Iranian Center—Don Lafoon: LaFoon stated that Iran had 1 professional theatre for youth through a special state institute, but will have 3 additional professional theatres within the next year. The Institute for the Intellectual Development of Children and Young Adults had been funded under the Empress of Iran. It began with a children's literature and library project, but now included film, music, and phonograph records, and will soon include puppetry.

Eek asked the following three 3 questions: 1) Is there a professional theatre? 2) Is there a corresponding address? and 3) Will dues be paid? LaFoon answered yes to all three questions. Moudoués requested that the proposed Center send her the aims and objectives of the Institute and the proposed Iranian Center to the Paris office.

LaFoon gave some background on the Institute: There are 80 libraries, 22 of which are in the capital of Teheran. Plays are presented in libraries, schools, and orphanages. The project has been able to attract 7 top actors and one of them accompanied LaFoon to the London Meeting. Finances are not a problem, since this project is one of the favorites of the Empress of Iran. Three plays are now on tour. Original material is frequently sought. The leading playwright of Iran has written for this theatre. One major large stage play is planned for each year. A pre-play to explain theatre conventions to the children begins each performance. For example, the actors put on their makeup in front of the audience. Theatre-in-a-Bus soon will leave on tour. The special bus was manufactured in Germany.

Lucian voiced his support of the Iranian application, since it was an area in the world about which ASSITEJ knew little. LaFoon responded that Afghanistan would be included in their touring, and an appearance at the Brussels Congress would be a possibility.

The application of Iran was accepted unanimously by the EXCOM. LaFoon then offered an invitation for the EXCOM to meet in Iran in either April or August of 1975, and he hoped for local financial support for such a project. If the EXCOM met in either of those months, they could also visit festivals in Persepolis and attend activities in Teheran.

Problems of the Spanish Language Nations: Sunyer reported that she had undertaken a considerable amount of work in connection with the Spanish-speaking countries, particularly South America. She had translated Rodenberg's speech in Montreal, and sent a Spanish language brochure to all Centers. In Buenos Aires, Argentina alone there were 12 theatre troupes, and 6-8 additional ones in the rest of the country.

Since 1962 there have been yearly festivals for all of the troupes. Sunyer had contacted twelve people in Argentina to try to form their own proper Center, but there are problems of distance, rivalry, and the instability of the politics. Hopefully they will send a representative to the Brussels Congress. Except for Costa Rica most work in children's theatre in South America is in the schools.

Among the Argentinean troupes only 2 were professional, which were not of great quality so far, but they did exist. The instability in South America forced troupes to go abroad to perform, and once there, they perform well, and then decide not to return to Argentina.

Pugh asked for information about Peru, but there was none. Rodenberg reported that Chile and Cuba do a great deal of work for children. Eek said that any valuable contact should be sent to Sunyer, whose special responsibility was the Spanish-speaking nations. Doolittle moved acceptance of the resolution which was unanimous. The EXCOM discussed and passed the resolution on the use of Spanish as a fourth language of ASSITEJ. This resolution had been originally discussed at the London EXCOM Meeting in 1973. A copy was appended.

Lastly both the FGR and the GDR withdrew their application for German as a fifth official language.

The Book on World Theatre for Children: Rodenberg reported that so far materials had been received from the USSR, USA, Peru, Czechoslovakia, Bulgaria, Israel, Yugoslavia, Canada, with promises from France and the GDR. Countries still missing were Great Britain, Romania, Italy, Netherlands, and Spain. Biotto said Italy had sent material and hoped that it had not been lost. Voronov (USSR) asked if an editorial board of ASSITEJ would help in the final selection of materials. Rodenberg said that the publishers could come to Spain if they had all the material by that time, and there would be an editorial board.

New Centers: Sunyer reported on the peculiar situation with the Portugal Center. She had talked to students at the Institute of Dramatic Art of Portugal and the President of the Portugal Center, Lilia de Fonseca. There was confusion; there were only twenty members in all of Portugal. Fonseca said there were no statutes, but Moudoués had statutes on file from Portugal. Moudoués would write to the Center to try to resolve the difficulty.

Klaus Urban (GDR) reported great success in his visit to Ceylon, which was approved as a new Center at this meeting. He hoped the same for Egypt where he had spent much time discussing ASSITEJ, and had appeared on television and radio, given magazine interviews, and had met the Under-Secretary of State for Culture of Egypt, all of whom had promised him that they would create a Center. So far nothing had been heard.

Future EXCOM Meetings: The next EXCOM Meeting would be in Madrid in 16-21 April 1974. EXCOM Meetings would be held in the mornings with performances in the Spanish festival of theatre for children in the afternoons. The Creative Drama Center of Madrid would be visited. An excursion to Seville and the bull fights would be planned for after the EXCOM Meetings on 23-26 April. Sunyer must know by the beginning of October at the latest, the numbers of people who would be coming to Spain, since hotel accommodations at Seville with their Feria were extremely difficult to obtain at this time of the year.

The following tentative schedule was agreed upon:
- 16 April am—Bureau Meeting
- 17 April am—EXCOM Meeting
- 18 April am—EXCOM Meeting
- 19 April am—EXCOM Meeting
- 20 April am—EXCOM Meeting
- 21 April am—EXCOM Meeting

Iran had invited the EXCOM to meet there in August 1975. Additional invitations for later meetings had been received from Leningrad, USSR; Bucharest, Romania; and Sophia, Bulgaria.

Moudoués also suggested that the 10th Anniversary of ASS'ITEJ might be celebrated in France, and a Bureau Meeting was always possible in France.

International Exchange of Scripts: Playwright M. Gridonis (Netherlands), author of *Two Buckets of Water*, was introduced. He proposed to travel the next year in order to write a book about theatre for the young. He wanted to investigate the possibility of arranging the project to lead to a greater circulation of plays. Spencer, his USA publisher, asked if he conducted such a project, would he own the rights to the plays and have the authority to negotiate a contract. Questions about language and translation were raised.

Inga Juul (Denmark) asked how often information about scripts would appear, and it was suggested that there be a bulletin six times a year; that money could come from the subscriptions and private enterprise; and that perhaps ASSITEJ would help to get subscribers. A subscription rate of £20 English was suggested.

Lucian asked if this bulletin would compete with the *ASSITEJ Bulletin* from Prague. Juul asked if there would be any conflict of interest with the *International Bibliography* as edited by Michael Pugh (Great Britain). Snoek asked if there might be a possibility of his serving as an international dramaturge. Spencer replied the possibility of exchange already existed. Pugh reiterated that the *Bibliography* consisted only of plays recommended by the Centers. No formal proposal came from the discussion.

Future Plans: Lucian (Romania) felt that at all the ASSITEJ meetings there never had been time for artistic discussions, and he proposed that at the time of each future meeting one person would present a paper on an artistic subject. He would be happy to present such a paper on the avant-garde at the EXCOM Meeting in Spain. He suggested other topics, such as: the relationship between improvisation and production; and classical texts in contemporary production. He also proposed that the Center's recommend the best play of each year, and send a copy to the other Centers, even if only in the original language. He felt the *Bulletin* needed development, and that the catalog of plays in translation no longer responded to the needs of ASSITEJ.

Moudoués suggested that the EXCOM decide on a topic after the plays had been selected for the Spanish conference. Voronov (USSR) agreed with Lucian that it was important also to discuss actual productions. Everyone on the EXCOM was an artist as well as an administrator, and they should be able to discuss as well as to legislate. It was proposed that Sunyer recommend a discussion topic once the plays had been chosen for the Madrid EXCOM Meeting in 1974.

Report from Italy: Biotto reported growing success in the past five years in the Italian Center. The Minister of Culture was beginning to understand and subsidize theatre for young audiences. Milan had recently recognized the *Angelicum Theatre* for twenty year's work in theatre for children, and especially praised their actors who were also given gold medals. Also, a gold medal was given to the Milan Company, which now had a permanent theatre performing for children of ages six to fourteen. Last season seven professional theatres for children performed throughout Italy.

Report from Denmark: Juul reported that Doolittle had visited her as a friend, and together they had gone to the Minister of Culture's office with inconclusive results on support for the creation of a Danish Center. Juul was also concerned that Jenner's death in England meant that plans for her Unicorn Theatre for youth would be cancelled. She felt that ASSITEJ should do something, if only to express concern.

Moudoués said she had spoken to an administrator of the theatre and had received a petition. Eek suggested that a letter from Moudoués on behalf of ASSITEJ to the Unicorn be written voicing concern for, and support of, the Unicorn Theatre for Children in London.

Special thanks were extended to Gerald Tyler (Great Britain) in acknowledgement for his work in planning the London meetings. There being no further business, the meeting was adjourned.

Performances: Concurrent with this meeting a large Festival of Theatre for Children was held at the Cockpit and the Young Vic theatres in London. Delegates attended as many of these plays as the meetings would allow. Following the London EXCOM Meeting, in adult theatre they attended a contemporary performance of Moliere's *The Misanthrope* with Diana Rigg at the National Theatre, and two other Shakespearean performances at Stratford and Birmingham.

1974
EXECUTIVE COMMITTEE MEETING
Madrid, Spain / 16-22 April 1974

The Executive Committee of ASSITEJ met in Madrid, Spain on 16-22 April 1974. Nat Eek (USA) as President presided, with Vladimir Adamek (Czechoslovakia) as 1st Vice-President, Ilse Rodenberg (GDR) as 2nd Vice-President, and Joyce Doolittle (Canada) as 3rd Vice-President, Rose-Marie Moudoués (France) as Secretary-General, and Ion Lucian (Romania) as Treasurer.

Other members attending were: José Géal (Belgium), Victor Georgiev (Bulgaria), Eberhard Möbius for Hanswalter Gossmann (FGR), Orna Porat (Israel), Benito Biotto (Italy), Maria Sunyer (Spain), Ivan Voronov (USSR), and Ljubiša Djokič (Yugoslavia). Co-opted members were Hans Snoek (Netherlands), and Advisory members were Michael Pugh (Great Britain), Ian Cojar (Romania), and Sara Spencer (USA). Jean Daconte (France), the ITI President was an invited guest.

Members absent: Great Britain had yet to appoint a representative to replace Caryl Jenner.

The Executive Committee Meeting in April 1974[114]

President Nat Eek presided at the meeting.

Cancellation of Brussels Congress: The most important item on the Agenda was making a decision related to the cancellation of the Brussels Congress. In November 1973 before this Madrid EXCOM Meeting, José Géal (Belgium) had informed the Secretariat that it would be impossible for Belgium to host the next International Congress. Moudoués informed President Eek immediately by letter. In a letter to the US Center Executive Committee Eek quoted from a copy of a letter from Géal which listed the reasons for the cancellation as " . . . Political complications of the several languages of the country and financial problems . . . ."[115]

Géal had sought his government's support in providing the required funds, but the support was offered with the provision that the program be presented in each of the official languages. This meant French, English, Russian, plus Flemish. Providing simultaneous translation was impossible from both a practical and financial standpoint. In addition, Géal who was the dynamic force of the Belgian Center became ill in 1973, and needed extensive hospitalization.[116]

A discussion of a location and dates for the next Congress ensued. The EXCOM realized that the new Congress could not be held until 1975 in order to provide time for the necessary preparation. Several countries made proposals that they might possibly be able to host the Congress. The GDR Proposal was the best prepared, followed by that of the FGR. However, politically the GDR always had the edge between the two countries, and had the strongest most artistic professional theatres for children.

The GDR Proposal: Rodenberg proposed that the Vth International Congress be held in either Berlin or Leipzig from 20-26 April 1975. She then itemized her recommendations:

- The Congress would be held in conjunction with a National Festival of Children's Theatres.
- They would like to invite 2 performing companies from abroad.
- They would emphasize comic opera and musical theatre.
- They would invite special groups to represent the amateur theatre.
- Delegates would be able to talk with the actors and children in the theatre and in the schools.
- The GDR would make a Report of their activities to the EXCOM at their meeting during the Berlin Congress.
- They would use the theme of the Brussels Congress.
- The foreign companies would be chosen by the GDR as they deemed appropriate.

The Spanish Proposal: Sunyer proposed that the Spanish Center withdraw its proposal to hold the Vth Congress in Spain in 1975, and postpone it until 1977. The proposed dates would be in March or April, depending on when Easter occurred.

The USSR Proposal: Voronov proposed that the Vth Congress could possibly be held in Moscow in 1977. At that time the new musical theatre of Natalia Sats would be open.

The Bulgarian Proposal: Georgiev proposed that the Vth Congress could possibly be held in 1977 or 1979 in Sophia. However, he was waiting for official confirmation.

The FGR Proposal: Eberhard Möbius of the FGR National Center proposed:

- That the Vth Congress be held in Hamburg the last week in August-September of 1975
- There would be over 50 theatres available, and meetings could be held in their new Palace of Congresses
- The theme could deal with new forms and new directions
- He would propose to invite 10 to 15 foreign troupes to perform, and 90 foreign countries would be represented.
- Herr Gossmann would be in Hamburg to help organize the Congress.

The informal minutes of Eek suggest that the EXCOM tentatively approved the holding of the VIth International Congress in 1977 in Spain; Sophia, Bulgaria; Moscow; or Israel. The EXCOM was still thinking in terms of having a Congress every two 2 years. Apparently no decision was made on a proposal for the Vth Congress at this time.

Dates of Future Meetings: Dates of other meetings were tentatively set as follows:

- January-February 1975, EXCOM Meeting in Dubrovnik, Yugoslavia or Amsterdam, Netherlands.
- April 1975, the Vth International Congress—location to be chosen
- September 1975, EXCOM Meeting in Hamburg, FGR
- April 1976, EXCOM Meeting in Israel or August 1976 – EXCOM Meeting in Iran
- If the 1977 EXCOM Meeting was held in Iran then January 1977, EXCOM Meeting in Israel
- Spring 1979, VIth International Congress—location to be selected

ITI Committee on Youth: Jean Daconte (France), President of the ITI, met with the EXCOM of ASSITEJ related to the ITI Committee on Young Theatre. He first suggested that ASSITEJ develop a more proper title such as "Young Theatre". Secondly, he suggested how ASSITEJ could cooperate with the Committee: allow each ASSITEJ National Center to establish contact with the ITI Committee, and then promote their international relationship.

A letter from ASSITEJ should be sent to Peter James, Chairman of the Committee, informing him that ASSITEJ wished to coordinate with the Committee. A meeting was suggested in Hamburg between ASSITEJ and the ITI Committee to clarify the roles of youth theatre. Letters needed to be sent to Daconte (ITI), Klaus Urban (Theater der Freundschaft), and the Hamburg representatives. James should be asked personally to help with the planning.

During the discussion one of the EXCOM members commented that ITI seemed to be getting smaller and smaller, and less affluent, and advised avoiding ITI altogether! Meanwhile ASSITEJ should create a list of countries wishing advice on children's theatre, and in turn create a committee of advisors. Also, a list of all ASSITEJ Centers should be sent to Hamburg. This discussion suggested that Hamburg was becoming an important theatre center. Nothing ever came of these contacts.

EXCOM Meeting / Thursday,18 April

The morning Agenda was set as follows:
1. Publications
2. Financial Report
3. New Centers
4. Museum
5. ASSITEJ Booklet
6. Statutes
7. FGR Report
8. The 1975 Congress

The afternoon Agenda included:
1. Géal request
2. Discussion of artistic matters by Lucian
3. Other business

Financial Report: Lucian as Treasurer gave the Financial Report, and indicated that the Romanian Center had a new address. He asked that each center identify exactly what the money was for when they sent him checks. This would avoid confusion in the payment of dues. Eek made a note to be sure that the US Center's dues for 1974 and 1975 were paid immediately, so that their delegates could vote at the Congress in April of 1975.

New Centers: Moudoués stated that Austria, Venezuela, Argentina, Denmark, and Australia had satisfied all requirements for membership except their sending of the statutes of their Centers. She also announced that the Minister of Culture for Sri Lanka had announced their first performance in children's theatre on 27 December 1973. Addresses for Centers in Austria, Venezuela, and Brazil were given. The USSR delegate announced contacts in Poland and Cuba, and that a Mr. Tarbour, who was trained in the USSR, would be establishing a Center in Turkey.

Publications: Moudoués announced that the Paris Office would be publishing an ASSITEJ History and Who's Who type of Biography as a brochure. There would be space for 50 names in each language, making a total of 150 pages. 1000 copies would be printed; 6" by 9" in size; and printing would be in black and white. This never happened, but in 1977 the Czech Center published the *Who's Who in ASSITEJ* in mimeographed form and distributed it to all the Centers in its *Bulletin.*

1975 Congress: In the EXCOM discussion, the following points were made:

1. The Congress would be for 7 days, allowing 1 day for arrival.
2. There would be room for 250 delegates. Of these 20 can come from the USA and 20 from Canada.
3. There will be a theme and sub-themes; the delegates would break into 3 groups for discussion.
4. Géal would be asked to give the major theme address since his Congress had been cancelled.
5. Topics would be announced ahead of time, and people would be notified accordingly.
6. Doolittle's speech topic would be "How Contact Is Made Between Professional Companies and the Schools".
7. Eek recommended that the planners use the Brussels format for the Bureau and EXCOM meetings. He also requested that his Presidential Address be made during the 1st Plenary Session of the General Assembly.

Lucian presented his paper on artistic concerns followed by discussion.

The Report of the Spanish Center (ATEIJ – Asociación del Teatro Español por Infantes y Juventudes) presented by Maria Sunyer:

1. The Spanish Center encourages the theatre arts on two levels: a) art in the schools, and b) art by adults.
2. They send specialists in creative dramatics to Salamanca, Barcelona, Tarragona, Seville, Madrid, and Tenerife.
3. Troupes that perform exclusively for children are in Madrid, Valencia, Malaga, etc. There are 25 different companies: 6 are professional; 2 are University; and 17 are amateur.
4. Currently it is felt that adults are incapable of understanding children. This contributes to the current crises among the younger generation.
5. There is a National Congress every two years. The next one is in March 1975.
6. They have created an Office for Research and Publications. This helps publish all aspects of children's theatre activity in Spain. Their budget for costs of translation is 300,000 pesetas annually.
7. Also, there are county ATEIJ committees who reproduce the information from the central committee. There is no link between theatre and education in the provinces without committees. To encourage them the Central Committee gives them extra votes.
8. The main problem is that they need more plays as well as needing to improve their quality. They hope to improve this by their next National Congress. Now there are good national authors, but unfortunately there is conflict between the taste of the directors and the individual author.
9. Performances are in the early afternoon, but only on holidays and weekends.
10. The actor is guaranteed a minimum number of performances. If the play is successful, more performances are scheduled.
11. Madrid and Barcelona have plays in repertory. Others do one play at a time.
12. They perform from October through April, and give approximately 48-64 performances a year, plus the city festivals.
13. The Center has a staff of one secretary and 2 typists who work from 4-7 pm.

14. The press does write critiques of the plays.

This ended her Report, and the EXCOM Meeting.

Meeting of the Bureau with AETIJ, 22 April 1974

Members of the ASSITEJ Bureau met to observe the meeting of the Asociación del Teatro Español por Infantes y Juventudes (ATEIJ)

SUNYER: Let us begin. We are grateful to have the ASSITEJ Bureau here to advise us in our deliberations.

THE SECRETARY'S REPORT: Three members of the Committee are absent. The Vice-President sent us a telegram regretting his absence. The work of the provincial boards is good on drama, schools, and teachers in Pamplona, Tarragona, Bilbao, Madrid, Tenerife, Toledo, Salamanca, and Barcelona. Courses in creative dramatics are taught in these various towns, and soon we will have these courses all over.

SRA. CONSUELA: On 25 February the 3rd Children's Theatre Conference in Barcelona was held at the Atheneo Cultural Center. Mr. Romero was the keynote speaker talking on "Theatre and the Child". 60 participants attended.

SECRETARY: The Center wants a new perspective; to foster new plays; to do better quality. Now authors are submitting plays, even one with a musical score. Archives of all theatrical activity are growing at a great rate. We would appreciate information from all foreign countries.

SRA. LUCAS: In a Financial Report the Ministry had recommended a budget of 975,000 pesetas for 1974, with 300,000 each for theatre and culture. In addition the Center would receive 200,000 in membership fees for 1974. This is impressive, and letters of thanks will be sent to the newly elected government. We recommend that we send a report to all those who have helped.

SECRETARY: Our national Congress for 1975 is proposed for 19-23 March. Malaga is a possible site. Torremolinos, Mucia, and Valencia are also possibilities. It will discuss the quality of children's theatre in Spain. We want authors and designers to participate, so please give me names. Also, we want to consider new forms and ideas. We suggest that all professional touring companies include in their repertory at least one play written for children. This will be presented to our General Assembly.

SUNYER: Apropos of the children's theatre festival in Madrid. It has professional companies as well as some amateur ones. Ticket sales would pay the costs, and we have the theatres available. There are two (2) companies of quality—Los Titeres and L'Oliva-Catalan. It is up to us to select the titles.

Sunyer then presented the information re: the 1975 ASSITEJ Congress. She introduced Rodenberg to the audience. Rodenberg presented gifts, slides, etc. to Sunyer and the Center.

SUNYER: Sr. Lopez y Arranda is a major author, who has written *The Bluebird* and *Don Quixote* for children.

ARRANDA: He had volunteered to write any plays for national theatres that they might want. He said the major problem of *Don Quixote* was transferring the language to the theatre for children. However, the children grasp the concepts and the plot immediately. An adaptation must be for the whole family, not just a child of a specific age. He decided on using a Chorus as an intermediary between the audience and the actor. He used the horse and the donkey as his Chorus, creating a dialogue between the horse, donkey, and the children. Dulcinea is a dream. When Don Quixote dies, all members are shown as members of a theatrical troupe.

Sunyer thanked Sr. Arranda, and asked if the Bureau had any questions?

LUCIAN: I am glad we are discussing quality in the theatre. Even today there are those who think children's theatre is only for children. I am also glad to see that you are seeking new forms, since some are opposed to this thinking. This is difficult, and I wish you luck! Thank you also for producing my play.

Creative Dramatics Demonstrations: The first demonstration purported to show the child who develops ideas after careful guidance by the teacher. The children were first graders—6-7 years old—and pantomimed to the music of the story of *Peter and the Wolf*. Sra. Perez said the children knew the music well and were on beat. Their costumes were leotards, tights, and ballet shoes. The movement was mostly circular and repetitive. The children were coached offstage by the teacher. The performance was formal, lacked invention, and little inspiration. Doolittle said to Eek *sotto voce* "This must be directed by a teacher. No child could be this dull!"

The next demonstration was of *The Firebird* with 12-13 year old children. The situation was dreamed up of different animals—a lop-sided bird, frogs, a slow bird, a centipede. Again repetitive movement. Better concentration. No one seemed to know how to develop the story. There was no reaction when a shoe was thrown as part of the action. Nice relationship between some of the animals. The finale showed all the animals at a watering hole playing. The performance ended with the boy being awakened by his brother.

The next demonstration was abstract. The children moved among a tangle of elastic lines to music. Again repetitive, but with a good sense of rhythm. Too long. Mixture of styles.

The Bureau next went to a private Ciudad Escolar (City School). They were told there were 1700 students, 16-18 years old. They would have one to two creative dramatics classes each week. Their gymnastic work was the best in the country. They gave formal presentations at the end of each semester, and formal plays at the end of the year.

In the first demonstration the teacher used a tambourine for musical accompaniment. All the children were dressed in black leotards and tights. They moved in rhythm first—walk, sit, jump, and then were ordered to be a window, be a tree, etc. All of them did things exactly the same way. Everything was totally memorized. They told the story of the scarecrow who gives pieces of himself away.

Next was *The Circus of CuCu* with 12-year-old girls performing. A piano played music from Mozart's *Toy Symphony*. Movement was all done in rhythm to the music. Costumes were black leotards and tights with pinafores, vests, and aprons. Enter the townspeople. Circus comes to town, sets up its tent. People pay and the acts begin. A wind blows the tent down. The townspeople help set up the circus, and the show goes on, a series of circus acts continue. Again Doolittle commented "All this is without joy!"

The children in the next performance had had creative dramatics for different lengths of time, the girls for 8 months, the boys for 2 months. This was a serious performance, and the children came from families with problems. The children lived in a boarding school. The music was played on a xylophone. Doolittle commented "Nice noises!" on the various sounds the children were improvising.

A storyteller entered on a horse. The actors went to a basket to get capes, animal masks, etc. The storyteller sat in an alcove narrating. Two sons set off to sell a horse, meet an old couple, a priest, two women, and comedians. A good sense of happiness. Well trained and lively. The story over, the group performed a stately dance with great ease.

The second tale concerned a man who became Pope by inspiration and magic. The third tale was Moorish in origin and concerned a shrewish daughter, her marriage, and her husband kills their dog, cat, and horse, and is in danger of killing his wife. The blocking kept grouping the actors so they could watch the action. Each tale was interspersed by music, a chorus and marimba orchestra. The final curtain was just one long line, but the performance was excellent.

The final demonstration featured 11 girls from Madrid who were 8-9 years old performing *Poems of Garcia Lorca*. The orchestra was a marimba, flute, drum, and tambourine. There was an overture, then the life of Lorca told in plain conversation, and then a recitation of the poems themselves. The girls wore black leotards with red checks. Well disciplined; the orchestra had memorized all the music. When the poems were finished, a puppet show was brought on. This completed the demonstrations, proving that they had an extensive creative drama program.

The EXCOM Meeting concluded with a farewell reception, and it was felt that the Spanish Center was indeed a very active and forward looking one.

Palacio Nacional de Congresos. VIth ASSITEJ Congress. Madrid,Spain. June 1978. Photograph courtesy of William Gleason, US Center for ASSITEJ.

"Asamblea General" by Lauro del Olmo. Produced by Los Titeres, Madrid, directed by Pilar Enciso. June 1978. Photo Courtesy of William H. Gleason, US Center for ASSITEJ.

1974
BUREAU MEETING
Paris, France / 11 November 1974

Members attending were: Rose-Moudoués (France) as Secretary-General, Vladimir Adamek (Czechoslovakia) as 1st Vice-President, and Ilse Rodenberg (GDR) are 2nd Vice-President were in attendance.

Members absent: Nat Eek (President), and apparently Ion Lucien (Treasurer).

The Secretary-General called a meeting of some of the members of the Bureau in Paris in November to discuss the location of the next Congress. In a letter from Moudoués to Eek dated 11 November 1974, she stated that there had just been a Bureau Meeting in Paris to try to solve the problems of a location for the next meeting.

In November of 1973 José Géal (Belgium) informed the Secretariat that it would be impossible for Belgium to host the next International Congress, and Moudoués had informed President Eek immediately by letter. Since there was no time for finding another site and for preparing a program for 1974, the International Congress was put off until 1975.[117] Though various countries had proposed having the next Congress in their countries, the EXCOM in Madrid had put off the decision until this EXCOM meeting in Zagreb.

This postponement of the Congress established the precedent that all future Congresses would be held every 3 years. While the cancellation seemed to be unfortunate, in reality it became an extremely intelligent precedent, since hosting an international meeting with its growing number of delegates and foreign productions was proving to be expensive and time-consuming in its planning and execution. It is interesting and sad to note that soon after this next Congress, Géal stopped attending the meetings, and Belgium became an inactive National Center, split by the Flemish and French languages.

Moudoués wrote that Rodenberg had proposed that the next International Congress be held in Berlin in the GDR, hosted by Rodenberg and her Theater der Freundschaft in April 1975. The Bureau had accepted her invitation, but there was no detailed Agenda as yet. However, Moudoués indicated that she had already made contacts for "rooms, theatres, and hotels." This would be presented at the Zagreb EXCOM Meeting in February 1975 for ratification. In the meantime she was sending "50 Inviting-booklets" to the US Center for distribution to their membership to encourage their attendance.[118]

This suggested that the planning of the Congress was well on its way, but unfortunately President Eek had not been informed of the meeting. It was a *fait accompli*. However, time had certainly been of the essence, and the resulting Congress in Berlin followed the Rodenberg proposal made to the EXCOM at the Madrid meeting in April 1974.

Group of Yugoslavian children in the Pioneer Palace, Zagreb, Yugoslavia, 1968. Courtesy of Yugoslavia ASSITEJ Center, 1968.

1975
EXECUTIVE COMMITTEE MEETING
Zagreb and Karlovac, Yugoslavia / 3- 9 February 1975

The Executive Committee of ASSITEJ met in Zagreb and Karlovac, Yugoslavia on 3-9 February 1975. Nat Eek (USA) as President presided, with Vladimir Adamek (Czechoslovakia) as 1st Vice-President, Ilse Rodenberg (GDR) as 2nd Vice-President, Rose-Marie Moudoués (France) as Secretary-General, and Ion Lucian (Romania) as Treasurer.

Other members attending were: Victor Georgiev (Bulgaria), Maria Sunyer (Spain), Ivan Voronov (USSR), and Ljubiša Djokič (Yugoslavia). Co-opted member was Hans Snoek (Netherlands). Observers were: Gerald Tyler (Great Britain) representing his Center, and Inga Juul (Denmark).

Members absent: José Géal (Belgium), Joyce Doolittle (Canada), Hanswalter Gossmann (FGR), Benito Biotto (Italy), and Orna Porat (Israel).

The EXCOM Meeting / Zagreb and Karlovac[119]

President Nat Eek presided at the meetings. Following are descriptions of these meetings.

*T*he first 3 days of the meeting were spent in Zagreb, and then the Committee moved to Karlovac for the rest of the meetings, returning to Zagreb for departures. The first meeting was on Tuesday, 4 February 1975 at 9:30 am. The delegates were welcomed by Milko Paravic and Ljubiša Djokič of the Yugoslavian Center.

The following Agenda was approved:
1. Minutes of the London and Madrid meetings
2. Preparation of the General Assembly for the Vth Congress in Berlin
3. Presentation of the candidates for the new EXCOM
4. Amendments to the Statutes

5. Special publications for the 10th Anniversary of ASSITEJ
6. Invitations for the next meetings of the EXCOM
7. Financial Report
8. New National Centers
9. Relations with ITI
10. Publications
11. Televised events
12. New Plays
13. Relations with UNESCO
14. The process of taking minutes of the EXCOM and General Assembly meetings
15. Report of the Yugoslavian Center
16. Miscellaneous business

There was considerable discussion over word meanings in the Minutes of the London and Madrid meetings. Eek proposed to ask Doolittle to redo the Minutes in brief, and to write out succinctly the decisions taken by EXCOM which were to be presented to the General Assembly in Berlin. Lucian was appointed as secretary of the current meeting to take notes in French. He would then send the Minutes to Doolittle to have them translated into English. This way the Secretary-General would be assured of their accuracy at the Berlin Congress.

The Berlin Congress: Rodenberg presented the following information about the Berlin Congress on 19-26 April 1975:
- A delegation from each National Center had been invited to attend by the GDR Center.
- 13 productions would be presented in 7 theatres in Berlin during the Congress.
- The program would include two speakers on the Theme of the Congress "The Professional Actor and the School"—Christel Hoffmannn (GDR) and José Géal (Belgium).
- 3 discussion groups would consider the following themes: Public Participation in the Professional Theatre, Differences Between Plays of the Theatre Performed by Professional Actors and that of Creative Drama, The Role of the Professional Theatre in the Education of Children.
- Many brochures and pamphlets would be available in 4 languages for the delegates, English, French, and Russian, with German

for the German delegates. These would be prepared by a large number of German institutions.

- 2 different exhibits would be in place during the Congress: 1) at the Theater der Freundschaft—"The Development of Children's Theatre in the GDR"; and 2) at the locations of the Congress— "Artistic Activities in the Schools".
- At all meetings delegates would need to have their personal ID for the Congress available.
- All delegates would have to have a visa and a hotel reservation.
- Simultaneous translation would be available in all meetings.
- Invitations had been sent to: a delegate from UNESCO; the President of ITI; and the International Association of Critics, which will be having a Symposium in Berlin at the same time as the Congress.
- As of that day 23 countries had registered for the Congress.
- The following Agenda for the General Assembly had been adopted by the EXCOM in Madrid including requests made in writing by the National Centers:
  1. Report Morale
  2. Financial Report
  3. Amendments to the Statutes
  4. Candidates for the new EXCOM
  5. Invitations for the next Congress
  6. List of activities
  7. Elections
  8. Miscellaneous questions

In discussion Moudoués said that the National Centers should send the Report of their activities to the Secretary-General by 1 April for inclusion in the Report Morale.

Also, she informed the EXCOM that Peru had sent in a written request that a discussion of the creation of a Center for Latin America be put on the Agenda. Moudoués said there was nothing in the Statutes for or against this concept. The Statutes only mentioned that National Centers belonged to ASSITEJ, not groups. However, Peru had not paid its dues, so this should be considered.

Maria Sunyer assured the EXCOM that there was liaison with Peru, and that they had received the ASSITEJ publications edited in

Spanish by the Spanish Center.

Candidates for the new EXCOM: Moudoués announced that in conformity with the Statutes 13 countries had written announcing their desire to be a candidate for the EXCOM. They were: Bulgaria (Victor Georgiev), Canada (Joyce Doolittle), Czechoslovakia (Vladimir Adamek), France (Rose-Marie Moudoués), GDR (Ilse Rodenberg), Great Britain (John English), Benito Biotto (Italy), Netherlands (Hans Snoek), Romania (Ion Lucian), Spain (Maria Sunyer), USA (Nat Eek), USSR (Ivan Voronov), and Yugoslavia (Ljubiša Djokič). In addition, she said the USA had sent a letter recommending 15 countries as candidates: the above 13 countries plus Iran and FGR. She then quoted the Statutes (Article X, Sec. 1): The Executive Committee is composed of a maximum of fifteen members, having the right to vote, including: The Chairman and Vice-Chairmen; the Secretary-General and the Treasurer, appointed by the General Assembly.

Amendments to the Statutes: Adamek presented the work on the revision of the Statutes recommended by the Committee to create the proper agreement among the English, French, and Russian texts. Further, amendments to the Statutes had been proposed by the GDR, Czechoslovakia, the USSR, and France. The following changes in the texts were to be proposed to the General Assembly at the Berlin Congress for their vote.

- Chap. II, Art. 5, Paragraph 3. . . . in compliance with the decisions taken by the Association, add the following: *to send once a year to the Secretary-General a written Report of the Center's activities.*
- Chap. IV, Art. IX, Paragraph 4. Change *2 years* to *3 years.*
- Chap. IV, Art. IX, Paragraph 13. . . . after it names the Secretary-General and the Treasurer on recommendation of the EXCOM, add: *retiring.*
- In the same location at the end, add: *The General Assembly on recommendation of the EXCOM is able to give the title of Honorary President and in a general manner recognize the honoree for exceptional services rendered to the Association. Members of Honor have a consultative voice, but do not have the right to vote nor can represent their country.*
- Chap. IV, Art. IX, Paragraph 16. . . . add: *only written questions written in the Agenda are able to be submitted to the General Assembly for voting.*

- Chap. IV, Art. X, Paragraph 12. . . . add at the beginning: *propose a plan of activities to the General Assembly*, and at the end: replace *two years* with *three years*.

Special Publications for the 10th Anniversary: Eek presented a copy of a booklet about the first ten years of ASSITEJ prepared by Doolittle and the Canadian Center for approval. The text would be printed in black in the three official languages with montages of photographs in blue or green. Each Center must send to Doolittle, before 1 March, a photograph of the Center's choice. She will make the final choices. A total of 3,000 booklets would be printed, and part will be distributed at the Berlin Congress, and the rest would be for distribution by the Centers. Eventually the booklet was completed and made available by the Canadian Center for international distribution at the 1975 Berlin Congress.

"Who's Who in ASSITEJ": Adamek would distribute the format for the biographies in Berlin for the brochure, and requested that each Center present no more than 5 persons who had worked for the past ten years on the international level. Late materials would appear in a supplemental edition.

The History of ASSITEJ: Eek spoke of his writing a history of ASSITEJ from 1960 to 1970, and that it was about 27 pages at the moment. He would bring the first draft in English to Berlin for additions and corrections. After that he will write a final draft. This never was done. Also, he informed the EXCOM that Frederick Scott Regan (USA Graduate Student) was working on a Dissertation covering the first ten years of ASSITEJ. Eek had sent him archival materials, and Regan had contacted the Secretariat.

Places and Dates of Next Meetings: The Spanish Center had invited ASSITEJ to have the next Congress after Berlin in 1977 or 1978 in Spain depending on the 2- or 3-year modification of the Statutes. This invitation would be presented to the General Assembly in Berlin for approval.

Although the FGR had invited EXCOM to hold a meeting in Hamburg in 1975 during their international festival, that festival had been cancelled, and Moudoués had notified the FGR that the EXCOM could not meet there because of that cancellation. Also, she said it was too costly to have too many meetings in one year. It was proposed to establish a required meeting calendar, and then to present it in Berlin for approval by the EXCOM. In August of 1976, Iran had proposed to host an EXCOM meeting there. [The monarchy in Iran was overthrown within the year!]

In the event that they could not hold the meeting, the USSR proposed to hold the meeting in Leningrad. There would be a meeting in 1977 or in 1978, depending on the changes in Statutes, and the EXCOM would require three months prior to prepare the Agenda for a Congress.

National Centers: Moudoués stated that after an examination of their candidacy, she had determined there were 4 new Centers to be accepted: Algeria, Cuba, Finland (Eastern in political attitude), and Australia (Western in political attitude).

Questions were raised concerning what other centers were having difficulties or were in the process of reorganization. Snoek stated that the Netherlands Center, after a meeting in December, had decided to change their statutes in order to admit a larger number of groups, primarily those which were not supported by the government. Max Wagener, Secretary of the Netherlands ITI, had offered to be the Secretariat for one year.

The Portugal Center was reorganizing to have its Statutes written in Portuguese. The Statutes would be the same as the prior ones. [The conservative, colonialist government was overthrown in April 1974 which had caused this re-writing.]

The Belgian Center had become a federation of the French and the Flemish. Eventually a third section in German would be formed under their new government. Belgium had recently gone through four different governments in as many years.

In the FGR the Statutes were unchanged, but the Center's Committee had been completely replaced with new and different members.

In the Swiss Center the Theatre of Lausanne had disappeared, but the other groups were still active. However, it would be necessary to clarify the position of the Swiss Center since they had not paid their dues.

EXCOM was happy to hear of the possible emergence of the first African Center in Zaire [previously the Congo]. Lucian had been invited to attend a conference in Brazzaville on 26-27 February, and had promised to send them information about the forming of an ASSITEJ

Center. He had assured them of ASSITEJ's desire to have the third world represented in the Association. EXCOM heartily approved this initiative.

Publications: Moudoués said there had been difficulties in assembling the manuscripts for the *Review* since the Centers had not sent in their promised materials by the deadline. Hopefully this would be resolved by the time of the Berlin Congress, and 5 issues will appear at the same time. On the other hand the first issue of 1975 was at the printers. She again asked the Centers for materials for the 1975 issues, and for précises in the other languages for each article.

She also urged the Centers to purchase more issues of the Review. Only Canada and the USA gave great financial support, and costs were increasing. Ultimately the French Center might have to resort to a publication only in French. The Soviet Center proposed to print the Review in Russian for the Berlin Congress, and distribute the copies there. They were thanked for their generosity.

The Czech Bulletin: Adamek had not received any information from the Centers for the last issue of the *Czech Bulletin* in 1974, which was to feature the history and origins of ASSITEJ in the first ten years. He stated that the Centers sent whole journals, but did not indicate the most important items for him to print. Also, he wondered if just an exchange of Bulletins among the Centers would not be sufficient. Despite these problems he hoped that the *Czech Bulletin* would be continued. He concluded by asking Centers to submit information for the *Bulletin* by the end of February, the end of June, and the end of October.

UNESCO: There had been a recent exchange of views with UNESCO about their relationship with ASSITEJ. The Soviet Center had asked about their Statute B prior to the EXCOM Meeting of UNESCO. Sunyer had participated in that conference and expressed severe doubts about any collaboration with UNESCO. Nine other associations had approached UNESCO about their working relationships with UNESCO with little result.

UNESCO had replied that:
1. Each organization should make contact with their national UNESCO delegation.
2. After that, make an approach to the General Director.
3. There appears to be a working plan for UNESCO throughout

the world using the country's departments of education, and contact that way would provide prompt action.

For years ASSITEJ had tried to establish contacts with UNESCO and ITI but to little avail. Many Centers felt that there would be financial support forthcoming from UNESCO if any rapport could be established. Some Centers had good working relationships with their National ITI Centers, but rapport was sporadic and varied greatly from country to country.

Creative Drama: Tyler once more addressed the proposal on Creative Drama to establish a committee or working group to prepare a report on creative dramatics and its relationship to ASSITEJ. This Committee was to present a recommendation to the General Assembly in 1977 or 1978 as part of the official Agenda.

Adamek stated that the characteristics of ASSITEJ were defined in Article II of the Statutes, and they did not seem to include Creative Drama. Voronov agreed, and said that ASSITEJ needed to guard its quality as an association. This was merely a continuation of the argument which emerged in 1964 at the London preparatory meeting about the place of Creative Drama in ASSITEJ. The lines were usually drawn along East-West divisions; the West regarding it as essential and appropriate, and the East regarding it as "amateur" and inappropriate for a professional association.

There was a lengthy discussion, after which President Eek decided to create, after discussions with the individuals concerned, a Presidential Commission to define the position of Creative Drama in ASSITEJ, and to present a solid proposal to the EXCOM in Berlin. Tyler accepted this suggestion.

Financial Report: Lucian reported that a very small number of Centers had paid their dues for 1975, although the Treasurer had requested payment, and had reminded the Centers that the right to vote in the General Assembly depended upon financial regularity. Also, Moudoués requested that because of the inevitable financial delay in the transfer of funds, when a Center pays its dues, it should send the Secretariat a copy of their order of payment by check to prove the payment.

Television: Doolittle had requested a discussion about the use of television in ASSITEJ deliberations, but since she was absent, there was no discussion. However, Snoek commented that the Netherlands used television extensively, and she would discuss this with each Center, and bring a report to the Berlin Congress.

Miscellaneous: Moudoués announced the number of votes that each Center had in the General Assembly (2 votes for professional and 1 vote for amateur).

Adamek announced that on the occasion of the tenth anniversary of ASSITEJ, it would be desirable to honor a number of people who had spent their lives in children's theatre. He proposed the following names:

- The title of Founding President in memory of Léon Chancerel who opened the Constitutional Congress after having actively prepared the foundation of ASSITEJ. 1975 was the tenth anniversary of his death.
- The title of Member of Honor in memory of Mila Melanova, who had worked forty years in the Czechoslovakian theatre, and Alexander Briantsev, who had founded the TUZ Theatre in the USSR.

The recommendations were placed on the Agenda for the General Assembly in Berlin. This concluded the Minutes of the meetings in Zagreb.

Activities planned for the delegates during the EXCOM meetings included a visit to the Studio of Creative Drama by the Youth Theatre of Zagreb, a visit to the National Park "Lakes of Plitvice", visits to Stubica and Kumrovec, and opportunities to see 10 different productions.

Performance of "Snoopy!!!", based on the comic strip "Peanuts" by Charles M. Schulz, Book by CMS Creative Associates, directed by John Tolch and performed by the University Theatre, University of Wisconsin, Madison, Wisconsin, USA, at the 24th International Children's Theatre Festival in Šibonek, Yugoslavia, 16-30 June 1984.

1975
VTH INTERNATIONAL CONGRESS OF ASSITEJ
Berlin, GDR / 19-26 April 1975

The Vth International Congress of ASSITEJ met in Berlin, GDR on 19-26 April 1975. Nat Eek (USA) presided as President, Vladimir Adamek (Czechoslovakia) as 1st Vice President, Ilse Rodenberg (GDR) as 2nd Vice President, Joyce Doolittle (Canada) as 3rd Vice President, Rose-Marie Moudoués (France) as Secretary-General, and Ion Lucian (Romania) as Treasurer.

Other members attending were: José Géal (Belgium), Victor Georgiev (Bulgaria), John English (Great Britain), Maria Sunyer (Spain), Ivan Voronov (USSR), and Ljubiša Djokič (Yugoslavia). Co-opted: Hans Snoek (Netherlands). Gerald Tyler was present as Honorary President (Great Britain), and Michael Pugh (Great Britain) as guest presenter of his Bibliography of Plays.

Members absent: Hanswalter Gossmann (FGR), Benito Biotto (Italy), Orna Porat (Israel) as EXCOM members, and Ian Cojar (Romania) and Sara Spencer (USA) as Advisors.

A total of 36 countries attended with 24 National Centers of ASSITEJ represented.

Also attending were official representatives: Hans Rodenberg, member of the GDR State Council; Hans-Joachim Hoffmann, Minister of Culture; and Radu Beligan (Romania), President of ITI. Organizations represented besides ITI were: International Association of Theatre Critics (AICT); International Organization of Theatre Designers and Technicians (OISIT); International Union of Puppeteers (UNIMA); and International Association of Amateur Theatres (IATA).[120]

The first of the delegates arrived on Saturday, 19 April 1975, and with excellent organization were given copies of the entire program, a list of participants, tickets, name tags, a narrative of the plots of the plays to be seen, and many informational brochures— all printed in the 3 official languages.

The next day Ilse Rodenberg, President of the GDR National Center, greeted the delegates, followed by a luncheon where they were welcomed by Kurt Löffler, State Secretary in the Ministry of Culture and Werner Engst, Deputy Minister of Education. In the morning there were a special welcome and an excellent concert by the Young Pioneer Orchestra of Berlin for the entire Congress featuring works of Schubert and Shostakovich.

The EXCOM Meeting / Sunday, 20 April 1975

According to the duplicated Program with Eek's hand-written notes, an EXCOM meeting was scheduled for 5:00 pm that day, but there seem to be no Minutes of it extant. Based on previous experience, it probably consisted of setting the Agenda for the first meeting of the General Assembly.

While this EXCOM met, the other delegates attended performances of *Three Fat Men* by Vladimir Rubin, directed by Natalia Sats, with a large cast, which the child audience enjoyed because its concept of authority was so frequently thwarted. It was performed by the Komische Oper of East Berlin, with a full orchestra in the pit with a safety net over it to protect it from flying properties. In the evening the performance of *Don Quixote* by Mikhail Bulgakov seemed conventional and very long.

The 1st Meeting of the General Assembly / Monday morning 21 April 1975

Rodenberg began the morning session of the Congress at 9:00 am with an official welcome, recalling the world-wide defeat of fascism in WWII, and the creation of a new social system in the GDR, a humanistic culture that included theatres for children from the very beginning.

Nat Eek, President of ASSITEJ, officially opened the Congress, describing its most important goal as greater understanding and cooperation among its members. If those working in children's theatre could come closer together as a result of this Congress, that goal would have been achieved.

Hans-Joachim Hoffmann, the Minister of Culture, stressed the high regard for ASSITEJ. He said the GDR Center's goal was to create the best conditions for the younger generation to develop into all-round personalities. In the GDR 50 percent of all audiences were 25 years old and younger, and ASSITEJ provided the venue for artistic discussion and scientific work for youth theatre in a larger context. The delegates' enthusiasm, creativity, and love of children united all the participants.

Eek thanked the Minister and then commented on the program of this Congress. Delegates had complained that past Congresses never seemed to be able to discuss important artistic and social questions, so this Congress specifically scheduled major speeches to set the theme, discussion groups afterword, and reports at the end of these discussions as handouts for delegates.

Since the Brussels Congress had had to be cancelled, it was most appropriate that its host José Géal (Belgium) gave a major address entitled "The Professional Actor and the School".

Géal opened his speech by underlining the fact that the theatre and the school were separate entities, and theatre must remain the concern of the professional workers and not defer to the so-called "pedagogues". However, collaboration is desirable, and having seen productions at the Theater der Freundschaft, he complemented their artistry and professionalism. This was possible since the plays were performed in a properly equipped theater, not a classroom. He stressed the value of arousing enthusiasm in the young audience by introducing them to theater properly, and he closed quoting the Belgian educator Jeanne Cappe about children's theatre: "It must use the simplest means for the most effective results. Nothing is good for our children that is not done with great honesty.

Christel Hoffmann (GDR) then gave an address on the effects of theatre and school on the development of the personality in young people.

Theatre speaks its own language of art, and it is not a classroom. However, the actor and the teacher are partners in developing the socialist personality and agree on content and purpose, and it is important for the actor and the child to interact. Voluntary study groups between actors and pupils are a useful tool in exploring the aesthetics of theatre for the child. She closed her speech by saying that "The actor and the teacher are, for the children, perfectly normal creative people who do good work, each in his own way."

Copies of both the speeches were handed out to the delegates for future discussion.

The 2nd Meeting of the General Assembly / 21 April 1975

The second session of the General Assembly occurred on Monday afternoon at 2:00 pm, with Eek presiding. There were 6 items on the Agenda:

- Approval of the Minutes of the General Assembly meeting in 1972
- The Secretary-General's Report Morale
- The Treasurer's Financial Report
- Modification of the Statutes
- Nominations for the new EXCOM
- General activities

The Minutes of 1972 had been sent previously to all the National Centers, and they were approved without discussion.

Report Morale: The Secretary-General gave a brief history of the first ten years of ASSITEJ, and stated that a more detailed document would soon be published. She announced that since the IVth General Assembly, 8 new national centers had joined: Algeria, Australia, Cuba, Finland, Iran, Peru, Sri Lanka, and Switzerland. She spoke at length about Publications, appealing to all centers to support the *Review* and the *Czech Bulletin* with their contributions.

Moudoués urged the Centers to choose 10 plays from their respective countries, and send in a brief description of each one. She also noted that the Czech Center was preparing a *Who's Who in ASSITEJ*, and that each Center could propose 5 people. She also reported on the work of the EXCOM, the Bureau, and the relations of ASSITEJ with other organizations.

Financial Report: Lucian distributed copies of the Financial Report, and in the discussion that followed the delegates voted to increase the membership dues for each Center from 75 to 100 USD. The Centers were instructed to send their dues in at the beginning of each year, and to indicate how the monies should be applied (for dues or for subscriptions) since some Centers would send a single undesignated check. Both the Report of the Secretary-General and the Treasurer were approved.

Statutes: President Eek then explained the proposed modification in the Statutes:

1) Chap. II, Art. V, Sec. 3: ". . . and to send a written report on their activities to the Secretary-General once a year."

2) Chap. IV, Art. IX, Paragraph 4: "The General Assembly shall meet at least once every *three* years."

3) Chap. IV, Art. IX, Paragraph 13: "The General Assembly appoints the Secretary-General and the Treasurer of the Association on the recommendation of the *outgoing* Executive Committee."

Add to the same paragraph: "The General Assembly on the recommendation of theExecutive Committee can give the title of President of Honor for exceptional service given to the Association. The Members of Honor have a consultative voice, but no right to vote, and they cannot represent their country."

4) Chap. IV, Art. IX, Paragraph 16: "Only questions which are on the Agenda can be submitted to the General Assembly to be voted on."

5) Chap. IV, Art. X, Paragraph 12: "The Executive Committee... proposes a plan of activities to the General Assembly . . . ." It [the plan] "shall remain in office [effect] for three years."

The amendments were voted on and approved by the delegates. There was considerable discussion over the change to meet every three years instead of two. Delegates pointed out that the Congresses were important to preserve contacts, but others stated that their countries would only pay for trips to Congresses, not special meetings. In the future it was decided to send invitations to the Congresses to National Centers and the Secretariat, as well as individual delegates.

Nominations: Moudoués then announced the nominations for the new EXCOM: Bulgaria (Victor Georgiev), Canada (Joyce Doolittle), Czechoslovakia (Vladimir Adamek), France (Rose-Marie Moudoués),

GDR (Ilse Rodenberg), Great Britain (John English), Italy (Benito Biotto), Netherlands (Hans Snoek), Romania (Ion Lucian), Spain (Maria Sunyer), USA (Nat Eek), USSR (Ivan Voronov), and Yugoslavia (Ljubiša Djoki!).

The USA delegation protested that they had presented a list of 15 names of countries, and that two were missing. Moudoués explained that every country which wished to be represented on the EXCOM could only propose its own candidacy. The USA proposal to amend this to the full fifteen centers failed by majority vote.

The invitation of the Spanish Center to hold the VIth Congress in the last week of April 1978 in Madrid was accepted.

Miscellaneous Business: Canada announced it had completed the printing of its booklet on the first ten years of ASSITEJ activity, and distributed information about purchases in the three official languages. The USA proposed creating a center for arranging exchanges of artists and ensembles for guest performances in other countries. A representative of the IATA requested that closer ties be established between ASSITEJ and their organization.

This concluded the General Assembly session. That evening the delegates attended a performance of *Robby Kruse* by Hans-Dieter Schmidt, an adaptation for youth of Robinson Crusoe, presented by the Theatre der Jungen Welt from Leipzig.

Tuesday, 22 April 1975

The day was given over to three discussion groups on "The Role of Professional Children's Theatre in General Arts Teaching in Schools", Acting by Actors and Play-Acting by Children", and "The Participation of Audiences in Professional Children's Theatre". A final report by the leader of each group would be given first to the combined discussion groups that day, and then to the General Assembly the next day. The Minutes on the final reports were extensive, so only a short précis of each leader's report has been written into the report of 23 April.

General Assembly / Elections / Wednesday, 23 April

President Eek opened the General Assembly by proposing on behalf of the EXCOM that 5 persons from theatres for children be named

Honorary Members of ASSITEJ:

1) Léon Chancerel (France), co-founder of ASSITEJ, died in 1965
2) Alexander Bryantsev (USSR), founder of the Leningrad Theatre for Young Spectators, died in 1961
3) Mila Milanova (Czechoslovakia), founder of the Czechoslovakian Children's Theatre, died in 1964
4) Victor Ion Popa (Romania), author of children's plays of high quality, died in 1946
5) Charlotte Chorpenning (USA), playwright and founder of the Goodman Children's Theatre in Chicago, Illinois, died in 1952

The General Assembly approved the naming of these five, and recommended that the EXCOM make further nominations by the next Congress.

The General Assembly by vote then approved the re-appointment of Rose-Marie Moudoués as Secretary-General and Ion Lucian as Treasurer, which automatically seated France and Romania on the EXCOM. The Assembly then elected the following countries to the EXCOM: Bulgaria (Victor Georgiev), Canada (Joyce Doolittle), Czechoslovakia (Vladimir Adamek), GDR (Ilse Rodenberg), Italy (Benito Biotto), Spain (Maria Sunyer), USA (Nat Eek), USSR (Ivan Voronov), and Yugoslavia (Ljubiša Djokič).

Although both Great Britain (John English) and the Netherlands (Hans Snoek) had been nominated, they failed to receive a majority vote, so they were not elected.

The New EXCOM Meeting

In the new EXCOM meeting they discussed nominations for the President and Vice-Presidents. Adamek and Rodenberg were nominated for the Presidency, and Doolittle, Rodenberg, Sunyer, and Eek were nominated for the Vice-Presidencies. Eek declined the nomination stating that his new position of Dean of the College of Fine Arts at the University of Oklahoma could not allow him to take on the duties of Vice-President. Also, he said that another representative from the USA could not be named until the next meeting of his National Center. In addition, he commented that being President had been a distinct privilege, but that now with the three year period between Congresses, a single term presidency would be most desirable in order to provide constantly new and fresh leadership.

The names of the proposed officers were presented to the next General Assembly, and the delegates elected the following officers: Vladimir Adamek (Czechoslovakia) as President, Ilse Rodenberg (GDR) as 1st Vice-President, Joyce Doolittle (Canada) as 2nd Vice-President, and Maria Sunyer (Spain) as 3rd Vice-President.

Adamek thanked the Assembly for his election and asked for the support of all the National Centers in his work which he said would not be easy. He also thanked Eek for his long-standing work and stressed that the name Eek would remain forever linked with ASSITEJ.

While the elections went on, the other delegates visited schools in Berlin, saw a children's group perform at the Academy of Arts, saw *Poor Konrad* by the Theater Junge Garde from Halle, attended Eugen Eschner's *King Jörg*, or saw a performance of *Die Horatier unde die Kuriatier* by Bertold Brecht at the Theater der Freundschaft.

General Assembly / Thursday, 24 April

The delegates met in the assembly hall of the People's Chamber to listen to reports on the individual group discussions of the previous day.

Secretary-General Moudoués announced the results of the elections from the previous day, and President Adamek announced the nominations of the honorary members. Past President Eek expressed his thanks for the support and the friendship accorded him while in office, and gave a final address. (See Appendix G). He closed his speech expressing the hope that ASSITEJ in the future would focus its attention on artistic questions, and that its younger members would acquire more influence so that the Association would not become isolated. According to the Doolittle Minutes, he received a standing ovation amidst great applause at the conclusion of his speech.

The speech was followed by the Reports of the three Group Discussions:

Group I discussed: "The role of professional children's theatre in general arts teaching in schools" led by Natalia Sats (USSR).

There were 75 people in her group, of whom 12 spoke. The discussion was lively, and she would see that it would be published in the Soviet magazine *Teatr*. Sats, after citing some personal examples, said the general aim of the theatre and the school was to bring up the "new man" who stood for peace, international friendship, and the goals of humanism. While the school opened the treasures of the past, it was the theatre's task to fill young people with enthusiasm for the ideals of the past. Theatre must awaken the creative instinct in people, so they not only followed others but would take the lead themselves.

Group II discussed: "Acting by actors and play-acting by children" led by Zvjezdana Ladika (Yugoslavia).

Ladika in her summary emphasized that very different attitudes towards actors' work with children had been expressed. The discussion was by no means ended, but one important problem must be stated: there were communication problems, and there was no standard terminology available for the discussion. She requested that EXCOM consider the question of standard and unambiguous terminology, and report on it in an article in *The Review*.

Group III discussed: "The participation of audiences in professional children's theatre" led by Brian Way (Great Britain).

Way stated that in his group there were too many topics to be discussed, so the session was primarily one of questions, for which there was no time for answers. In final summary, he said he had been impressed by the Congress, but many of the questions asked had been answered in London twenty years ago. There was need for a special, one-day seminar, and he seconded Ladika's request for standard terminology, adding that new terminology should always be given to the interpreters.

A general discussion followed these reports: Moudoués said Ladika's request would be considered by the EXCOM, and informed the Assembly that Denmark had been accepted as a new National Center.

Miscellaneous discussion: Future discussions should be in smaller groups, or broken up by languages. Pugh said the new *Bibliography of Plays* would be mailed by the end of the year. Snoek gave information on a film project on professional theatre for children. Legrave (France) informed the delegates of the Bordeaux Conference for playwrights in February 1976, and supported the plea for standard terminology.

Doolittle announced a Children's Theatre Conference in Canada in May 1976, and said invitations would go to every center. She also requested that because the EXCOM was smaller EXCOM now that the full fifteen members be elected next time. Also, she suggested that each Center nominate two delegates, one of which is younger than 35 years of age. She also felt there should be more use of film, since language could be a barrier for third world countries. Spanish as a fourth official language should be examined again.

Tyler informed the Assembly of a festival in Great Britain planned in the fall of 1975 to celebrate the 10th Anniversary of ASSITEJ. He supported both the standard terminology request as well as the increase in size of the EXCOM. He felt that the current Statutes were too narrow, and their vagueness needed to be clarified.

Raoul Carrat (France) criticized the Minutes of the IVth Congress because the critiques of the plays did not present the views of all the delegates. He felt the themes of the current Congress were not sufficiently related to each other, and their topics were not announced in sufficient time for proper preparation. Juul (Denmark) requested time for more discussion in future Congresses. Moudoués answered questions on the theatre festival planned for Hamburg in the FGR [which was later cancelled].

President Adamek concluded the session expressing his gratitude for the faith and honor which his election had granted to the children's theatre in Czechoslovakia. This year of the 30th Anniversary of the end of WWII contained a special duty for ASSITEJ: it had brought people together, and he emphasized the need for artistic contact, since theatre best expressed itself on the stage, not in discussion.

He continued that a new era was beginning for ASSITEJ. Theatres were springing up everywhere, and there were now 28 Centers in ASSITEJ. Room must be made for youth on the EXCOM, and suggested that representatives from 3-4 Centers not elected to the EXCOM be invited to attend each EXCOM Meeting. Contacts between Centers must be improved.

He thanked the Past President, the hosts and organizers of the Congress, and noted this was International Woman's Year and congratulated the three newly elected Vice-Presidents accordingly. He concluded quoting Léon Chancerel ten years ago about the unifying element: "...love of and respect for art, the child, the youth, and of oneself...we must better come to know each other for we can only work usefully if we trust one another."

That afternoon delegates saw *Cinderella* by Yevzenij Shvarts. In the evening the Berlin Deutsche Statsoper presented two children's ballets, *Peter and the Wolf* by Prokofiev and *The Emperor's New Clothes* by J. Francaix. The evening concluded with a reception for all participants in the Ministry's banquet hall.

Friday, 25 April 1975

This morning *The Little Hump-Backed Horse* by E. Erb and A. Endler was presented by the Theater der Freundschaft. In the afternoon delegates again visited schools in the city. In the House of Young Talent a children's group showed its music and movement program. Films were also shown which delegates had brought from their countries. That evening the Theater für Junge Zuschauer from Magdeburg presented *The Playboy of the Western World* by J. M. Synge. Another play seen during the Congress was *The Broken Doll* from Chile. The next day the delegates departed.

The Vth Congress had been an unqualified success in its organization, its variety, its artistic discussions, the shear number of events planned for the delegates, the number of delegates, the number of countries present, the presence of high officials, the international organizations represented, and the respect in which ASSITEJ was held: all were impressive factors in its success.

Hotel Beroliner, Berlin, GDR. February, 1966. Where the EXCOM members and delegates to a Congress were housed. Personal photograph.

A SUMMARY OF 1972-1975

<u>1972</u>

*B*ordeaux, France was an ideal place to have the first ASSITEJ meeting following the IVth Congress in North America in June of 1972. The mid-October weather was gloriously warm and pleasant, the meals of fresh seafood delectable, and the sense of success carried over from the IVth Congress made for an excellent meeting.

The Bureau: The original Statutes of ASSITEJ (1965) do not identify the Bureau. It was created out of necessity when Gerald Tyler (Great Britain) was Acting President in 1966. It allowed the elected officers of the Association—President, Vice-Presidents, Secretary-General, and Treasurer—to meet separately and make decisions that would then be recommended to the entire EXCOM at their first meeting following the Bureau Meeting for their acceptance or rejection. The Bureau decisions could not be binding by the Constitution (see Constitution [1965], Article X, Section 7). Much later the Bureau and its powers would be defined by an amendment to the Constitution, and its concept became a permanent part of the Association's *modus operandi*.[121]

Many times Bureau meetings were prompted by an emergency, such as the cancellation of the Congress in Belgium in 1974. A Bureau Meeting allowed it to clear the next Agenda, so that the EXCOM was not tied down by long discussions and perhaps endless wrangling. A Bureau Meeting could also be misused by only the members who could attend on the date designated. Thus decisions could be made that did not have the input of the entire Bureau.

Tyler as President used the Bureau primarily as a means of clarifying the Agenda the day or so before the regular EXCOM Meeting. However, Moudoués as Secretary-General used it as a means of discussing personal agendas. While these were not formally called Bureau Meetings, she would announce their recommendations at the next full Bureau Meeting, citing difficulties of getting everyone together and the urgency of the current problems.

Later members of the EXCOM began to object to the pre-conceived decisions of the Bureau, feeling that the Bureau was deliberately by-passing the input of the EXCOM for proper discussion. This forced the

Bureau to pull back on their discussions, and to keep their meetings primarily for organization and clarification. Eek was conscious of being ignored at least twice by not being invited or informed about Bureau Meetings held in Europe. He received a letter announcing the meeting after it was held that included the decisions that were recommended. Usually the Secretary-General cited the inconvenience, costs, and delay of Eek having to come from the USA for the meeting. However, decisions were not official until they were approved at the next EXCOM meeting, although Bureau decisions thus made were never reversed.

Only the Bureau met in Bordeaux, France in October of 1972. Maria Sunyer (Spain) had been invited to attend to present her Center's request that Spanish become a fourth official language of ASSITEJ which had been tabled at the IVth Congress in North America.

Statutes: The Secretary-General recommended that a meeting of the Statutes Committee be held before the Bureau and EXCOM Meetings in London in 1973. The EXCOM could make recommendations for Statute changes, send them to the Centers for discussion and eventual approval, and then forward them to the General Assembly for final acceptance. Since only the General Assembly could make changes in the Statutes, she propsed that recommendations could be sent by the Statutes Committee in their final report to the next EXCOM Meeting in London. These recommendations would in turn go to the 1975 Congress for approval.

Centers: The Secretary-General reported that the legality of the Portugal Center had been questioned. There was the possibility of two national centers. However the Statutes specify only one center per country, and so Portugal would have to solve this problem internally. She had also written to Australia, with no reply. Rodenberg reported that Egypt, Mongolia, and Ceylon had all expressed interest in ASSITEJ and in forming centers.

Minutes: Doolittle was appointed Recording Secretary for the Minutes of the Bureau and the EXCOM, replacing Eek.

ITI Committee on Youth: The ITI of UNESCO had recently created a new committee for youth and young adults, and each country had been asked to form a commission on this subject. Those representatives would meet in Budapest, Hungary in December 1972. The Secretary-General of ITI had visited Moudoués to explain that no duplication of

ASSITEJ was intended, and had invited her to attend that meeting as ASSITEJ's representative. Others in the EXCOM indicated that the ITI in their countries had invited them also. In the animated discussion that followed the EXCOM decided that ASSITEJ should be represented. The ITI meeting was later held in Moscow, USSR in November 1973, and many ASSITEJ members attended.

For years ASSITEJ had tried to court support from UNESCO, but even with the ITI Center in Paris, nothing ever came of these approaches. The history of ASSITEJ's finances is primarily one of self-financing through the support of the national centers in the form of dues as well as considerable subsidization by the French center and the specific government hosting each particular meeting. For twenty-five years the French Center gave remarkable financial support to the international office through Moudoués and ATEJ (the French national children's theatre association founded by Léon Chancerel). After 1990 considerable support came from the Scandinavian Centers. As of 2005 ASSITEJ was still not financially secure and independent of governmental subsidies.

Brussels Congress: José Géal presented the proposed program for the Vth Congress in Brussels, Belgium which would start on Monday, 1 July 1974. However, all his careful planning was for naught since he had to cancel the Congress in Belgium as of November 1973. (See EXCOM Meeting in Madrid, Spain on 16-22 April 1974.)

Spanish as a 4th Language: Sunyer presented the case for the inclusion of Spanish as a 4th official language by reading from a brief that stated: 25 nations, particularly in Central and South America, speak Spanish as their primary language; 240,000,000 people in the world speak Spanish; Spanish is the second most used language in the world after English; if Spanish is not included as a 4th language, the Spanish-speaking nations will create their own ASSITEJ. She closed her remarks recommending the possibility of only having Spanish as an official language at the International Assemblies.

Sunyer suggested that in *The Review*, which her Center now distributed, she could add an editorial in Spanish to say what she was doing. She also proposed to make a Spanish edition of *The Review* available, and was preparing a Report in Spanish about the IVth Congress in North America.

The Spanish Language Sub-Committee recommended to the

EXCOM that the Spanish Resolution be voted upon in June 1973 in London. The Secretary-General meanwhile was to inform the Spanish-speaking countries of this resolution, and the appointing of the Spanish Center as liaison to all Spanish-speaking countries. Sunyer finally requested that President Eek appoint her officially as the liaison between ASSITEJ and the Spanish-speaking countries, and to send copies of this letter to Brazil, Venezuela, Peru, and Puerto Rico. Politically Sunyer was moderately right under a benign older Franco, but this did not sit well with the Eastern countries and the Paris office, even though Sunyer spoke French fluently and supported ASSITEJ whole-heartedly with many Spanish theatres as members of that Center.

In an unofficial Post Script Eek wrote to the members of the US Center for ASSITEJ that the most important part of the decisions made was that Sunyer and the Spanish Center could now become the official communicant to all Spanish-speaking nations. Up to this point the Paris office had kept them in low priority. However, Adamek had correctly raised the question that German as another official language would have to be dealt with by the Sub-Committee.

For several years the Spanish Center continued publication of journals and information, and distributed them to all Spanish-speaking centers and interested countries, probably much to the relief and possible dismay of the Paris office. With the retirement of Maria Sunyer, who had proved to be an energetic, efficient, and positive administrator with extensive governmental contacts as well as her own personal funds, the Spanish Center gradually declined for a lack of strong leadership, the publications stopped, and the Center became much less active in ASSITEJ.

1973

The entire EXCOM met in London in June of 1973. The major item of discussion was the program for the Brussels Congress of 1974, and Géal gave a complete report showing imagination and careful planning. but with its cancellation in late 1973, these details became moribund.

As a person Géal was an excellent actor, had a very good, though small, performing company. He was a man with considerable charm and know-how, fluent in several languages. He also seemed to have the right political connections, and he had been involved in ASSITEJ before and since its inception in 1965. He had obviously done an excellent job of planning the Brussels Congress, and he had had the complete cooperation of the Paris office. However, the Congress could only happen with considerable subsidy.

When the Brussels Congress was officially cancelled in 1973, it was a result of a complete lack of governmental subsidy. Belgium had been through three separate governments in a short time, and Géal had had to present his requests three separate times. The Congress would also have the expensive complications of providing multiple languages, including Flemish. Géal stated this in a letter which Eek quoted to his center. In addition, Géal had become ill and required extensive hospitalization.

ITI Committee on Youth: In the fall the ITI held its Meeting on Youth in Moscow, USSR. Its theme was "The Progress of the Theatre in Modern Society." 52 countries were represented by 572 delegates, one half of them from the USSR. Other organizations that had been invited were: UNIMA, ASSITEJ, The Critics Organization, and the Student Theatres International Organization. The third world countries were well represented for the first time at an ITI Congress.

In the discussion at the London EXCOM Doolittle commented that she felt cooperation, not competition, was to be encouraged with the ITI Youth Committee. While there was considerable confusion in the Committee, Rodenberg acknowledged that ITI was bigger and more powerful than ASSITEJ, and the Association should keep track of their activities and invite them to the Brussels Congress in 1974. This summed up the EXCOM's reaction.

Publications: Moudoués, Editor of *The Review*, announced a new editorial policy: in the future two different National Centers would be responsible for the contents of each issue, which came out four times a year. The articles would be in the language of the Center with a précis printed in the three official languages. This only continued for a year or two, and was an attempt to salvage and solidify the struggling *Review*.

On the financial front, the Treasurer announced a surplus in the bank, and requested permission, which was granted with enthusiasm, to invest 5% of that surplus in a French interest-bearing account.

Centers: The Sri Lanka Center had sent their Statutes with everything in order. They were waiting for admission before they paid their dues. A man named Garcia would probably form a Brazilian Center, and would come to discuss its creation in Spain in 1974. Poland had not yet created a Center [even though it had been accepted previously!], although the country had many activities for youth, particularly puppet theatre. Apparently both the Secretary-General and Rodenberg consistently blocked the acceptance of a Polish Center as "...not being serious about the professional theatre." The Secretary-General also said that Mr. Jurkowski of the Polish Ministry of Culture told her that there were only 2 professional children's theatre troupes in Poland, so why bother to create a Center?

In representing a proposed Iran Center, Don LaFoon gave some background on the Institute for the Intellectual Development of Children and Young Adults: "There are 80 libraries, 22 of which are in the capital of Teheran. Plays are presented in libraries, schools, and orphanages. The project has been able to attract 7 top actors and one of them has accompanied me [LaFoon] to the London Meeting. Finances are not a problem, since this project is one of the favorites of the Empress of Iran. 3 plays are now on tour."

The applications of Sri Lanka and Iran were accepted unanimously by the EXCOM.

Don LaFoon (Iran) was a USA citizen who was fluent in Farsi, and who had established the children's theatre and the Iran Center with the support of the Empress of Iran. When the Shah was overthrown in 1977, LaFoon returned to the USA, and the Iran Center and its children's theatre program collapsed. Much later in the 1990s a new Iran Center was established.

Artistic Discussions: The next EXCOM Meeting was set for Madrid in 16-21 April 1974. Then a long discussion ensued on the need to discuss artistic matters in ASSITEJ. No ASSITEJ meeting ever seemed to have time enough for artistic discussions, and it was proposed that at each meeting in the future one person should present a paper on an artistic subject. This was a continuing complaint of the membership, and was intermittently solved by individual papers and some enlivened discussions at the various Congresses. The purpose behind having a theme for each Congress was to allow a focus for such artistic discussions. Many of the discussions fell into predictable camps, but occasionally there would be flashes of interesting controversy that would move the art of children's theatre forward.

Probably the ultimate answer to artistry would always remain with the viewing of various productions at each Congress. Here would always be proof of artistic decisions for everyone to see and digest and discuss with each other. For many delegates this was the best part of any Congress, and many productions sparked controversy. This would always be the *raison d'être* of international conferences-this and personal contacts.

Performances: The London theatre had provided excellent diversion as well as controversy for the delegates. Not only was there a wealth of theatre for young people, but there were three planned performances for the delegates after the meeting was over. A contemporary performance of Moliere's *The Misanthrope* with Diana Rigg was at the National Theatre. With actors lolling around on cushions drinking champagne and eating caviar, the sparkling dialogue came across brilliantly. Then an excursion to Stratford-on-Avon to see a production of Shakespeare's *As You Like It* produced an anti-romantic version of the comedy in modern dress with a balding Orlando, a skinny Rosalind, and a fat Phoebe inhabiting a stark skeletal aluminum forest that destroyed any laughter that might have been present. Fortunately the Birmingham Rep rescued the Bard with a first rate production of *Twelfth Night* that let the poetry take flight and the comedy prove to be really funny rather than forced.

1974

In November 1973 before the Madrid, Spain EXCOM Meeting of April, José Géal (Belgium) informed the Secretariat that it would be impossible for Belgium to host the next International Congress. The Secretary-General informed President Eek immediately by letter.

1975 Congress: The most important item on the 1974 Madrid Agenda was to make a decision about where and when to hold the next Congress. The EXCOM decided that with so little preparation time, a Congress could not be held that year. This postponed the Vth Congress to 1975, with a hiatus of 3 years between Congresses becoming the norm hereafter.

At this EXCOM meeting in Spain 5 different centers proposed to host the next Congress: the GDR Center in Berlin in April 1975; the

Spanish Center in Madrid in 1977; the USSR Center in Moscow in 1977; the Bulgarian Center in Sophia in 1977 or 1979; and the FGR Center in Hamburg in 1975. The decision to accept one of these offers was put off until the next meeting in Zagreb in February 1975. This would allow those countries making the offers to get their details together. It also allowed the Bureau to make a decision without the EXCOM, and in turn announce it as a *fait accompli* because of the emergency.

ITI Committee on Youth: Jean Daconte (France), President of the ITI, met with the EXCOM of ASSITEJ about the ITI Committee on Young Theatre. He first suggested that ASSITEJ develop a more proper title such as "Young Theatre". Secondly, he suggested how ASSITEJ could cooperate with the Committee: by allowing each ASSITEJ National Center to establish contact with the Committee, and then promote their international relationship. It was suggested to have a Hamburg meeting between ASSITEJ and the ITI Committee to clarify the roles of youth theatre. It should be remembered that Gossmann and the FGR had offered to hold the next Congress in Hamburg. During the discussion one of the EXCOM members commented that ITI seemed to be getting smaller and smaller, and less affluent, and advised avoiding ITI altogether!

Meanwhile ASSITEJ should create a list of countries wishing advice on children's theatre, and in turn would create a committee of advisors. Also, a list of all ASSITEJ Centers should be sent to Hamburg. This discussion suggested that Hamburg was becoming an important theatre center, but nothing ever came of these contacts.

New Centers: The Secretary-General stated that Austria, Venezuela, Argentina, Denmark, and Australia had satisfied all requirements for membership except their sending of the statutes of their Centers. The Minister of Culture for Sri Lanka (formerly Ceylon) also had announced their first performance in children's theatre on 27 December 1973. The USSR delegate announced contacts in Poland and Cuba, and that a Mr. Tarbour, who was trained in the USSR, would be establishing a Center in Turkey.

The Madrid Meeting: In addition to the business meetings and concerns about the next Congress, this EXCOM featured visitations to several schools and creative drama workshops. Those delegates opposed to the concept did not attend, but it was a worthy attempt, since Spain had an active creative dramatics program. In retrospect one admired the magnitude of the Spanish creative drama movement, that these formal classes were available to many children, that they were government supported, and that this was a recent new direction. However, one regretted the fact that the classes were held under strong control by the teachers, and seemed to leave little room for the child to be creative on his or her own. Canada, Great Britain, the Netherlands, Scandinavia, USA, and Yugoslavia were much further along in the development of this form of creative improvisation.

Performances: The Congress also featured both adult and children's theatre productions: *Alice in Wonderland*, Lope de Rueda's *Marta La Pieta*, *Don Quixote*, and *Los Communeros. Don Quixote* was costumed in masks and grotesquely wired costumes which distorted the natural silhouettes. One scene which held the attention of the children very well was a marionette play performed with visible manipulation and creation of sound effects. When Quixote destroyed the marionettes, it was a poignant moment. The performance was in the afternoon for the children, and the play had to use the same set as that for the adult play that evening.

Los Communeros dealt with Carlos V as both a young and an old king, and their acting personas talked to each other during the course of the play. Well performed by the National Theatre with a huge cast, it concerned the uprising of the nobles against the king in the 16th Century, protesting the influence of the Flemish Advisors to the court who seemed to be ruling the country. Colors were in black, white, and grey, with huge drawbridges that were raised and lowered to form different aspects of the scenery. A very impressive production of a remarkable play written by the daughter, Anna Diosdada, of the leading actor of the company.

Interim

Although various countries had proposed having the next Congress in their countries, the EXCOM in Madrid had put off the decision until the next EXCOM meeting in February 1975 in Zagreb. But by this time the Secretary-General and Rodenberg had already made the decision to hold it in Berlin, and plans were well on the way.

This postponement of the Congress established the precedent that all future Congresses would be held every three 3 years. While the cancellation seemed to be unfortunate, in reality it became an extremely intelligent precedent, since hosting an international meeting with its growing number of delegates and foreign productions was proving to be very expensive and time-consuming in its planning and execution. Soon after the Belgian cancellation regrettably Géal stopped attending the meetings, and Belgium became a less active National Center, split by the Flemish and French languages.

There were other changes taking place in ASSITEJ. Some of the National Centers were in difficulty. The Netherlands Center was changing its statutes to admit more theatre groups. Portugal was rewriting their statutes in Portuguese. [Their conservative government would be overthrown in April 1974.] Belgium was becoming a federation of French, Flemish, and possibly German languages, having gone through 4 different governments in as many years. The FGR Center had completely replaced their membership. The Swiss Center had disappeared, but there was a possibility of a new Center in Zaire.

Meanwhile, the Secretary-General called a meeting of some of the members of the Bureau in Paris 1974 in November to discuss the location of the next Congress. Eek was not informed of the meeting until afterwards. In a letter from Moudoués to Eek dated 11 November 1974, she stated that there had just been a meeting in Paris of members of the Bureau to try to solve the problems of a location for the next meeting. The letter indicated that Moudoués, Adamek, and Rodenberg were in attendance. Lucian apparently was absent.

The Secretary-General wrote Eek that Rodenberg had proposed to hold the next International Congress in Berlin in the GDR, hosted by Rodenberg and her Theater der Freundschaft in April 1975. The Bureau had accepted her invitation, but there was no detailed Agenda as yet. However, Moudoués indicated that she had already made contacts for "rooms, theatres, and hotels." This would be presented at the Zagreb EXCOM Meeting in February 1975 for ratification. In the meantime she was sending "50 Inviting-booklets" to the US Center for distribution to their membership to encourage their attendance.

The planning of the Congress was well on its way, but unfortunately President Eek had not been able to attend any of the meetings since he wasn't informed. It was a *fait accompli*. However, time had certainly been of the essence for planning the Berlin Congress. It should be noted that all members of the Bureau who met were sympathetic to or were from the Eastern countries, so there was probably little consideration of the other offers. Also, a representative from the USSR was not present whose invitation could have overridden any decision. Also, the FGR offer to hold the Congress was the last heard from their Center, Hamburg declined in its activities, and the FGR Center under new leadership became a rubber stamp for the decisions of the GDR.

1975

The February 1975 EXCOM meeting in Zagreb, Yugoslavia was well attended, and Rodenberg gave a complete report on the organization and planning for the Berlin Congress to take place in April. Absent were representatives from Belgium, Canada, FGR, Italy, and Israel. With plans for the Berlin Congress in 1975 accepted, the EXCOM approved the Spanish invitation for the next Congress to be held in Madrid in 1978, to be presented for acceptance by the General Assembly at the Berlin Congress.

In the discussion of candidates for the next EXCOM to be elected at the Vth World Congress, the USA delegation had asked to be able to nominate centers other than their own. Once more the Secretary-General stated that only a single Center could nominate itself, and that finished any further discussion. Apparently this may have been normal procedure in Europe, but in the USA multiple nominations were allowed as long as the nominator had obtained the permission of the individual nominee. The USA Center was particularly interested in this possibility hoping to maintain an East-West balance.

The Zagreb EXCOM Meeting was obviously affected by the changes in world events. With the financial downturn, monies were difficult to obtain. The Vietnam War was being regarded as an American disaster. Religious fervor and extreme nationalism was gaining a more dominant place in world politics. The world was becoming more conservative, which in turn brought forth entrenched attitudes and ideas, making the leaders hold onto the "known" rather than seek new directions in the arts. The separation caused by the cold war was even more intense and in evidence.

Vth International Congress: The Vth International Congress was held in Berlin, GDR from 19-26 April. Most of the EXCOM members were in attendance with the exception of the representatives of the FGR, Italy, Israel, and two of the Advisors. A total of thirty-six (36) countries attended, as well as many representatives from other theatre associations. Rodenberg had planned well, and upon arrival delegates were given copies of the entire program, a list of participants, tickets, name tags, a narrative of the plots of the plays to be seen, and many informational brochures—all printed in the 3 official languages!

President Eek (USA) officially opened the Congress, describing its most important goal as one of greater understanding and cooperation among its members. The Minister of Culture in his welcome stressed their high regard for ASSITEJ, and the fact that the GDR Center's goal was to create the best conditions for the younger generation to develop into all-round personalities. In the GDR 50 percent of all audiences were 25 years old and younger, and ASSITEJ provided the venue for artistic discussion and scientific work for youth theatre in a larger context. The GDR delegates' enthusiasm, creativity, and love of children united all the participants.

Since the Brussels Congress had had to be cancelled, it was most appropriate that its host José Géal (Belgium) gave a major address entitled "The Professional Actor and the School". Géal opened his speech by underlining the fact that the theatre and the school were separate entities, and theatre must remain the concern of the professional workers and not defer to the so-called "pedagogues". However, collaboration was desirable, and having seen productions at the Theater der Freundschaft, he complemented their artistry and professionalism. This was possible he said since the plays were performed in a properly equipped theater, not a classroom.

Report Morale: The Secretary-General gave a brief history of the first ten years of ASSITEJ. Since the IVth Congress, 8 new national centers had joined: Algeria, Australia, Cuba, Finland, Iran, Peru, Sri Lanka, and Switzerland. She spoke at length about Publications, appealing to all centers to support the *Review* and the *Czech Bulletin* with their contributions.

Moudoués urged the Centers to choose 10 plays from their respective countries, and send in a brief description of each one. She also noted that the Czech Center was preparing a *Who's Who in ASSITEJ,* and that each Center could propose 5 people. She also reported on the work of the EXCOM, the Bureau, and the relations of ASSITEJ with other organizations.

In order to comply with the delegates' request for more artistic discussions, the Assembly broke into 3 discussion groups, each led by a member of the EXCOM, who then later reported on the results of the discussions. This proved to be an excellent and lively solution to the need to have discussions on the art of the theatre.

1978 Congress and the 1975 Elections: The invitation of the Spanish Center to hold the VIth Congress in the last week of April 1978 in Madrid was accepted. The Assembly approved the changes in the Statutes with no controversy, and in the elections the following countries became the new EXCOM: Bulgaria (Victor Georgiev), Canada (Joyce Doolittle), Czechoslovakia (Vladimir Adamek), GDR (Ilse Rodenberg), Italy (Benito Biotto), Spain (Maria Sunyer), USA (Nat Eek), USSR (Ivan Voronov), and Yugoslavia (Ljubiša Djokič).

Although both Great Britain (John English) and the Netherlands (Hans Snoek) had been nominated, they failed to receive a majority vote, so they were not elected. Clearly votes had been deliberately *not* cast to defeat Great Britain and the Netherlands. Thus the EXCOM for the next three years comprised a total of only 11 members, although the Statutes authorized a total of 15. Of the East-West orientation the totals were 7 East and 4 West. Politically the organization had shifted radically. If Great Britain and the Netherlands had been elected, the vote would have been 7-East to 6-West. Several years earlier Tyler had tried to get the EXCOM to approve the concept that the delegates *must* vote for a total of 15 countries in order to avoid this kind of negative voting, but the proposal failed.

The General Assembly by vote then approved the re-appointment of Rose-Marie Moudoués as Secretary-General and Ion Lucian as Treasurer, which automatically seated France and Romania on the EXCOM, making a total of 11 centers on the EXCOM. The votes of these 2 Centers would be considered "Eastern" in loyalty. This made the final tally of seven—East to four—West.

Adamek and Rodenberg were nominated as President, but Rodenberg declined claiming that Adamek had prior claim since he had stood for President in 1968, and could not accept that responsibility because of the burden of his theatrical duties. A more valid excuse might have been the political unrest brought on by the "Prague Spring" and the ensuing occupation of Czechoslovakia. The Soviet Center certainly could not have supported a defecting country's candidature.

Doolittle, Rodenberg, Sunyer, and Eek were nominated for the Vice-Presidencies. Eek declined stating that his new position of Dean of the College of Fine Arts at the University of Oklahoma could not allow him to take on the duties of Vice-President. He commented that being President had been a distinct privilege, but that now with the 3-year period between Congresses, a single term presidency would be most desirable in order to encourage constantly new and fresh leadership. Up until that time two terms as President were almost assured. In the future this advice was ignored, and Rodenberg became the first President to serve a total of three terms.

The names of the proposed officers were presented to the General Assembly, and the delegates elected the following officers: Vladimir Adamek (Czechoslovakia) as President, Ilse Rodenberg (GDR) as 1st Vice-President, Joyce Doolittle (Canada) as 2nd Vice-President, and Maria Sunyer (Spain) as 3rd Vice-President with Rose-Marie Moudoués as Secretary-General and Ion Lucian as Treasurer.

Adamek thanked the Assembly for his election and asked for the support of all the National Centers in his work which he said would not be easy. He also thanked Eek for his long-standing work and stressed that the name Eek would remain forever linked with ASSITEJ.

President Adamek concluded the session expressing his gratitude for the faith and honor which his election had granted to the children's theatre in Czechoslovakia. This year of the 30th Anniversary of the end of WWII contained a special duty for ASSITEJ: it had brought people together, and he emphasized the need for artistic contact, since theatre best expressed itself on the stage, not in discussion.

He continued that a new era was beginning for ASSITEJ. Theatres were springing up everywhere, and there were now 28 Centers in ASSITEJ. Room must be made for youth on the EXCOM, and suggested that representatives from 3-4 Centers not elected to the EXCOM be invited to attend each EXCOM Meeting. Contacts between Centers must be improved. This was a valid recommendation since many of the centers had become conscious of the aging of its leaders after ten years. However, nothing was ever made of bringing younger people into the main stream.

Eek's nineteen-year-old son Konrad attended the Congress with him, and they both clearly remembered one night awakening at 2 a.m. in their hotel on Karl Marx Strasse to the sounds of tanks, armored vehicles, and heavy motors on the move. Looking out the hotel room window, they saw what looked like an entire army proceeding down the boulevard. At first concerned as to how they would get out of East Berlin if a war had been declared, they were relieved to find out that it was just the GDR army returning from spring maneuvers.

The Vth Congress had been an unqualified success in its organization, its variety, its artistic discussions, the shear number of events planned for the delegates, as well as the number of delegates. The number of countries present, the presence of high officials, the international organizations represented, the respect in which ASSITEJ was held were all impressive factors in its success. In retrospect each of the five Congresses had increased in size and activity since the previous one, a good sign that ASSITEJ was growing, not only in size but importance.

As usual, the elections were controversial. The with-holding of votes to defeat certain countries was appallingly political. The election of only 11 countries to the new EXCOM severely restricted international involvement and exchange of ideas. The East-West split became solidified with the majority of political power now on the side of the East side. It would not be until 12 years later in 1987 at the Australian Congress in Adelaide that the power would begin to shift, and ASSITEJ would become a sizeable and more truly international organization. The final shift in that direction would not occur until the Stockholm, Sweden Congress in 1990.

Finally ASSITEJ, after 10 years of idealistic growth and development was facing an entirely different world and future. The many changes need to be placed in a historical context of the mid 1970s. The world was in a period of great upheaval and disillusionment.

The World in 1975: The economy was sluggish, and there were energy and resource shortages, and big government was mistrusted. The USA was evacuating the civilians from Vietnam in April 1975 because of the communist take-over, exactly the same month as the meeting of the

Vth International Congress in Berlin, GDR. Also, the Watergate scandals had forced President Richard Nixon's resignation in August 1974, there was a recession in Europe and the USA with the bust of the oil boom and the decline of the dollar, along with a severe international questioning of the moral and financial leadership of the USA.

However, the 1972 Berlin Pact and the SALT talks had created a political détente between East and West, only to be broken by Russia's invasion of Afghanistan in 1979. In Latin America conservative regimes regained control with a 1973 military coup in Chile and one later in Argentina in 1976.

The colonialist government of Portugal had been over-thrown in April of 1974, and all non-Communist Europe came under democratic rule after free elections were held in Spain in June 1976, seven months after the death of Franco. In Africa the last European colonies were granted independence.

However, in China less that a year after the Berlin Congress, in 1976 Mao Tse-tung and Zhou Enlai were dead, the power struggle was won by the pragmatists, ending in a purge of the orthodox Maoists, and a year later the notorious "Gang of Four" was arrested. As a result the new leaders modified Maoist policies in education, culture, and industry, and sought better ties with non-communist countries in Europe, plus Japan, and the USA.

Lastly, religion was into politics with the rise of Evangelical Protestant groups in the USA, the religious wars in North Ireland, and the Muslim countries experiencing a rise in religious militancy as a result of the growth of Arab oil wealth.

Essentially the world was growing smaller and more interactive caused by the ease of communication and travel, while at the same time becoming more conservative and less tolerant. This was the new world that ASSITEJ would be facing in the next fifteen years, a new generation, and new concepts and challenges to theatre for young audiences.

(Left to right) The authors: Nat Eek, Ann M. Shaw, Katherine Krzys.

A SUMMING UP
by Nat Eek

*J*n a letter dated 7 April 1975 and sent to all the members of the current EXCOM of ASSITEJ, Sara Spencer (USA) wrote of her concerns about the upcoming Berlin Congress that month, as well as the future of ASSITEJ.

She stated that the achievements of ASSITEJ in ten years had been indeed remarkable: yearly international theatre festivals; production exchanges; seminars, colloquies, and workshops; publications of articles; visiting speakers; and private studies and researches utilizing contacts made through ASSITEJ. She expressed hope that soon it would be possible to exchange repertory more easily among the national centers, and as a Publisher of plays for young audiences, this was dear to her heart.

However, she expressed grave concern that there was "...no new blood coming on, nor have we developed any means of capturing the interest of new people."[122] She felt it essential that the National Centers make strong efforts to broaden the bases of their memberships, and actively to recruit young blood and new ideas.

Knowingly, she had put her finger on the status of ASSITEJ in 1975. The Association was a *fait accompli*, and it had survived and shown modest growth in its first ten years. It had hosted 6 international Congresses—Paris, Prague, The Hague, Venice, Canada and the USA, and now Berlin—all in different venues and on two continents, a sizeable achievement. Thanks to the French Center, ASSITEJ had had continuity through its Paris office as a Secretariat, and while its finances were questionable, the bills were being paid, most correspondence was being answered, and a future was being planned. While the results of many of the elections were politically manipulated, there had been a continuing leadership, and there were other leaders waiting in line to succeed to office.

However, the world had changed. The optimism and promise of the 1960s had been replaced by the cynicism, the divisiveness, the financial down-turn of the 1970s, and ASSITEJ had been affected accordingly. The Association was still Euro-centric. There was little growth and development in the National Centers. As to political philosophy, the majority of the membership had grown more "East" in its outlook. On the whole the same leadership was still in place ten years later, and growing older and more conservative. The East-West division had intensified, and ASSITEJ seemed determined to maintain the status quo. It would not be until the 1980s that the Association would reap the benefits of phenomenal growth, new National Centers—especially in the third world, new leadership, and a financial stability that would aid in its growth and development.

Meanwhile with twenty-five years to go before the arrival of the new century, ASSITEJ had survived and had become a stable, articulate, and vital voice for theatre for young audiences, and was gaining respect among the professional and non-professional theatres of the world. A formidable achievement in ten years!

An Afterword
by Nat Eek

*T*his concludes *The History of ASSITEJ, Volume I (1964-1975),* and the first ten years in which I was most involved as a delegate and then later as an officer. The *History* is projected to be written through 2005, the date of the Montreal Congress, which will complete its forty (40) years of existence. I have written and asked the following participants to help in the writing of these next thirty years: Ann M. Shaw (USA), Michael Ramløse (Denmark), Michael FitzGerald (Australia), Harold Oaks (USA), Niclas Malmcrona (Sweden), Kim Peter Kovac (USA), and others.

Having already started on Volume II, I have now found it necessary to divide it into two volumes. Consequently I project that Volume II will cover the period from 1975 to 1990, and Volume III, from 1990 to 2005, ending with the XVth World Congress in Montreal, Canada. God willing and if the creeks don't rise, Volume II will be completed before the next XVIth World Congress in Adelaide, Australia in 2008.

APPENDIX A
List of Officers and
Honorary Members
(1965-1975)

Presidents of ASSITEJ

1965-1968	Gerald Tyler (Great Britain), 2 2-year terms
1968-1972	Konstantin Shakh-Azizov (USSR), 2 2-year terms
1972-1975	Nat Eek (USA), 1 3-year term

Vice-Presidents

1965-1968	Vladimir Adamek (Czechoslovakia), 2 2-year terms
	Konstantin Shakh-Azizov (USSR), 2 2-year terms
1968-1972	Vladimir Adamek (Czechoslovakia), 2 2-year terms
	Nat Eek (USA), 2 2-year terms
	Ilse Rodenberg (GDR), 2 2-year terms
1972-1975	Vladimir Adamek (Czechoslovakia), 1 3-year term
	Ilse Rodenberg (GDR), 1 3-year term
	Joyce Doolittle (Canada), 1 3-year term

Secretary-Generals

1965-1975	Rosemarie Moudoués (France), 10 years

Treasurers

1965-1968	José Géal (Belgium), 3 years
1968-1972	Ian Cojar (Romania), 4 years
1972-1975	Ion Lucian (Romania), 3 years

Honorary Presidents

As of 1966	Gerald Tyler (Great Britain)
As of 1972	Konstantin Shakh-Azizov (USSR)

Honorary Members

As of 1975	Léon Chancerel (France)
As of 1975	Alexander Bryantsev (USSR)
As of 1975	Mila Milanova (Czechoslovakia)
As of 1975	Victor Ion Popa (Romania)
As of 1975	Charlotte Chorpenning (USA)

APPENDIX B
BIOGRAPHIES
Volume I
Of Principal Officers, Leaders, and Members in alphabetical order

What is most impressive about these Biographies is the fact that these people, without an exception, represent a remarkable group of well educated, well qualified, well practiced, professional leaders in the art of theatre for children and young people, who were dedicated to the realization of that art.

Vladimir Adamek (Czechoslovakia)[123]

Dr. Vladimir Adamek was born in Prague on 1 February 1921. He studied at the Conservatory of Prague and the Theater Institute of Moscow. He was an actor and director of the Army Theatre in 1945-46 and the Realist Theatre from 1951-57. He became the Artistic Director of the Jiří Wolker Theatre in Prague from 1957 to 1974 for which he directed many productions.

He was a Professor of Directing at the Academy of Arts in Prague. He wrote many articles and presented papers at conference on children's theatre, both in Czechoslovakia and abroad. He was Editor-in-Chief of many books and publications. He traveled abroad extensively, and was the organizer of many colloquies.

Adamek was a highly respected member of the children's theatre community by both the East and West. His Jiří Wolker Theatre did plays from both the East and the West with impeccable casts, and imaginative design, giving a theatrical experience to young people that was professional in every sense. As a person he was reserved, modest, had an excellent sense of humor, and was personally dedicated to the sense of the "art" in theatre. From the Western viewpoint he was able to skate the differences in the opposing "cold war" philosophies extremely well.

He was involved from the beginning in the creation of ASSITEJ (1960-63), and was appointed to the Preparatory Committee. His country was elected as a member of the first EXCOM, and he continued as its representative through the 1970s. He hosted the Ist International Congress of ASSITEJ in Prague in 1966. He was elected Vice-President for 4 terms (1966-1975), and was President from 1975-78. With Ján Kákoš he founded the National Center of Czechoslovakia, and served as its President from 1965-1973.

He received many awards and decorations—Honored Artist of Czechoslovakia, Prize of the Capital of Prague, etc. He died in Prague on 20 March 1990.

Benito Biotto (Italy)[124]

Benito Biotto was born on 19 November 1927 at Moriago della Battaglia, Italy, and was a resident of Milan. He began his activities in children's theatre in 1953. In collaboration with the Angelicum, he established the first permanent professional theatre for children in 1957. In 1958 he began writing theatrical transcriptions for children on Italian Radiotelevision. Then in 1964 he started making recordings of plays for children.

He promoted national Festivals of Plays for Children, and promoted many tours to Switzerland and performed in many play festivals in Venice. He was author of plays transmitted on television. He wrote many articles and publications. He attended the Constitutional Conference in Paris, France in 1965, and with Don Raffaello Lavagna established the Italian National Center in 1965. He took over as representative of the Italian National Center for ASSITEJ from Maria Signorelli, whose profession was primarily puppetry, and Don Rafaello Lavagna from the Vatican, whose interest was youth theatre and as a playwright. Bioto was a member of the EXCOM of ASSITEJ from 1966 to 1975, and attended all the International Conferences.

Biotto had his own professional company, Teatro dei Ragazzi, which performed primarily in Milan for young people. He invited ASSITEJ to hold its 3rd Congress in Venice, Italy in 1970, and was able to able to obtain funding from the Cini Foundation to support the meeting. That same Foundation supported the Preparatory Conference of ASSITEJ in 1964 which wrote the first Constitution for ASSITEJ.

He was a respected colleague, well organized, consistently cheerful, and participated fully in all the meetings and discussions.

Léon Chancerel (France)[125]

Léon Chancerel was born in Paris on 8 December 1886. The son and grand-son of doctors, he came from a notable Parisian family, but he renounced a career in medicine, receiving his degree in Letters. He first published several literary works, of which a novel inspired by WWI entitled *Le Mercredi des Cendres [Ash Wednesday]* (1919) was awarded a prize by l'Académie Française.

In 1920 he met Jacques Copeau, then at le Théâtre de Vieux-Columbier, and became one of his closest collaborators. In 1924 Copeau retired with his students to Bourgogne and Chancerel followed him. While Chancerel participated only a few months in Copeau's new venture by writing songs and one act plays, this experience left him with an indelible theatrical and communal impression. He decided to dedicate himself to the task of changing drama to that as conceived by Copeau. Eschewing professional theatre, he turned his attention to the theatre of social action. He clung to this ideal during his lifetime, in the hopes of giving birth to a dramatic art of quality "in all sectors of social life".

On returning to Paris in 1925 Chancerel collaborated with Dullin, Pitoëff, and Jouvet. But his most important meeting was with the Boy Scouts of France with whom he established *la Compagnie des Comédiens Routiers (1929)*, an amateur theatre that continued to grow until 1939 with the advent of WWII. Chancerel pursued two objectives with the children: 1) a basic technique, founded on bodily training, and improvisation of drama, and 2) the creation of an appropriate repertory of dramatic pieces with choral recitations, small farces, and religious celebrations. He stated: "This Company has as its goal to establish comic or tragic productions everywhere there is a need for social action, more particularly in the suburbs and in the country." For ten years, the troupe gave hundreds of presentations throughout France.

At the same time Chancerel, tried hard to develop the practice of dramatic play in the scout community and a group of organizations for young people. He edited a Newsletter (1932-1950), and established a Center of studies and dramatic presentations (1933) that offered courses and plays regularly. In 1937 on the occasion of the World's Fair, he obtained the building Porte d'Italie as a "Center specializing in information and addressing the rearing of young people, to educators and fighters for the People's Culture."

In 1935 he created with the Comediens Routiers an artistic theatre for children, le Théâtre de l'Oncle Sébastien, based on the principles of Commedia dell'Arte, but the Company was broken up by WWII. Finding refuge in Toulouse, Chancerel reinstituted his association, under the auspices of Jeune France, and organized cultural performances at the Théâtre du Taur, between 1941 and 1942. After the war he began to recreate a new traveling troupe: le Théâtre de la Ville et des Champs. It ceased its activities in 1947 for lack of financial support, and without his company Chancerel was not able to continue his revival of the people's theatre. After the Liberation of France, he favored establishing regional centers of dramatic art based on the model of his Parisian Center, giving a strong stimulus to amateur theatre and recreating a dramatic life in the provinces.

In 1951 he succeeded Jouvet as the President of la Société d'Histoire du Théâtre and took over the responsibility for the Review d'Histoire du Théâtre, and the publication of "Famous Theatres throughout France". From 1951 to 1955, he was artistic director of the Festival de Sarlat. In November 1953, he was named Advisor on the techniques of the People's Culture. At the end of his life, theatre for children occupied the center of his attentions: in 1957 he founded l'Association du Théâtre pour l'Enfance et la Jeunesse (ATEJ) in France.

For the next seven years he worked with other European leaders in children's theatre to form a professional association that culminated in the creation of ASSITEJ. Although severely ill at the time in 1965 at the Paris, France Constitutional Conference, he delivered the welcoming address to the delegates at the first General Assembly of l'Association Internationale du Théâtres pour l'Enfance at la Jeunesse (ASSITEJ). In recognition of his importance as one of its founders, he was named an Honorary Member of ASSITEJ in 1975. He died 6 November 1965.

Ian Cojar (Romania)[126]

Ian Cojar was born in Recas, Romania on 9 January 1931. He studied at the Theatre Institute of Bucarest and the Max Reinhardt Seminar in Vienna. He was a director at the National Theatre, at the Theatre for Children and Young People, the Theatre Mic, and the Children's Theatre at the town of Piatra Neamtz. He served as the Conference Host of the Institute of Theatrical Art and Cinematography in Bucharest.

He is an excellent stage director, and he has made many foreign trips for study, as well as theatrical tours. He has written various articles and collaborated on the publication "Manual of the Art of the Actor" in 1973.

He was a member of the ASSITEJ EXCOM from 1966-1972, served as Treasurer of ASSITEJ from 1968-1972, an Advisor to EXCOM from 1972-1975, was President of the Romanian National Center from 1965-1970, then Vice President from 1970.

He received the Order of Cultural Merit from his government.

Orlin Corey (USA)

Orlin Corey received his BA and MA degrees from Baylor University. He studied at the Central School of Speech in London. He was a Professor of Drama and Director of Theatre at the Marjorie Lyons Playhouse, Centenary College of Louisiana (1960-68). He was Founder and Producer of the Everyman Players as of 1959, which toured internationally.

He was President of of CTAA (1971-73), a member of the Theatre Production Staff of the JFK Center for the performing Arts from 1974-75. He was author of several stage adaptations and of books, lectured around the world, and was script advisor for the Anchorage Press, Inc.

He was an official delegate (USA) at the Sophia EXCOM (1968), and attended the ASSITEJ Congresses since 1968, and was Program Chairman of the IVth Congress of ASSITEJ in Albany, New York, USA. He was President of the US Center for ASSITEJ from 1972-75.

Ljubiša Djokič (Yugoslavia)[127]

Ljubiša Djokič received his degree in Letters from the Faculty of Dramatic Arts as a Director. He was a Professor at the University of Belgrade and Dean of the Faculty of Dramatic Arts. He has directed many plays, a considerable number of them for children. He wrote ten plays for children performed both in Yugoslavia and abroad. He made many trips abroad, and wrote many publications on the theory of creative dramatics for children.

He was a member of the ASSITEJ EXCOM from 1967-1976, and Vice-President (1966-1968) and President (1968-1975) of the Yugoslavian Center for ASSITEJ.

Joyce Doolittle (Canada)[128]

Prof. Joyce Doolittle was born in 1928 in the USA. She first taught child drama in Indiana, Wisconsin, and North Dakota. She was appointed to the faculty of the Department of Drama at the University of Calgary, where she initiated and taught first courses in Developmental Drama, Theatre for Children, Playwriting and Studies in Canadian Drama. She has acted in and directed over 100 plays, often in collaboration with well known Canadian composer-husband Quenten Doolittle.

She is co-author, with Zina Barnieh, of *A Mirror of Our Dreams—Children and the Theatre in Canada*, and was Drama Editor of the Red Deer Press for fifteen years. In 1972, she founded the Pumphouse Theatres, saving an historic, river-edge pumping station from demolition and helping raise over a million dollars to renovate it into two performing arts spaces, one of which bears her name. She returned to acting after retirement, winning an award for best actor for her performance of Mag in *The Beauty Queen of Leenane* at Alberta Theatre Projects (ATP).

Prof. Joyce Doolittle attended her first ASSITEJ meeting in Moscow in 1968 where she was appointed as an official observer. She served as Canada's official representative on the EXCOM from 1969-1978, and as Vice-President of ASSITEJ from 1972-1978. In 1972 she was Chairman of the IVth International Congress of ASSITEJ in Montreal, Canada.

As of this writing, she lives in Calgary, Alberta, Canada with her husband Quentin, a major Canadian contemporary composer, and continues in her acting career.

Nat Eek (USA)

Nat Eek (PhD) was born on 16 October 1927 in Maryville, Missouri. He obtained his degrees from the University of Chicago (PhB), Northwestern University (BS, MA), and Ohio State University (PhD). He taught theatre arts, children's theatre, art administration, and directed plays at the University of Kansas, Michigan State University, and the University of Oklahoma. He was Director of the School of Drama at the University of Oklahoma from 1962-1975, and then Dean of the College of Fine Arts from 1975-1991. He retired from the University of Oklahoma in 1993, and was named Regents Professor Emeritus of Drama and Dean Emeritus of Fine Arts.

He was the USA representative at the Founding Congress of ASSITEJ in Paris, France in 1965, and served on the Executive Committee from 1965-1975 at which time he retired from active participation in the international Association.

He was the USA representative to ASSITEJ, was twice elected as Vice-President from 1968-1972, and was elected President serving from 1972-75. In 1981 he was made an Honorary President of ASSITEJ. From 1988-1994 he was producer and director of the professional Southwest Repertory Theatre in Santa Fe, New Mexico.

During his career he directed over 100 plays, musicals, operas, and did the *mise en scene* of several ballets. He was a Board Member of the American Theatre Association, President of their national Children's Theatre Association, and President of the International Association of Fine Arts Deans. He was named a Fellow of the American Theatre in 1985.

He continues to be active in his professional associations, and began the writing of *The History of ASSITEJ* in 2002. His current address is in Norman, Oklahoma, USA with a second home in Santa Fe, New Mexico.

José Géal (Belgium)[129]

José Géal was born in Hingene, Belgium on 11 March 1931. He was founder and Director of Théâtre de l'Énfance of Belgium in 1954. As an actor, he performed at many Belgian theatres—National, Parc, Poche, Galeries. He toured many foreign countries, and was author of a series of plays for children, performing in Belgium and abroad, as well as film presentations for television. As a puppeteer he founded the Belgium Center of UNIMA, and since 1962 has been a member of their Presidium. He served as Director of Théâtre Toone in Brussels.

He was involved in the creation of ASSITEJ as of 1962. He attended the London Conference in 1964, was on the Preparatory Committee, and his

Center, with him as its representative, were elected to the EXCOM. He was a member of the EXCOM from 1965-75, and served as Treasurer for one two year term from 1966-1968. He was Founder and President of the Belgian National Center.

He received a Gold Medal at the Brussels World's Fair in 1958, and was President of the Chamber of the French Language of Theatre for Children and Young People in Belgium.

He originally was to host the Vth International Congress in 1974, and had planned an excellent program. However, in 1973 he had to cancel his center's invitation for lack of financial support as well as the Flemish language problems. The Congress was moved to Berlin, GDR, in 1975, and at that time he was invited to make a major address. After that time he became less involved in ASSITEJ, and eventually stopped his membership.

Victor Georgiev (Bulgaria)[130]

Victor Georgiev was born in Plovdiv, Bulgaria on 8 May 1919. He finished his studies at the Academy of Theatre Art, and began his acting career at the National Theater of Sophia. He was appointed Director of the Theater of Young People in Sophia in 1966. He was Founder and Host of the International Festivals of Theatres for Children and Youth in Sophia, hosting in 1968, 1972, and 1976. He has performed in many foreign countries.

He was made a Member of the EXCOM of ASSITEJ in 1968, having established the Bulgarian National Center one year before and was serving as its President. He was widely recognized and respected as an excellent actor in the National Theatre of Bulgaria.

After the political change in the late 1980s, his theatre was shut down, and perhaps because of this he died soon after.

His awards include Artist of the People, and the G. Dimitrov Prize Laureate.

Hanswalter Gossmann (FGR)[131]

Hanswalter Gossmann was born in Nuremberg on 28 February 1920. He studied German, History of Arts, Music, and Theory and Psychology. He was a Professor of Speech Training.

He was Founder and Head of the Theater Workshop at Erlangen University from 1946-48. He was co-Founder of the Theater der Jugend and the Städtischen Bühnen Nürmberg-Fürth in 1948, and he was Head of this Theatre from 1948 to 1975. His theater made many foreign tours, and he organized six

International Theatre Festivals for Young People in Nuremberg from 1960 to 1973.

He was a play director and author of many plays for children, gave lectures and wrote articles on children's theatre.

He served on the Preparatory Committee (1964-1965), attended the Constitutional Conference in Paris in 1965, was elected to the EXCOM of ASSITEJ from 1965-1975, and attended all the Congresses since 1966 as the Head of the West German National Center. He was co-Founder of that center with Volker Laturell in 1966 and served as its President from 1966 to 1974. He hosted the EXCOM of ASSITEJ in Nuremberg in 1967. He was bearer of the Schiller Prize of the City of Nuremberg.

He died in the 1990s.

Caryl Jenner (Great Britain)

Caryl Jenner was born in London on 19 May 1917 and died on 22 January 1973.

She was educated at Norland Place School and St. Paul's Girls School, studied at Central School of Speech Training and Dramatic Art in London, and received University Diplomas in Dramatic Art. She began her career as an actress in 1935. She formed the Mobile Theatre Ltd. in 1951 performing plays for young people on tour, the English Theatre for Children (1960), and directed plays for children in various London theatres.

In 1962 she launched the Unicorn Theatre Club for Young People, which became Caryl Jenner Productions Ltd. and the Unicorn Theatre for Young People as of 1964. She was Chairman of the Young People's Theatre Executive of the Council of Regional Theatres, and representative of the Council of Regional Theatres (CORT) in 1979. She was a member of the Young People's Theatre Panel of the Arts Council of Great Britain (1967-69).

She represented Great Britain at the ASSITEJ EXCOM from 1968-1972, attending many meetings and Congresses.

Inga Juul[132]

Mrs. Inga Juul was born in Odense, Denmark on 25 October 1928. She studied at the University of Copenhagen, and did specialized study in children's theatre in Great Britain and Scotland, and all over Europe. She came to Dansk Skolescene in 1963, and created a division that produced regular professional performances for children. From 1968 on performances were given for various age groups of young people in "Inga Juul's Børnetheater".

She gave lectures, wrote articles, and made translations of plays for children and youth. She headed workshops and seminars for teachers and students. With two others she founded the Danish Drama Teachers' Society in 1968. She also founded and built a private library with archives covering children's and youth theatres from all over the world, open to interested specialists.

She attended the Constitutional Conference in 1965, the Congresses since 1966, and many of the EXCOM meetings. She was appointed an Advisor to the EXCOM from 1968 to 1972. She died in the 1990s.

Galina Kolosova (Russia)[133]

Mrs. Galina Kolosova was born on 11 May 1940 in Moscow. She graduated in 1965 from Moscow State University majoring in the Department of Philology specializing in Romantic and Germanic Languages and Literature. She worked for the Soviet Women's Committee (International Department) as of 1969 at the Pan-Russian Theatrical Society. She functioned as Secretary and Translator for the Soviet Center of ASSITEJ from 1969, and attended many sessions of the EXCOM and Congresses from 1970 on.

In 1975 she was invited to join the Theatre Association of Russia (STD) where she was designated Secretary of the Soviet ASSITEJ Center (later ASSITEJ/Russia), whose main task was the development of international relations for 60 Russian professional repertory companies for young spectators.

While in that position she organized and coordinated the committee that was responsible for the VIIIth (Moscow) and XIIth (Rostov-on-Don) World Congresses of ASSITEJ and their corresponding Festivals. She remained in that position until 1996.

Since 1980 she has been a translator of English, American, Canadian, and French plays into Russian, and these translations have been performed in Moscow, Rostov-on-Don, Oryol, Nizhny Novgorod, and many other cities in Russia and CIS.

She initiated and coordinated the first Russian International Theatre Festivals for children and young people (MINIFEST) in Rostov-on-Don (1989, 1991, 1993, 1995, and 1996). With her Netherlands counterparts, she organized in Russia the first International Seminar for Theatre Managers which dealt with problems of marketing and management (1990, 1991, and 1992).

She created a special volume of the leading theatre magazine based in Moscow entitled *Theatre Life (Teatralnaya Zhizn)* dedicated to problems of survival of theatres for young spectators in new Russian and to ASSITEJ activities (published July 1996).

From 1996 to 2000, she was a member of the Advisor's Council of *Theatre Life* Magazine, a member of the "George Soros" Foundation (Open Society Institute) as an expert on cultural programs, a member of the editorial Board of the new Moscow Quarterly *Theatre for Children and Young People* (affiliated with *Contemporary Playwriting* Magazine), and Advisor to the EXCOM of ASSITEJ.

Since 2000 she has been Projects Coordinator with English-speaking countries for the Organizing Committee of the Moscow Chekhov International Theatre Festival, a member of the Theatre Association of Russian, and a member of the EXCOM of ASSITEJ/Russia.

Zvjezdana Ladika (Croatia)[134]

Mme. Zvjezdana Ladika was born in Karlovac, Croatia 1921, but moved to Varazdin in her early childhood where she received her secondary-school education. At the University of Zagreb, she completed the studies of the literatures of the nations—the former Yugoslavia, French language and literature, and Russian language and literature.

After graduation, she spent a short time teaching at a secondary school, but resigned in order to study directing at the Film Studio, which she completed in 1950. In addition, she graduated in staging from the Academy of Dramatic Arts in Zagreb.

After her second graduation, she found employment at the Zagreb Theatre for Young People as both a director and theatrical educator. It was there that she staged Shakespeare's *Romeo and Juliet* as her graduation piece. Over the years, she staged more than a hundred performances for and with children and young people at the same theatre.

In the year 1956 she went on a study tour to Prague and in 1960 to France where theatre for children developed as creative dramatics for children and young people.

With her plays she took part in numerous theatre festivals throughout Europe. Her international theatre exchange also included an exchange with the professional theatre for children and young people in Brno (Prague, Bratislava, Brno, 1956).

Mme. Ladika published a large number of writings on children's dramatic creativity—in her own book *The Child and the Dramatic Art*, and as a co-author of the books *Theatrical Plays; The Child and Creativity;* and *I'm Bored, I Don't Know What to Do*. She published her writings in professional periodicals and publications in Croatia and abroad.

She was a long-standing member of the ASSITEJ Executive Committee, where she left an indelible imprint through her activity and influenced the development of the world's theatre for children and young people. As a result she was named an Honorary Member of ASSITEJ in 1996. She was one of the founders of the *Mala Scena* Theatre in 1989, where she was active as a director, writer, and head of its drama studio.

Mme. Ladika received numerous rewards for her artistic work, the most important of them being *Young Generation* in 1972 for direction of the play *Tomcat Genghis Khan and Miki Trasi*; an award from the Dramatic Artists' Society for direction in 1984; *Dubravko Dujsin* Award in 1988 for her long productive theatrical work with children and young people at the Zagreb Theatre for Young People; and the *Vladimir Nazor* Life Achievement Award.

She died on 17 August 2004 at the age of 82.

Ion Lucian (Romania)[135]

Ion Lucian was born on 22 April 1924 in Bucharest, Romania. He received his Baccalaureate Degree in the Humanities from the Royale Academy of Arts.

He is a noted actor, stage director, and playwright. He was a Professor at the Royale Academy of Arts and Hyperion University in Bucharest. He is so well known as a major performer that strangers stop him on the street to praise and congratulate him.

He was Founder and Manager of the Ion Creanga Theater in 1964. Since 1965 he has been President of the Romanian Center for ASSITEJ, and continues to this day. He served ASSITEJ International as its Treasurer for fifteen years from 1972 to 1987. He was on the ASSITEJ Executive Committee from 1966 to 1990.

Since 1990 he has been the Manager of the Excelsior Theater in Bucharest, and is currently the Supervisor on the construction of a new 11-story building which will house the Excelsior Theater. He continues to perform with the National and Comedy Theaters, and has directed plays in Romania, Italy, Belgium, Canada, Japan, France, and Israel.

Plays for which he is noted include: *The Disobedient Little Cock, Free Voice, The Musketeers of Her Majesty, Donkey, Cinderella*, and *Tales With Masks* (for young people), and *Fight Against TA-GA-TA, Humorous Variations*, and *Humorous Stars* (for adults). He performed in his play *Tales With Masks* at the IVth International Congress in Canada/USA to universal acclaim. He has also written translations of the plays of Moliere, Goldoni, Feydeau, and Labiche among others.

He has received many distinctions: the Title of Honored Artist of

Romania, a Member of Honor of the Romanian National Theater, the Order of Cultural Merit, an Officer of the French Legion of Honor, and a Chevalier of the Cultural Order. He has also received the Cultural Merit Medal-First Class for his artistic and cultural achievements.

Rose-Marie Moudoués (France)[136]

Mme. Rose-Marie Moudoués was born in Castejaloux, France on 28 November 1922. She did superior work in Letters, History, and History of Art at the University of Toulouse. She became a teaching professor in the Paris region as of 1945. She first worked with Léon Chancerel (1945-1965) and then with Louis Jouvet (1945-1951) at the resumption of the Society of the History of Theatre which had been interrupted during WWII. From 1948 on at this same time she served as *Engineer to the C.N.S.R. for Theatrical Sciences.*

In 1948 she left this association, and for several years helped integrate the National Center of Scientific Research and the Society of the History of Theatre. She became Director of the Documentation Center of the Library of the Society of the History of Theatre and of the Association of Theatre for Children and Young People (ATEJ), which she had helped create as an organization.

She also participated in the creation of the *Review d'Histoire du Théâtre* (she is still an editor today), and was an author and translator of programs on the theatre for the radio titled *Prestige du Théâtre.* She has published numerous articles in both French and foreign publications. She was the author of the Biography of Theatrical Arts in France, and Editor-in-Chief of the *History of Theatre Review,* and *Theatre—Children and Youth.* She has given many lectures in France and abroad.

She established and edited an annual international bibliography of shows, and was actively involved in the founding of the International Federation of Theatrical Research (FIRT) of which she became co-secretary for many years. She was also a founding member and vice-president for the Institute for Theatrical Research in Venice, Italy.

Attentive to the development of the contemporary theatre, under the Ministry of Culture she was a member of the Commission to assist local theatrical companies with the creation of theatres, and she was and is to this day an expert on the local administration of cultural affairs (DRAC). As a major reader of contemporary dramatic authors, under the Ministry of Culture from 1980 to 2000 she headed the Commission to help with the creation of dramatic works and specifically to promote the production of unpublished works.

As a collaborator with Léon Chancerel, founder in France of the first artistic theatre for children, Moudoués assisted him in his activities favoring young people's companies, and participated in the founding of the French Association of Theatre for Children and Young People (ATEJ), as well as the International Association of Theatre for Children and Young People (ASSITEJ). The first meeting she attended took place at ATEJ in Paris in 1963 which brought together representatives from Great Britain, Italy, Netherlands, Belgium, and Rumania. Later she attended the London Conference in 1964, the Preparatory Conference in Venice in 1964, and was Secretary of the Preparatory Committee in 1964-1965. As a result of these meetings, Moudoués drew up the Constitution of ASSITEJ (based on that of ATEJ) for discussion, amendment, and adoption by the Constitutional Congress in Paris organized by ATEJ in 1965. She presided at the Constitutional Congress in Paris in 1965, and was a member of the EXCOM from 1965 to 1990. In 1966 she established the French National Center for ASSITEJ.

At the 1965 Paris Conference Moudoués was elected Secretary-General, an election which was confirmed at the Ist International Congress in Prague, Czechoslovakia in 1966. She held this position for 25 years up to the Xth International Congress in Stockholm, Sweden in 1990. Leaving this position with grace, she put at the disposal of ASSITEJ the technical assistance of ATEJ and the publication of the Review of ATEJ *Théatre, Enfance, Jeaunese.*

She was named a Member of Honor of ASSITEJ at the General Assembly in Seoul, Korea on 20 July 2002. She continues to be active in theatre research and writing.

Orna Porat (Israel)[137]

Mrs. Orna Porat was born in Cologne, Germany on 6 June 1924.

She attended the Drama School "Städische Bühnen der Stadt Köln" from 1940 to 1942, had various acting engagements in Schleswig, Koblenz, Eutin, and Cologne, and immigrated to Palestine in 1947. She was a permanent member of the Cameri Theatre in Tel-Aviv since 1948. She performed many major roles, and appeared in Zürich, Paris, London, and Montreal. She was the Founder and Director, with the Cameri Theatre, of the National Theatre for Children and Youth from 1970 on. In 1973 she was appointed Lecturer to the Faculty of Drama at Tel-Aviv University.

She has been considered the "grande dame" of theatre in Israel until today. In addition to her many successes on the stage, she was also noted as one of the best actresses in Israeli cinema.

She attended the Constitutional Conference in Paris in 1965. She was a Member of the EXCOM of ASSITEJ from 1970 to 1975. She participated in several Congresses and EXCOM Meetings. She was made an Honorary Member in ASSITEJ in 2002.

Ilse Rodenberg (Germany)[138]

Dr. Ilse Rodenberg was born in Düsseldorf on 3 November 1906, and died at the age of 99 on 6 January 2006 in Berlin.

She was born the illegitimate child of a serving girl in Düsseldorf. Self-supporting at an early age, she moved to Hamburg where she began her career as an actress at the left-wing Kollektiv junger Schauspieler from 1930 to 1933. Then from 1935 to 1945 she was banned from performing, but she established contacts with comrades working illegally and supported them with information from her job as switchboard operator in a hotel. From 1945 to 1947 she was Manager and actress at Kabarett "Laternenanzünder" in Hamburg. From 1949 to 1950 she was the head of the theatre in Neustrelitz, and from 1950 to 1957 of the theatre in Potsdam.

In 1959 Rodenberg became the head of "Theater der Freundschaft" (today Theater an der Parkaue) in Berlin, and through her marriage to Hans Rodenberg rose in the political establishment of the GDR. This theatre, which she now headed, had been founded by her husband in 1950.

In opposition to the provincial nature of the GDR elite, she was open to the world, and in children's and youth theatre she found a career that she loved. During her 14 years as Intendant she made the theatre an indispensable venue for children's and young people's culture due to her unprecedented competence and remarkable personality. She was Founder and Director of the Bureau for International Questions on Theater for Children and Young People in the GDR in 1973. She wrote many publications, made speeches, and traveled to countries in Europe, Asia, and America. In West Germany which she visited often she was a member of a Fraternal Party of the National Democratic Party of Germany, an association she found useful in the GDR.

She understood power but made it her own, coping emotionlessly and pragmatically with all problems, such as presenting a poor play by a politically-connected author in order to raise actors salaries to equal those of the great Berlin theatres at the time. Outwardly she showed complete trust of her cohorts, but she never allowed anyone to question her control. She cooperated with the major GDR theatres, putting her theatre on an equal level.

She was a Member of the Preparatory Committee in 1964-65, a member of the EXCOM of ASSITEJ from 1965 on, and served three terms as President from 1978 to 1987.

As Vice-President and later as President of ASSITEJ she contributed comprehensively to the development of children's and young people's theatre on a world scale. In 1973 on her retirement the GDR Center for ASSITEJ was established as an independent office, and she was placed in charge. Refusing a salary and relying on her pension, she devoted herself full-time to the Center and later to her office as ASSITEJ President. She established the bi-annual International Directors Seminar as well as the Hallenser Workshop Meeting and Playwright's Competition. She constantly developed creative exchanges among directors, playwrights, and educational theatre artists.

In 1987 she retired as President of ASSITEJ after three terms. Then in December of 1989 after the unification of Germany, she participated in the establishment of the Children and Youth Theater Center of Germany in Frankfort, making her theatrical legacy safe for future generations.

She maintained an active interest in world affairs and children's theatre, reading three papers a day, until her death in 2006.

Natalia Ilyinichna Sats (USSR)[139]

Natalia Sats was born on 27 August 1903. Ilya Sats, her father, was a famous composer, and as a young girl she remembered hearing music being played in the room next to her bedroom. She described the music as "...sometimes impetuous, sometimes shimmering like water and magically glimmering as if a fairy had arrived." It was the music composed by her father to *The Blue Bird* of Maurice Maeterlinck, the famous production by the Moscow Art Theater. Her great love of music for children dates from these early childhood experiences.

By the time she was 15 in 1918, she was running the Mossovet Theatre, the first theatre for children that was born of her initiative. People would refer to her as "the Mother of all the theatres for children in the world." The Moscow Theatre for Children, the Moscow Central Theatre for Children, and the Moscow Musical Theatre for Children, named and dedicated to her, were all a result of her efforts, including the first Theatre for Young Spectators in Kazakhstan. In the early 1920s she had become known as an outstanding theatre director, and her productions of *A Little Negro and a Monkey, About Dzyuba, The Golden Key,* and *Seryozha Streitsov* were highly acclaimed by both the press and the public.

On the opera stages of the world she collaborated with conductor Otto Klemperer in productions of Verdi"s *Falstaff* at the Crollopera in Berlin, Germany in 1931, and Mozart's *The Marriage of Figaro* at the Teatro Colon in Buenos Aires, Brazil that same year.

Tragically she fell afoul of the governmental authorities, and she was exiled to Siberia soon after. But even in exile she created a theatre in the gulag in which she was imprisoned. In the early 1960s she was rehabilitated under Premier Nikita Khrushchev, and began a new life in Moscow. She immediately created a musical theatre for children that had no venue at first, but by 1983 she had succeeded in building the State Musical Theatre for Children in Moscow, which was later named in her honor. After her reappearance, she immediately became involved in ASSITEJ, and during the 1980s she served as head of the USSR National Center and was elected to the Executive Committee of ASSITEJ. During her long career she was given many awards—*People's Artist of the USSR, Hero of the Socialist Labor,* and a winner of the *Lenin and State Prizes of the USSR.*

She died at the age of 100 on the 18th of December 1993.

Konstantin Shakh-Azizov (USSR)[140]

Konstantin Shakh-Azizov (1903-1977) merited artist of Georgia and Russia, dedicated himself to theatre from his early years. He played in amateur and young people productions in Tiflis (now Tbilisi) in the 1920s. His life then developed in such a way that theatre became his true vocation for his entire life.

In 1927 at the age of 24 he started his first theatre for children in Transcaucasia. It was named the Russian Theatre for Young Spectators. He was Chairman of their Board, and played many roles since he was a striking actor with a great flair for comedy.

A year later following this example, the Georgian Theatre for Young Spectators was opened, an indication that the "children's theatre movement" had come to Tiflis. Young people were invited to experience this theatrical art form, and this became the starting point of a creative life for many major artists, e.g. Georgy Tovstonogov, later one of the greatest Russian stage directors.

In 1933-1945 Shakh-Azizov was Managing and Artistic Director of the Griboedov Russian Drama Company in Tbilisi, a company of the highest artistic standards with a rich repertory. After WWII he moved to Moscow, and returned to theatre for children. He was appointed the Managing Director of the Moscow Central Children's Theatre, and remained in this position for 29 years (1945-1974). From time to time he also served as Artistic Director of the Company.

During the 1950s the Moscow Central Children's Theatre became one of the leading companies in the USSR. Maria Knebel, Stanislavski's pupil and teacher of the Moscow Art Theatre method of acting, Oleg Yefremov and Anatily Efros, both future leaders of the Russian stage started their artistic life at this theatre. Also, Russian playwright Victor Rozov (famous author of the screenplay *The Cranes Are Flying*) made his artistic debut on this stage.

The Moscow Central Children's Theatre with its high quality, with its wide repertory of both contemporary and classic plays was easily accessible to its young spectators. The youngest were charmed by the beautiful and poetic tales, and by the theatrical style. The company spoke a language comprehensible to teenagers on topical and difficult themes related to their lives. This experience of running a theatre for children which never sacrificed artistic quality while becoming a colleague of youth proved useful during the third part of Shakh-Azizov's career which started in the mid 1960s.

In 1963 a group of children's theatres from the USSR, Bulgaria, the German Democratic Republic, and Czechoslovakia started preliminary work on the creation of the International Association of Theatre for Children and Young People. In the West other countries also worked in this same direction, and they all got together at the London Conference in 1964 to form ASSITEJ. This creation was ratified at the Constitutional Conference in Paris in 1965. The aim of ASSITEJ was to develop theatre art for children, to unite those who were working for that aim, and to exchange experience, to organize tours and festivals.

From the beginning of ASSITEJ's existence, Shakh-Azizov was elected Vice-President twice (in 1966 and 1972). He was elected President in 1968 and 1970, a total of two terms. In 1965-1974 he was head of the Soviet ASSITEJ Center. In 1972 at the IVth International Congress held in Canada and the USA he was awarded the title Honorary President of ASSITEJ.

Ann M. Shaw (USA)

Dr. Ann M. Shaw (EdD) was born on 26 June 1930 in Wilsonville, Nebraska, USA. She received degrees from Northwestern University (BA, MA), and Columbia University (EdD). Her dissertation was considered seminal in creative drama.

Beginning in 1952 she taught creative dramatics in the Evanston, Illinois public schools, and then continued her academic career at Western Michigan University, Hunter College and Teachers College, Columbia University. She retired in 1990 having taught for 22 years at Queens College, City University of New York.

Author of many publications on children's theatre, theatre and the handicapped, her works have been translated into many languages. For the American Theatre Association (ATA) she served on their Board of Directors, key committees, organized two national conferences, and founded their handicapped program (ATD).

Early professional theatre activities included Head, Wardrobe Department of the Central City Opera (Colorado); Box Office Manager, D'Oyly Carte Opera Co. (Colorado); costume execution of new productions, New York City Opera; and study at the Berghoff Studio.

Shaw's honors include a CTAA Special Citation, Kennedy Center's Outstanding Educator Award, and Northwestern University's Award of Merit, a

Medallion from the Children's Theatre Foundation, and ASSITEJ/USA named the Ann M. Shaw Fellowship Awards in her honor.

She attended her first meeting of ASSITEJ at the IVth International Congress in Canada and the USA where she programmed the Creative Drama sessions. She was the USA representative to the ASSITEJ Executive Committee from 1978-1987. In 1981 she created the new US Center for ASSITEJ, known as ASSITEJ/USA and was its President until 1987. She initiated Pacific Rim TYA exchange (1984) and Mexico-USA Exchange (1985). She directed the World Theatre Festival for Young Audiences and Symposium at the New Orleans World's Fair (1984).

She was twice elected ASSITEJ International Vice President, 1981-84 and 1984-87 and served as a USA voting delegate at eight Congresses from Madrid in 1978 through Trömso in 1999. In 2002 at the XIVth World Congress in Seoul, Korea she was made an Honorary Member of ASSITEJ. She has attended every international Congress from 1972 to 2005, with the exception of the Vth Congress in Berlin, GDR in 1975.

She currently lives in Santa Fe, New Mexico, USA, and is active in St. Bede's Episcopal Church there.

Hans Snoek (Netherlands)[141]

Dame Hans Snoek was born in Geertruidenberg, Netherlands, and was married to Erik de Vries, a noted writer and expert in television.

Snoek was founder, dancer, choreographer, artistic leader of the Scapino Ballet Amsterdam (with the Scapino School for children and amateurs) from 1945 to 1970. Scapino was the only dance theatre for children in Europe, and it was large with 37 dancers and a total of 60 members in the company. She founded "Jeugdtheater Amsterdam" in 1971, and was founder and member of the board for the Individual Secondary and Art Education Schools of Amsterdam. She served as Chair of the Dutch Dancers Union from 1948 to 1952, and was a Board Member of the Netherlands Councils and Committees on the Arts, as well as ITI and the Netherlands Dance Council.

She created many ballets for children, was the author of *Ballet in Dance*, gave regular lectures on dance, and traveled abroad extensively.

She attended the London Conference in 1964 and was appointed a member of the Preparatory Committee from 1964 to 1965, served as a member of the EXCOM from 1965 to 1975, attended all the Congresses and EXCOM Meetings, and was founder and Chair of the Netherlands National Center from 1967 to 1975.

Her government named her an Officer of the Order of Orange – Nassau.

The Netherlands theatre for children and youth honor her annually by awarding a prize given in her name.

An elegant, graceful woman, she was an excellent colleague, well organized and considerate, and always championed liberal causes, taking a new and welcoming view of innovation in the arts.

She died in the 1990s.

Sara Spencer (USA)[142]

Miss Sara Spencer was born and bred in Kentucky, USA. Despite having polio in her infancy, she acknowledged no insuperable obstacles. She nurtured artists and theatre all her life.

She received her BA degree from Vassar in 1930 where she studied with Hallie Flanagan. She founded the Children's Theatre of Charleston, West Virginia in 1932. Then to provide plays for theatre for children she founded the Children's Theatre Press in 1935, which was located in Anchorage, Kentucky since 1945, and has published over 100 plays. It changed its name to The Anchorage Press, Inc. in 1968.

She was a devoted theatre patron, founding and sustaining the Children's Theatre of Anchorage, Kentucky, Stage One of Louisville, Kentucky, and the world renowned Actor's Theatre of Louisville.

Her life was devoted to quality theatre which won audiences to life-long theatre-going. As a publisher she constantly looked for new plays, for translations of foreign plays, and wrote several dramatizations herself. She was a Member of the College of Fellows of the American Theatre Association, and for two years the Director of the Children's Theatre Conference. She was Chair of the Board of Trustees of the Children's Theatre Foundation of America, Inc. and traveled abroad extensively.

She received many awards: a Famous Woman Designation from the Kentucky Chamber of Commerce; the Jennie Heiden Award for theatrical excellence from the Children's Theatre Association of the USA; and the Distinguished Service Award from the Southeastern Theatre Conference.

She was a tireless Advocate of the founding of ASSITEJ. She served ASSITEJ as a member of the Preparatory Committee from 1964 to 1965, attending the Founding Conference in Paris in 1965 as a delegate, was a member of the ASSITEJ EXCOM from 1965-67, and served as Advisor to the EXCOM from 1972-1975. She was a Founding member of the US Center for ASSITEJ in 1965 and served on its first Board. She attended several ASSITEJ Congresses and EXCOM meetings as a US delegate.

She died on 9 February 1977, the week after she sold The Anchorage

Press, consigning its proceeds to the Children's Theatre Foundation of America, Inc.

Maria Nieves Sunyer y Roig (Spain)[143]

Sra. Maria Sunyer was born in Barcelona on 31 October 1925.

After 1942 she centered her activities in the area of theatre for children and youth. In 1960 in Madrid she organized the first professional theatre troupe called "Los Titeres" which performed only for children and young people, and has played at five national meetings of Spanish theatres. Los Titeres appeared in a special performance at the Constitutional Conference in 1965 in Paris and again at the VIth Congress of ASSITEJ in 1978 in Madrid. She has written extensively, organized numerous conferences, and travels widely abroad.

She first attended the Constitutional Conference in Paris in 1965, and then all the Congresses since then to 1975. Since 1968 she has edited and distributed free to all Spanish-speaking centers a Newsletter in Spanish that features ASSITEJ news and reviews. She was a member of the EXCOM from 1970 on, was elected Vice-President in 1975, and hosted an EXCOM meeting in Madrid in 1974 and the VIth International Congress in Madrid in 1978. She also served as the President of the Spanish National Center.

She received the Honorary Orders—Isabel the Catholic, Cisneros, and Mérite Naval.

Gerald Tyler (Great Britain)[144]

In 1930, Thomas Edward Tyler met Emily Briggs at Leeds Art Theatre in a production of Oscar Wilde's *A Woman of No Importance*, with Gerald in the juvenile lead as Gerald Arbuthnot. Two consequences followed. 'Thomas Edward' became known as 'Gerald' thereafter and three years later in 1933, he and Emily were married. For the next 40 years, they devoted themselves to all aspects of theatre—as actors, directors, and teachers—with Children's Theatre at the centre.

Tyler was instrumental in forming the Leeds Children's Theatre in 1936 and produced plays for that group, for the Brighouse Amateurs (the Leeds Branch of the National Union of Teachers), as well as many other local groups.

During WWII Tyler served in the Royal Artillery on the Home Front, and then for three years in India and Burma. Even there, he organized drama and concert parties for his troops.

He returned to England in 1946 to resume his teaching, and began organizing the Brighouse Children's Theatre with his wife Emily, both of them directing plays. Brighouse quickly earned a reputation for producing excellent children's theatre, utilizing regular children and teenagers as their company, achieving with zest and enthusiasm high standards of dramatic excellence.

In 1948, he was appointed County Drama Adviser to the West Riding Education Committee and served in that capacity until his retirement in 1973. During that period, he promoted youth drama groups and youth theatre festivals throughout the County. His International Theatre Month Festivals did much to widen understanding of other countrys' cultural traditions. Many professional actors, Patrick Stewart and Brian Blessed among them, owe their early introduction to theatre to his summer theatre schools for young people.

Tyler helped found the British Children's Theatre Association (BCTA), and served as its Secretary for many years. He was closely involved in the early meetings abroad that culminated in the creation of ASSITEJ. In 1965 at the Paris, France Constitutional Conference, he was elected Provisional President. In 1966 at the Prague, Czechoslovakia Congress he was elected President. He served two terms, and in 1966 he was elected Honorary President along with Léon Chancerel as the two significant founding fathers of the Association.

Tyler felt that his greatest achievement was helping found ASSITEJ, and as an officer of the Association, he traveled extensively to Europe, the Eastern Block, and the USA to promote international relations and coordinate its work. His many efforts were the glue that held the Association together. In all his endeavors, he was supported by Emily, always there to give advice and encouragement.

Tyler always came across as a true "gentleman", constantly willing to help and encourage others in the service of children's theatre. As an officer of ASSITEJ, he will be remembered particularly for his tact and diplomatic handing of moments of conflict and his innate sense of fair play in international affairs. His receiving of the first title of Honorary President of ASSITEJ in itself is testimony to the high regard in which he was held. He died on 2 July 1984.

APPENDIX C
List of World Congresses of ASSITEJ
(1965-1975)

4-9 June 1965	The Constitutional Conference of ASSITEJ / Paris, France
26-30 May 1966	Ist International Congress of ASSITEJ / Prague, Czechoslovakia
27-31 May 1968	IInd International Congress of ASSITEJ / The Hague, Netherlands
19-24 October 1970	IIIrd International Congress of ASSITEJ / Venice, Italy
14-25 June 1972	IVth International Congress of ASSITEJ / Montreal, Ontario, Canada and Albany, New York, U.S.A.
19-26 April 1975	Vth International Congress of ASSITEJ / Berlin, GDR

APPENDIX D
List of Executive Committee Meetings of ASSITEJ
(1965-1975)

Executive Committee Meeting of ASSITEJ / Berlin, GDR / 19-26 February 1966

Executive Committee Meeting of ASSITEJ / Nuremberg, FGR / 6-11 March 1967

Executive Committee Meeting of ASSITEJ / Moscow, USSR / 1-10 March 1968

Executive Committee Meeting of ASSITEJ / Sophia, Bulgaria / 21-28 October 1968

Executive Committee Meeting of ASSITEJ / Šibenik, Yugoslavia / 25 June-3 July 1969

Executive Committee Meeting of ASSITEJ / Bucharest, Romania / 7-10 June 1970

Bureau Meeting of ASSITEJ / Paris, France / 3 May 1971

Executive Committee Meeting of ASSITEJ
Bratislava, Czechoslovakia / 17-18 October 1971
Prague, Czechoslovakia / 20-22 October 1971

Executive Committee Meeting of ASSITEJ
Berlin and Leipzig, GDR / 4-11 March 1972
Dresden, GDR / 10 March 1972

Bureau Meeting of ASSITEJ / Bordeaux, France / 16-21 October 1972

Executive Committee Meeting of ASSITEJ / London, England / 11-17 June 1973

Executive Committee Meeting of ASSITEJ / Madrid, Spain / 16-22 April 1974

Bureau Meeting of ASSITEJ / Paris, France / 11 November 1974

Executive Committee Meeting of ASSITEJ / Zagreb and Karlovac, Yugoslavia / 3-9 February 1975

The First Constitution (1965)

Approved at the Constitutional Conference in Paris, France on 9 June 1965.

CONSTITUTION OF ASSITEJ

INTERNATIONAL ASSOCIATION OF THEATRE FOR CHILDREN
and YOUNG PEOPLE

CHAPTER I

CREATION

Since theatrical art is a universal expression of mankind, and possesses the influence and power to link large groups of the world's peoples in the service of peace, and considering the role theatre can play in the education of younger generations an autonomous international organization has been formed which bears the name of the International Association of Theatre for Children and Young People.

ARTICLE I

1. This Association proposes to unite theatres, organizations, and individuals of the world, dedicated to theatre for children and young people.

2. This Association is free from political, religious, or racial commitment of any kind.

3. Official languages in constitutional meetings will be English, French, and Russian. On the occasion of international conferences, the languages of the inviting country will be added.

ARTICLE II–AIMS

This Association is created to facilitate the development of theatre for children and young people, on the highest artistic level. Its aims are:

1. To promote contacts and interchange of experience between all countries, encouraging theatre artists to become mutually acquainted so as to estimate their own work, and in this spirit influence their own public.

2. To promote study tours for individuals and groups, as well as engagements for producing companies traveling abroad.

3. To introduce and support, at its discretion, proposals made to competent national authorities, for the furtherance of its work.

4. To promote the formation, in countries where there is none, of national associations uniting all organizations and persons interesting themselves in theatre for children and young people.

ARTICLE III–MEANS

The means of achieving these aims are:

1. Organizations of international congresses, conferences, festivals, study courses, exhibitions and other activities, and participation in such projects.

2. Assistance in the publication and distribution of books, magazines, legitimate stage plays, musical plays, and other literary works, dramatic or musical, to do with theatre for children and youth.

3. Promotion of theatre for children and young people through the press, films, radio, recording, television, and other means.

4. Encouragement of translation and exchange of plays, texts, or other literature pertaining to theatre for children and young people.

5. Foundation of institutions for research and study purpose—such as libraries, museums, collections of records, etc.—on the subject of theatre for children and young people.

6. Participation in the studies of other international organizations with related interests.

7. Acquisition of the necessary property and equipment.

CHAPTER II

ARTICLE IV—MEMBERS

Members of this Association are National Centers of Theatre for Children and Young People. The following categories of membership for National Centers are acceptable to the International Association:

1. Professional companies of adult actors playing for children and young people.

2. Adult non-professional companies, community theatre companies, college and university theatre companies playing for children and young people.

3. Institutions, organizations or individuals actively engaged in the work of theatre for children and young people.

4. Supporting organizations—institutions, associations, or persons interested in theatre for children and young people.

To qualify for Full Membership in the Association a national Center must have at least one member as defined in Category 1 or 2.

Other National Centers are Corresponding Members.

ARTICLE V—RIGHTS AND OBLIGATIONS

1. **Full Members** have the right to participate in activities mentioned in Article III, to make proposals in constitutional meetings, to allow their representatives to elect, to be elected, and to vote according to the rules declared in Article IX.

2. **Corresponding Members** have the right to participate in the activities mentioned in Article III, and have a consultative voice in the General Assembly, but have no right to vote.

3. **All Members** have the obligation to work to achieve the aims defined by the Association, to maintain its statutes, to act upon the decisions taken by the Association, and to pay their membership fees.

ARTICLE VI—APPLICATION, RESIGNATION, EXPULSION

1. Written applications for membership shall be addressed to the Secretary-General. In the case of a denial by the Executive Committee, the candidate may appeal to the next General Assembly.

2. Any member who wishes to resign should inform the Secretary-General in

writing for it to take effect from 1ˢᵗ January in the following year.

      3. The Executive Committee may decide, by a majority of two-thirds, on the rejection or expulsion of any member whose work conflicts with the fundamental aims of this Association, or who has failed several times in one of the obligations mentioned in Article V.

      4. Any rejected or expelled member may appeal to the General Assembly.

CHAPTER III

ARTICLE VII–FINANCE

      1. This Association is financed from the subscriptions of members, as well as from bequests, gifts, and subsidies accepted by the General Assembly.

      2. The fiscal year of this Association runs from 1ˢᵗ January to 31ˢᵗ December.

      3. Membership fees, which are determined by the General Assembly, are due to 1ˢᵗ January of each year, and are payable to the Treasurer.

CHAPTER IV

ARTICLE VIII–STRUCTURE

      The governing body of this Association consists of:

The General Assembly
The Executive Committee
The Officers

ARTICLE IX – FUNCTIONS OF THE GENERAL ASSEMBLY

      1. The General Assembly consists of delegates of all National Centers.

      2. Each national delegation has three (3) votes:

Two (2) votes for its professional companies
One (1) vote for its non-professional companies

      3. Voting by proxy is permitted.

      4. The General Assembly shall meet at least once every two years, and will be called at least six months in advance by the Secretary-General upon instruction of the Chairman. Normally it will decide the location where the next General Assembly shall meet—but if it should be unable to take a decision on this matter, or if a change of location should prove necessary, this decision may be left to the Executive Committee.

      5. An extraordinary meeting of the General Assembly will be called by the Secretary-General three (3) months in advance on the request of two-thirds of the members or at the discretion of the officers of the Executive Committee in the case of an emergency.

      6. The General Assembly has final control over the Constitution, and decides on any changes or additions necessary. Any member wishing to amend the Constitution must give notice in writing to the Secretary-General at least three (3) months before the date of the General Assembly. Any decision taken upon a proposal to amend the Constitution shall require a majority of two-thirds of the members of the Association.

      7. The General Assembly establishes the broad outlines of the Association's policy.

      8. The General Assembly receives for approval the report of the activities and the financial report which are submitted by the Executive Committee.

9. The Chairman of this Association is by right Chairman of the General Assembly. In the event of his absence, he will be replaced by a Vice-Chairman, or in the absence of all the Vice-Chairmen, by a member of the Executive Committee elected for this purpose by the General Assembly.

10. All decisions unless otherwise stated are taken by simple majority vote. In the case of a tie the Chairman will cast the deciding vote.

11. The General Assembly determines the membership fees and other charges to be levied on the members of the Association.

12. A meeting of the General Assembly can only be held if the delegates of half the National Centers express in writing to the Secretary-General their determination to be present and to participate, either in person or by proxy. This decision must be sent to the Secretary-General three (3) months in advance of the meeting. The General Assembly can only take decisions if half the members participate.

13. The General Assembly shall *elect* the Executive Committee and out of their members the Chairman and three Vice-Chairmen. Nominations must be submitted to the Secretary-General three (3) months before the date of the meeting of the General Assembly for circulation to the members. It appoints the Secretary-General and the Treasurer on the recommendation of the Executive Committee. The officers and members of the Executive Committee shall be chosen to represent all the interests as fairly as possible.

14. The General Assembly shall decide upon the acceptance of, and shall hold, all gifts, bequests, and subsidies made to the Association.

15. The General Assembly shall appoint two professional auditors to the Association.

ARTICLE X–FUNCTIONS OF THE EXECUTIVE COMMITTEE

1. The Executive Committee is composed of a maximum of fifteen members, having the right to vote, including:

> The Chairman and Vice-Chairmen
> The Secretary-General
> The Treasurer, appointed by the General Assembly

2. In the event of the death or resignation of one of its members, the Executive Committee shall authorize the National Center which nominated the member, to appoint a deputy for the remaining period of his office.

3. The Executive Committee has the power to co-opt up to two additional members. It also has the power to co-opt advisors.

4. Any member who cannot attend a meeting of the Executive Committee may appoint a deputy, by giving notice to the Secretary-General, in writing.

5. A meeting of the Executive Committee may be called only if at least half of the members express in writing to the Secretary-General their determination to be present and participate, either in person or represented by a deputy. The presence of half the members shall constitute a quorum.

6. The Executive Committee will meet at least once a year: the Committee will decide by majority vote if it is necessary to hold additional meetings, and will choose the places and dates of such meetings. The Committee must be called three months in

advance. Meetings will be called by the Secretary-General at the request of the Chairman.

7. The Executive Committee may decide upon urgent matters by correspondence if it proves impossible to hold a special meeting. In this case the Secretary-General, by agreement with the Chairman, shall send to each member of the Executive Committee a questionnaire, to which each member will reply in writing. Decisions will be made by two-thirds majority. The decisions will come before the Executive Committee at their next meeting for ratification. The replies will be placed in the records of the Association where they will be available for examination by members of the General Assembly.

8. Each member of the Executive Committee possesses one vote which he can use in person, or by deputy, or by letter. Voting by proxy is not permitted.

9. The Chairman of this Association is also Chairman of the meetings of the Executive Committee. In the event of his absence, he will be replaced by a Vice-Chairman, or if all Vice-Chairmen are absent, by a Chairman elected for this purpose by the Executive Committee.

10. All decisions are taken by a simple majority vote, except decisions taken by correspondence.

11. The Chairman of the meeting has the right to vote in his own right as a member of the Committee. If a majority decision cannot be established by this means, the Chairman may cast a second vote to decide the issue.

12. The Executive Committee shall deal with the affairs of the Association between meetings of the General Assembly and carry out the decisions taken by the General Assembly. The Executive Committee shall remain in office for the two years or thereabouts and its members shall be eligible for re-election.

13. The Executive Committee will accept or reject new applications for membership made to the Secretary-General.

14. The budget is administered by the Executive Committee according to a program established by the General Assembly.

15. The Executive Committee entrusts to the Treasurer the administration of funds, the preparation of the budget, and the accounts. The accounts of the Association must be audited every two years by two professional auditors, appointed by the General Assembly on the recommendation of the Executive Committee.

16. The Executive Committee may take the initiative in matters not anticipated by the General Assembly, providing that these matters are in keeping with the aims and character of this Association, and providing that the Executive Committee takes the first opportunity to report on these matters to the General Assembly.

ARTICLE XI–THE OFFICERS

The Officers of this Association are elected for two years or thereabouts and as follows:

> The Chairman, elected
> The Vice-Chairmen, elected
> The Secretary-General, appointed
> The Treasurer, appointed

1. The Officers are charge with carrying out the Association's program and

rendering reports to the Executive Committee.

2. In the case of any urgent matters not foreseen by the Executive Committee, the Officers are given power to act at their discretion and will take the first opportunity to report on these matters to the Executive Committee.

CHAPTER V

ARTICLE XII—DURATION

1. This Association is created for an unlimited period.

2. This Association shall cease to function when, for any reason, three-fourths of the members (National Centers) on the basic number of votes shall express in writing to the Secretary-General, the desire to dissolve the Association. In this event, the Executive Committee shall be authorized to declare the Association dissolved, and any funds remaining in the Association's treasury shall be given to international organizations pursuing similar aims.

ARTICLE XIII—ADOPTION OF STATUTES

This Constitution shall come into force at the moment of its approval by a Constituent General Assembly of delegations from all interested countries called for this purpose. From that moment the Association may accept as members the national Centers who send their applications to the Secretary-General.

APPENDIX F
THE ELECTION PROCESS OF ASSITEJ / 1975
By Nat Eek

During the first ten (10) years, an election process emerged and was codified by practice:

1. At the beginning there was no indication in the Statutes that Centers were supposed to nominate themselves to stand for the EXCOM. So, in the earliest elections, the EXCOM decided that all present EXCOM Members were automatically nominated. However, there could be nominations from the floor.

2. By the Constitution of 1965 there could only be 15 members on the EXCOM, each representing his or her official dues-paying national center. All EXCOM members were to be elected by majority vote. If less than fifteen were elected by majority vote, the EXCOM would only consist of that number for the next term. Then all officers had to be elected by majority vote in the General Assembly, and only from among the newly elected EXCOM members. However, there could be nominations from the floor, provided the nominee was on the newly elected EXCOM. The Secretary-General and the Treasurer had to be elected as part of the 15 members.

3. In the General Assembly with the Elections on the Agenda, after presentation to the Bureau and the EXCOM in separate meetings, the Secretary-General announced those centers present that were eligible to vote, and how many votes each center had (2 votes for professional theatres as center members and 1 vote for amateur theatres as members). This meant that each center had acceptable statutes in conformity with the ASSITEJ Constitution, had a corresponding delegate and address, and had paid its dues. Each center so approved was either present in person, or may have given its proxy to another center. There was no limit on the number of proxies held by one center.

4. At first the delegates voted on the member-centers to be on the new EXCOM, and then they elected all the officers from those so elected to the EXCOM. Later the Secretary-General and the Treasurer were elected first, so that their countries could always be represented on the EXCOM. Otherwise it would be possible to have two persons from the same country sitting on the EXCOM. This never happened, but there was concern that Belgium, France, and Romania could possibly have had two members on the EXCOM.

5. Later the Secretary-General would read in English the names of the National Centers, in alphabetical order, who had nominated themselves and who were willing to stand for election. This could be any number. At this same time the Secretary-General announced any proxies and which Centers held them. The total number of votes was announced, as well as the majority of votes required for election. In order to be elected a Center had to receive at least a majority of the votes eligible to be cast (51%). This meant that by not voting for all 15 Centers or by not voting for a particular Center, a Center could be defeated for election by not having a majority vote (51%). Several times there had been a proposal to require all Centers to vote for a total of the current 15 places on

the EXCOM, but it had been defeated twice. On the positive side, this voting procedure guaranteed that every Center on the EXCOM had a majority vote of confidence.

6. 3 identical ballots with the name of each nominated Center on them were distributed to each Center, one for each of their potential 3 votes (2 professional and 1 amateur), again in alphabetical order.

7. Each center marked the ballots accordingly, and the ballots were deposited in the ballot box, again each center being called to the ballot box for deposit in alphabetical order. The ballot box varied from a cardboard box, a hat, or an empty waste-basket. Finally there was a proper one with a closed top with a slit for the deposit of the ballots.

8. The President appointed 3 tellers to count the ballots, and to report the results to the Secretary-General who in turn announced the results to the General Assembly. The Secretary-General announced those elected by starting with the greatest number of votes received, continuing until a total of 15 Centers was reached. Ties were automatically accepted within the fifteen. If there was a tie at 15, then a run-off election was held between the two. If less than 15 Centers received a majority vote, the EXCOM would be comprised only of the number that had received a majority vote. The original EXCOM was only 12 and at another election only 11 received a majority.

9. A recess was declared; the *new* EXCOM retired; and in executive session they selected a slate of officers by name, not by country: a President and 3 Vice-Presidents from among the fifteen individuals on the EXCOM. They could present more than one name for each office. These names were then presented by the Secretary-General to the General Assembly. There could be nominations from the floor; ballots were prepared; and the Centers voted on those names. Again each name had to receive at least 51% of the total eligible vote. If a name received less than the majority vote, the EXCOM retired to come up with a new slate; or additional nominations could be made from the floor; or if it is among the Vice-Presidents, they could just have fewer than three. The Vice-Presidents become 1st. 2nd, and 3rd in order of the majority of votes received. For the first few years there were only two vice-presidents.

10. Only the EXCOM could co-opt (or appoint) a Center to sit on the EXCOM with vote. The Constitution limited the number of co-options to 2. However, in practice the EXCOM at times co-opted three or more. The co-options were usually made at the first meeting of the "new" EXCOM. There was no limit on Advisors or Counselors. There was no limit on how often a center or an individual could be appointed. However, co-opted Centers and Counselors did not have to be appointed. If it so wished, the EXCOM could do without, or might appoint them at a later date as need arose. Several times a center that had been defeated in the general election was immediately co-opted at the first "new" EXCOM meeting, usually maintaining the East-West balance.

APPENDIX G
Final Speech by President Nat Eek, Vth International Congress
Berlin, GDR, 24 April 1975

In 1965, ten years ago as a delegate, I addressed the Constitutional Assembly in Paris regarding actor training in the United States. In 1975, ten years later as your outgoing President, I now wish to address this Fifth General Assembly regarding the art and purpose of children's theatre. I am extremely grateful for being allowed to serve ASSITEJ, and I thank you for the support and friendships given me during these ten years. May I share a few final thoughts with you which I hope will help us all to rededicate ourselves to the original purposes of ASSITEJ, which are: 1) to promote contacts and interchange of experience between *all* countries, and 2) to promote tours of individual artists and companies.

I fear we have become entangled in statutes, special allegiances, ego trips, and trivia which have nothing to do with children's theatre. Let me remind us of what children's theatre is all about by asking a series of five questions and trying to provide the answers.

What is the *strength* of children's theatre? Its strength is multiple. It is immediate and alive. What the audience sees is happening as it watches. As an art it is temporal; it exits only while it continues, and once the curtain falls it ceases to exist. It has a unique one to one ratio between the actor on stage and the audience member. Film is larger than the audience member, while television is smaller, but theatre approaches you on an equal basis. Theatre presents subjective experience in a very objective way. The audience is able to view the characters' actions and hear their ideas, and then in turn the audience draws its own opinion related to what it sees. The audience actually participates in the performance and affects its eventual success. There must be constant interchange between actor on stage and the response of the audience in the house. Lastly, I remember a child commenting that she liked theatre better than movies or television, because the actors were "round" rather than flat!

What is the *splendor* of children's theatre? Its splendor comes from its offer of a total visual experience to the audience. It is capable of mixing sight and sound, all in a three-dimensional response. While film can overwhelm us with the accuracy of its naturalistic style, children's theatre has the advantage of being able to create anything visually by calling on the child's imagination to fill in the spaces. At this Congress we were delighted with the antique ship in *Robby Cruse*[145] and its anchor made out of an old chandelier. There was also that marvelous postage stamp of a town complete with bridges and alleys white hot in the sun on the circular stage in *The Story of the Deserted Doll*[146] As Sir Tyrone Guthrie, the celebrated British Director, said: "Good theatre allows the audience to participate in glamorous goings on." Theatre should be more splendid than our everyday lives. Are we giving the children enough splendor? Are we enriching their visual experiences? Certainly the circus finale of *The Three Fat Men*[147] added a dazzle and excitement of its own that was excellent.

What is the *spirit* of children's theatre? It says all things are possible on the stage. It is positive—enquiring—surprising—joyous! It should lift you out of your seat and delight you. We haven't seen much of this spirit recently. The sight or action which suddenly makes the child shriek with laughter, or applaud spontaneously, or jump for joy, or shudder with fear seems to be missing. I am afraid we are taking ourselves too seriously, and consequently we are getting dull and talky. Theatre should be fun and fascinating, and serious plays can be just as much fun as comedies. *Poor Konrad*[148] was dull and didactic theatre, and the way the children behind me yawned and slumped in their seats confirmed my suspicions.

What are the *social aspects* of children's theatre? Theatre holds a mirror up to nature—the world—life around us! But all life—not just carefully selected elements. Children's theatre should help the child find his identity in the world and society; and by seeing what others do and say and think, children's theatre should make him want to grow up to accept adult responsibility. Through children's theatre he can experience the terrors and triumphs of life vicariously, and then he is ready to confront the real thing when it happens to him. Ideally, he should experience both formal theatre and informal creative drama. Children must experience all things. They cannot achieve knowledge by pooling ignorance. Watching the film of Robert Bolt's play *A Man for All Seasons*, I saw Sir Thomas More as a man of sincere belief who was capable of ignoring his private religious principles in order to approve a sacrilegious marriage for his king. At the end of the film as the ax fell beheading him, a teenager behind me turned to his companion and commented, "He really won, didn't he!"

What is the *soul* of children's theatre? It is the child himself—our most precious resource. He is our reason for existence, and only by serving his aesthetic, intellectual, and emotional needs are we justified in surviving. The drama critic Dan Sullivan has said that good children's theatre brings out the child in the man. As adults we should enjoy the plays as much as the child audience does, and hopefully recognize something of ourselves in the child's response. As producers and performers we have a greater obligation to the child audience than the adult audience. Why? Because the child is a captive audience—he is usually brought by someone else: his school, his parents, his friends—and we must be worthy of his attention. Our theatre must challenge and stretch his mind and his emotions, and not pander to cheap sensationalism or quick emotional effect or trendy sociologies. Then as the child grows, we must let go. Margaret Mead, the U.S. anthropologist, has said that each child must be free to choose a road of life, the end of which we need not know. We will never fully know how we have influenced the child through children's theatre, hopefully for the best, but if we err, let us err by pushing him forward rather than pulling him back.

I hope ASSITEJ in the next ten years will rediscover these truths. I hope ASSITEJ will hold a greater number and more varied discussions of artistic matters, and that we may see performances by more foreign companies and new companies doing different plays in different ways. I hope the leadership will have the courage to be challenged by youth, and to bring new and younger people into the Association. If we do not do this, we will become extinct like the dinosaurs, of interest only to ourselves and archaeologists.

Those of us in the theatre have the greatest power in the world—the power of giving pleasure. To be on stage or in the back of the theatre during a successful performance, immediately to see and hear the children respond as you had hoped, and to know that you are part of that entire creative process—is a *privilege* that very few people in the world have. To paraphrase Agnes DeMille, the U.S. choreographer, "This is power and this is glory, and it is ours nightly." We must be worthy of this privilege.

THE HISTORY OF THE FORMATION and
SUSPENSION OF NATIONAL CENTERS
(1966-1975)

ASSITEJ began with a total of twelve (12) National Centers whose representatives were elected to the Provisional Committee at the Constitutional Conference in Paris, France in May of 1965.

Year	Center	Status	Status—1975
1966—Founding Centers			*** Extant and Active**
	BELGIUM	Official thru 1975	*
	CANADA	Official thru 1975	*
	CZECHOSLOVAKIA	Official thru 1975	*
	FEDERAL GERMAN REPUBLIC	Official thru 1975	*
	FRANCE	Official thru 1975	*
	GERMAN DEMOCRATIC REP.	Official thru 1975	*
	GREAT BRITAIN	Official thru 1975	*
	ITALY	Official thru 1975	*
	NETHERLANDS	Official thru 1975	*
	ROMANIA	Official thru 1975	*
	USA	Official thru 1975	*
	USSR	Official thru 1975	*
1966	BRAZIL	Expelled for non-payment of dues	
	DENMARK	Forming by Juul Official in 1978	*
	ISRAEL	Forming but in and out	*
	POLAND	Forming but in and out	*
	SPAIN	Spain became Official, but no indication exactly when	*
	YUGOSLAVIA	Official thru 1975	*

The list of 6 centers above in 1966 was declared "Official" making a total of 18 Centers. However, in reality some were still forming and were *in and out* over the years.

Year	Center	Status	Status—1975
1967	BULGARIA	Official thru 1975	*
1968	CANADA	Official thru 1975	*
	CUBA	Forming	*
	HUNGARY	Forming	*
	INDIA	Forming	
	IRELAND	Forming	*
	JAPAN	Forming	*

	Country	Status		
	NORWAY	Official thru 1975	*	Represented Scandinavia
	POLAND	Forming		
	PORTUGAL	Forming	*	
	SWEDEN	Forming		
1969	HUNGARY	Still Forming		
	JAPAN	Still Forming		
	POLAND	Still Forming		
	PORTUGAL	Still Forming		
	YUGOSLAVIA	Official thru 1975	*	

For several years Yugoslavia had had a representative attending meetings as a co-opted Member. There is no record of when they became an official center. Probably around 1969 with their hosting of the EXCOM at Šibenik, Yugoslavia.

	Country	Status		
1970	ARGENTINA	Forming		*
	AUSTRALIA	Forming		*
	DAHOMEY	Forming	Non-existent	
	EGYPT	Forming	Non-existent	
	INDIA	Still Forming		
	IRELAND	Still Forming		*
	JAPAN	Still Forming		*
	HUNGARY	Still Forming		*
	POLAND	Still Forming		*
	PORTUGAL	Still Forming	Inactive	
	SENEGAL	Forming	Non-existent	
	SWITZERLAND	Forming		
	TUNISIA	Forming	Non-existent	

This made a total of 18 active centers with 13 forming.

	Country	Status	
1971	AUSTRALIA	Still Forming—Made an official presentation	*
	HUNGARY	Accepted provisionally	*
	IRELAND	Accepted provisionally	*
	ISRAEL	Though officially a Center it could not pay its dues	*
	POLAND	Accepted provisionally	*
1972	AUSTRIA	Expelled for non-payment of dues	*
	BRAZIL	Expelled for non-payment of dues, then a possible presentation for a new center	
	CEYLON	Possibly forming	*
	IRAN	Forming, and then official	*
	ISRAEL	Had not paid dues for 3 years	*
	JORDAN	Possibly forming	

	MONGOLIA	Possibly forming	Non-existent
	NORWAY	Expelled for non-payment of dues	
	PERU	Official—dues unpaid	*
	POLAND	Back to still forming	*
	SWITZERLAND	Official	
1973	SRI LANKA (CEYLON)	Forming	*
1974	AUSTRIA	Official (reinstated)	*
	ARGENTINA	Official thru 1975	*
	AUSTRALIA	Official thru 1975	*
	CUBA	Still forming	*
	DENMARK	Official thru 1975	*
	POLAND	Back to still forming	*
	TURKEY	Possibly forming	
	VENEZUELA	Official thru 1975	*
1975	ALGERIA	Official thru 1975	*
	AUSTRALIA	Official again thru 1975	*
	BELGIUM	Reforming as a federation	*
	ZAIRE	Forming	Non-existent
	CUBA	Official thru 1975	*
	FINLAND	Official thru 1975	*
	NETHERLANDS	Reforming under new statutes	*
	PORTUGAL	Reforming to use Portuguese as their official language	*
	SWITZERLAND	Center had disappeared, dues unpaid	

At the Berlin Congress in 1975 it was announced that there were 28 official Centers for ASSITEJ. These were the following:

ALGERIA	IRELAND
ARGENTINA	IRAN
AUSTRALIA	ISRAEL
AUSTRIA	ITALY
BELGIUM	JAPAN
CANADA	NETHERLANDS
CUBA	PERU
CZECHOSLOVAKIA	PORTUGAL
DENMARK	ROMANIA
FEDERAL GERMAN REPUBLIC (FGR)	SPAIN
FINLAND	SRI LANKA
FRANCE	USA
GERMAN DEMOCRATIC REPUBLIC (GDR)	USSR
HUNGARY	VENEZUELA

NOTES

Introduction
1. In 1972 the American Educational Theatre Association (AETA) changed its name to the American Theatre Association (ATA) and the Children's Theatre Conference (CTC) became the Children's Theatre Association of America (CTAA).
2. Ann M. Shaw, *The Formation of ASSITEJ*, ASSITEJ Annual 1996/97, Ed. Wolfgang Schneider, Druckerei Heinrich, Frankfurt am Main, Germany, p. 99.
3. *Ibid.*, p. 100.
4. Ann M. Shaw, *ASSITEJ—The First 30 Years*, ms, p. 3-4.
5. *Ibid.*

The Formation of ASSITEJ
6. Rosamund Gilder, "Foreword," in the *Official Report of the Fourth International Congress of ASSITEJ*, 18-25 June 1972 (State University of New York at Albany), p. 5.
7. Sara Spencer in a letter to Coleman Jennings quoted in Frederick Scott Regan, "The History of the International Children's Theatre Association From Its Founding to 1975", a dissertation to the Faculty of the Graduate School of the University of Minnesota, USA, July, 1975.
8. Rose-Marie Moudoués, Speech entitled "The Birth of ASSITEJ," *One Theatre World Symposium*, Seattle, Washington, USA, 10 May 1995 as printed in *ASSITEJ Annual 1996-97*, p. 92.
9. Shaw, *ASSITEJ Annual 1996-97*, p. 93-94.
10. Rose-Marie Moudoués, letter to Scott Regan as quoted in Regan, *op.cit.*, p. 11.
11. Shaw, *Formation op.cit.*, p. 94.
12. Nat Eek, telephone conversation with Ann M. Shaw, Norman, Oklahoma, Santa Fe, New Mexico, USA, 1 July 1996.
13. Agnes Haaga (USA) "Report on the International Conference of Theatre for Children—May 13-21, 1964." to CTC and AETA, Mimeographed, p. 1.
14. M. Pugh, British Children's Theatre Association, "Report on the International Conference and Festival of Theatres for Children, London, 13-21 May 1964." Mimeographed, p. 24.
15. Shaw, *ASSITEJ Annual 1996-97*, p. 95.
16. Haaga, op.cit.

The Preparatory Meeting
17. Pugh, BCTA, op.cit., p.1.
18. Pugh, BCTA, op.cit., p. 34-43.
19. Ann S. Hill, interview by Nat Eek on 15-16 June 2005 in Nashville, Tennessee, USA.
20. Haaga, op.cit.
21. Regan, op.cit., p. 18.
22. Haaga, op.cit., p. 2.
23. Michael Pugh, letter to Sara Spencer dtd 8 September 1964.
24. Janice C. Hewitt, "The Development of the International Association of Theatre for Children and Young People with Particular Emphasis on the United States Participation", MA Thesis, University of Kansas, 1966, p. 38.

25. Jed H. Davis, Letter to Nat Eek dtd 2 July 2005.

26. Ann S. Hill, interview by Nat Eek on 15-16 June 2005 in Nashville, Tennessee, USA.Davis, op.cit.

27. Haaga, op.cit.

28. Hewitt, op. cit.

29. Gerald Tyler, "Meeting of the Preparatory Committee held at the Cini Foundation, Isola, San Giorgio, Venice, September 1964," Mimeographed, p. 2.

The Preparatory Committee

30. Ibid.

31. Nat Eek, Speech entitled "The Formative Years of ASSITEJ", One Theatre World Symposium, Seattle, USA, 10 May 1995.

32. Moudoués, op.cit., Seattle, USA, 10 May 1995.

The Constitutional Conference, 1965

33. Sara Spencer, Official Report of the USA/Canada Congress, Albany, New York, USA, 1972, p. 29. Child Drama Collection. Dept. of Archives and Special Collections. University Libraries. Arizona State University, Tempe, Arizona, USA.

34. List taken from the *French language Minutes of the International Congress of ASSITEJ*, 3 pp. ASSITEJ Foundation, 1965, GS-96. ASSITEJ International Archives; Kinder und Jugend theaterzentrum in der Bundesrepublik, Frankfurt am Main; Federal Republic of Germany.

35. Gerald Tyler and Nat Eek, *History of the International Association of Theatre for Children and Young People (ASSITEJ)*, dated 1 June 1971. Child Drama Collection. Dept. of Archives and Special Collections. University Libraries. Arizona State University, Tempe, Arizona, USA.

36. *French language Minutes of the International Congress of ASSITEJ*, 3 pp. ASSITEJ Foundation, 1965, GS-96. ASSITEJ International Archives; Kinder und Jugend theaterzentrum in der Bundesrepublik, Frankfurt am Main; Federal Republic of Germany.

37. Hewitt, op.cit.

38. Virginia G. Michalak, "Notes on the International Conference on Theatre for Children and Youth, Paris, 1965," Mimeographed, p. 2.

39. Shaw, *Formation op.cit.*, p. 98.

40. Chapter I of The Constitution of ASSITEJ (1965).

41. Sara Spencer, "International Children's Theatre—ASSITEJ," *Children's Theatre Conference Newsletter*, XIV (November, 1965) p.14 as quoted in Janice C. Hewitt, op.cit., p.38.

42. Ann S. Hill, "At First International Session On Children's Theatre Ideologies Submerged By Interest in Youth," The Nashville (Tennessee) Banner, 26 May 1964.

43. Muriel Sharon, "International C.T. Meeting in Paris", *Children's Theatre News*, a Publication of Region 14, CTC, Vol. 5, No. 2, December 1965, p. 1-2.

EXCOM Meeting, February 1966

44. The following narrative was taken from Notes taken by Nat Eek (USA), 1966. Child Drama Collection. Dept. of Archives and Special Collections. University Libraries. Arizona State University, Tempe, Arizona, USA.

1st Congress, May 1966

45. The following narrative was taken from Notes taken by Nat Eek (USA) 1966. Child Drama Collection. Dept. of Archives and Special Collections. University Libraries. Arizona State University, Tempe, Arizona, USA.

Summary, 1965-66

46. Nat Eek, notes taken during the meeting, Paris, France, June 1965.

47. Nat Eek, *Report to the US Center on the Berlin Conference, 1966.* Special Collections, Dept. of Archives and Manuscripts. University Libraries, Arizona State University, Tempe, Arizona, USA.

48. *The Constitution of ASSITEJ (1965),* Chapter IV, Article XI, Section 2, Appendix E.

49. *The Constitution of ASSITEJ (1965),* Chapter IV, Article X, Number 3, Appendix E.

EXCOM Meeting, May 1967

50. The following narrative was taken in part from Notes taken by Nat Eek (USA) 1967. Child Drama Collection. Dept. of Archives and Special Collections. University Libraries. Arizona State University, Tempe, Arizona, USA.

51. Nat Eek, "Report from the Director—Executive Meeting, Nuremberg, 6-11 March 1967," Mimeographed.

EXCOM, March 1968

52. The following narrative was taken from Notes taken by Nat Eek (USA) 1968. Child Drama Collection. Dept. of Archives and Special Collections. University Libraries. Arizona State University, Tempe, Arizona, USA.

53. Prof. Joyce Doolittle attended her first ASSITEJ meeting in Moscow in 1968 where she was appointed as an official observer. She served as Canada's official representative on the EXCOM from 1969-1978, and as Vice-President of ASSITEJ from 1972-1978 (Joyce Doolittle in interview with Nat Eek 22 June 2005).

54. The CCDYA later in 1968 appointed Doolittle as Canada's official delegate to the EXCOM with the condition that any expenses incurred by the establishment of the Canadian Center for ASSITEJ at the University of Calgary and by her attendance at international meetings not be paid by CCDYA. The Department of Drama at the University of Calgary agreed to absorb costs of printing and distributing newsletters and reports. Doolittle was Canada's representative to ASSITEJ for ten years during which time she co-hosted the IVth International Congress in Montreal/Albany, and served as Vice-President from 1972 to 1979. (Joyce Doolittle in interview with Nat Eek 22 June 2005).

55. Ann S. Hill, *European Children's Theatre and the Second Congress of the International Children's Theatre Association* (Washington, D.C., ACTA Newsletter, 1968), p. 1.

56. Ann S. Hill, interview by Nat Eek on 15-16 June 2005 in Nashville, Tennessee, USA.

IInd Congress, May 1968

57. The following narrative was taken from Minutes and Notes taken by Nat Eek (USA) and the Official Program of the Hague Congress 1968. Child Drama Collection. Dept. of Archives and Special Collections. University Libraries. Arizona State University, Tempe, Arizona, USA.

58. Nat Eek, Minutes and notes of the IInd Congress of ASSITEJ, May 1968. Child Drama Collection. Dept. of Archives and Special Collections. University Libraries. Arizona State University, Tempe, Arizona, USA.

59. Ibid.

60. Ibid.

61. "Report of the Second Assembly of ASSITEJ" Author unknown (possibly British), p. 1. Child Drama Collection. Dept. of Archives and Special Collections. University Libraries. Arizona State University, Tempe, Arizona, USA.

62. Nat Eek, Minutes of the IInd Congress of ASSITEJ, May 1968.

Summary, 1966-1968

63. Galina Kolosova, Chekhov International Theatre Festival, Moscow, Russia. E-mail to Nat Eek dtd 22 May 2006.

64. Ibid.

65. Doolittle was an "observer" from Canada, pending her endorsement as an official representative by her national Center.

66. Joyce Doolittle, e-mail to Nat Eek dtd 24 June 2005.

EXCOM Meeting, October 1968

67. *The Constitution of ASSITEJ*, Article I, No. 2. "This Association is free from political, religious, or racial commitment of any kind."

68. Regan, op.cit., p. 132.

69. Orlin Corey, Complete Minutes of the Sophia EXCOM Meeting sent to the US Center EXCOM, dtd 26 December 1968, p. 2-3. Child Drama Collection. Dept. of Archives and Special Collections. University Libraries. Arizona State University, Tempe, Arizona, USA.

70. Ibid.

71. Ibid.

72. Bulgaria was appointed to the EXCOM (1967 in Nuremberg) almost the minute its national Center was formed.

73. Corey, op. cit.

EXCOM Meeting, June-July 1969

74. Nat Eek, Minutes of the Šibenik EXCOM Meeting, 27 June–1 July 1969, p. 1. Child Drama Collection. Dept. of Archives and Special Collections. University Libraries. Arizona State University, Tempe, Arizona, USA.

75. Ibid., p.1-2.

76. Ibid., p. 2.

77. Ibid.

EXCOM Meeting, June 1970

78. The Report of the Bucharest Meeting is taken from the excellent Minutes provided by the Czech Center under Adamek's direction. Because of disastrous flooding in Romania, the Meeting had to be postponed until the June dates. Vladimir Adamek, Czechoslovakian Center, "Minutes of the Bucharest EXCOM Meeting, 1970". Child Drama Collection. Dept. of Archives and Special Collections. University Libraries. Arizona State University, Tempe, Arizona, USA.

79. Ibid.

IIIrd Congress, October 1970

80. This narrative has been taken from Nat Eek, Minutes and notes of the IIIrd

Congress of ASSITEJ, October, 1970. Child Drama Collection. Dept. of Archives and Special Collections. University Libraries. Arizona State University, Tempe, Arizona, USA.

Summary, 1968-1970

81. *Outstanding Plays for Young Audiences* (An International Bibliography), edited by Patricia Whitton for ASSITEJ/USA. Funded by the Alcone Foundation, the ASSITEJ/USA Development Fund, and New Plays Incorporated.

82. Nat Eek, "Report on the Šibenik Meeting", *Children's Theatre Review* (USA), p. 3.

83. Ibid.

84. Ann S. Hill, *3rd Congress of ASSITEJ* as published in *The Nashville Banner*, 1970, pp. 1-8. Child Drama Collection. Dept. of Archives and Special Collections. University Libraries. Arizona State University, Tempe, Arizona, USA.

85. Ann S. Hill, interview by Nat Eek on 15-16 June 2005 in Nashville, Tennessee, USA.

86. Pat Ruby, assistant to the Canadian Correspondent, CCYDA, Canadian Center for ASSITEJ, Report on the IIIrd General Assembly of ASSITEJ, Venice, Italy, 19-24 October 1970, pp. 16-18.

87. Ibid.

88. Ibid.

89. Joyce Doolittle, interview by Nat Eek on 21-22 June 2005 in Calgary, Alberta, Canada.

Bureau Meeting, May 1971

90. Letters of Rose-Marie Moudoués and Nat Eek, May 1971. Child Drama Collection. Dept. of Archives and Special Collections. University Libraries. Arizona State University, Tempe, Arizona, USA.

EXCOM Meeting, October 1971

91. This narrative was taken from Nat Eek, Official Minutes of the EXCOM Meeting in Bratislava, 1971. Child Drama Collection. Dept. of Archives and Special Collections. University Libraries. Arizona State University, Tempe, Arizona, USA.

92. Ibid. They are completely presented in the Minutes of this Meeting, pp. 12-17.

EXCOM Meeting, March 1972

93. This narrative was taken from Nat Eek, Official Minutes of the EXCOM Meeting in Berlin, Leipzig, and Dresden, 1972. Child Drama Collection. Dept. of Archives and Special Collections. University Libraries. Arizona State University, Tempe, Arizona, USA.

94. Ibid.

IVth Congress, June 1972

95. The following narrative was taken from Minutes taken by Joyce Doolittle (Canada), Minutes and Notes taken by Nat Eek (USA) 1972, the Official Report of the IVth Congress in Albany, NY, published by the State University of New York in Albany. Child Drama Collection. Dept. of Archives and Special Collections. University Libraries. Arizona State University, Tempe, Arizona, USA.

96. Nat Eek, Minutes of the Bureau Meeting in Montreal, Canada, dtd 13 June 1972, 2 pages. Child Drama Collection. Dept. of Archives and Special Collections. University Libraries. Arizona State University, Tempe, Arizona, USA.

97. Richard Courtney, "Creativity and Theatre for Children", *the stage in Canada*, Vol. 7, No. 2, October 1972, p. 15.

98. Regan, op.cit.

99. Ibid.

100. Ibid.

101. Ann S. Hill, interview by Nat Eek on 15-16 June 2005 in Nashville, Tennessee, USA.

102. *Official Report, The Fourth International Congress of ASSITEJ*, published by the State University of New York at Albany, NY, dtd 18-25 June 1972, pp. 17-18.

103. Ann S. Hill, interview by Nat Eek on 15-16 June 2005 in Nashville, Tennessee, USA.

104. The following narrative was from Minutes taken by Joyce Doolittle (Canada) and Notes taken by Nat Eek (USA), June 1972. Child Drama Collection. Dept. of Archives and Special Collections. University Libraries. Arizona State University, Tempe, Arizona, USA.

105. Ibid.

106. Regan, op.cit. p. 214.

107. Ibid.

Summary, 1970-1972

108. See ASSITEJ Constitution, Article IV, Nos. 1 and 2 in Appendix E.

109. *Official Report, The Fourth International Congress of ASSITEJ*, p. 19.

110. *Ibid*, p. 21.

111. Ann S. Hill, interview by Nat Eek on 15-16 June 2005 in Nashville, Tennessee, USA.

Bureau Meeting, October 1972

112. The following narrative was taken from Minutes taken by Joyce Doolittle (Canada) and Notes taken by Nat Eek (USA). Child Drama Collection. Dept. of Archives and Special Collections. University Libraries. Arizona State University, Tempe, Arizona, USA.

EXCOM Meeting, June 1973

113. The following narrative was taken from Minutes taken by Joyce Doolittle (Canada) dtd 29 August 1973, 11 pages. Child Drama Collection. Dept. of Archives and Special Collections. University Libraries. Arizona State University, Tempe, Arizona, USA.

EXCOM Meeting, April 1974

114. The following narrative was taken from Minutes taken by Joyce Doolittle (Canada) and Notes taken by Nat Eek (USA). Child Drama Collection. Dept. of Archives and Special Collections. University Libraries. Arizona State University, Tempe, Arizona, USA.

115. Nat Eek, ltr to US Ctr EXCOM dtd 30 November 1973.

116. Interview between Patricia Snyder and Scott Regan, July, 1974.

Bureau Meeting, November 1974

117. The following narrative was taken from correspondence of Nat Eek (USA) in 1974 and 1975. Child Drama Collection. Dept. of Archives and Special Collections. University Libraries. Arizona State University, Tempe, Arizona, USA.

118. Letter from Rose-Marie Moudoués to Nat Eek dtd 11 November 1974.

Child Drama Collection. Dept. of Archives and Special Collections. University Libraries. Arizona State University, Tempe, Arizona, USA.

EXCOM Meeting, February 1975

119. This narrative is taken from the Minutes of the EXCOM Meeting in Zagreb and Karlovac, 3-8 February 1975, in French, apparently distributed by the Paris Secretariat, 1975. Child Drama Collection. Dept. of Archives and Special Collections. University Libraries. Arizona State University, Tempe, Arizona, USA.

Vth Congress, April 1975

120. The following narrative was from Minutes taken by Joyce Doolittle (Canada) and Notes taken by Nat Eek (USA) 1975. Child Drama Collection. Dept. of Archives and Special Collections. University Libraries. Arizona State University, Tempe, Arizona, USA.

Summary, 1972-1975

121. *The Constitution of ASSITEJ International (2005)*, Article 8, Number 3 and Article 11.

A Summing Up

122. Sara Spencer, Letter to EXCOM of ASSITEJ dtd 7 April 1975. Child Drama Collection. Dept. of Archives and Special Collections. University Libraries. Arizona State University, Tempe, Arizona, USA.

Appendix B

123. Adamek Biography. Taken in part from "Who's Who in ASSITEJ", the Czech Bulletin, 1977 (3). Edited by the Theatre Institute, 110 01 Prague 1, Celetná 17, for the Czechoslovak Centre for ASSITEJ.
   E-mail from Alena Kulanáková, ASSITEJ/Czech Republic dtd 13 January 2007.

124. Biotto Biography. Taken in part from "Who's Who in ASSITEJ", the Czech Bulletin, 1977 (3). Edited by the Theatre Institute, 110 01 Prague 1, Celetná 17, for the Czechoslovak Centre for ASSITEJ

125. Chancerel Biography. Nat Eek, e-mail from Maryline Romain, Société d'Histoire du Théâtre, dtd 20 November 2006, quoting Evelyne Ertel, Dictionnaire encyclopédique du théâtre. Maryline Romain, le Dictionnaire Biographique des Militants. XIX-XX siècles. Translated and edited by Eek.

126. Cojar Biography. Taken in part from "Who's Who in ASSITEJ", the Czech Bulletin, 1977 (3). Edited by the Theatre Institute, 110 01 Prague 1, Celetná 17, for the Czechoslovak Centre for ASSITEJ.

127. Djokič Biography. E-mail from ASSITEJ/Serbia.

128. Doolittle Biography. Mailed to author in June 2005.

129. Géal Biography. Taken in part from "Who's Who in ASSITEJ", the Czech Bulletin, 1977 (3). Edited by the Theatre Institute, 110 01 Prague 1, Celetná 17, for the Czechoslovak Centre for ASSITEJ.

130. Georgiev Biography. Taken in part from "Who's Who in ASSITEJ", the Czech Bulletin, 1977 (3). Edited by the Theatre Institute, 110 01 Prague 1, Celetná 17, for the Czechoslovak Centre for ASSITEJ.
   E-mail from Christel Hoffmann dtd 26 March 2007.

131. Gossmann Biography. Taken in part from "Who's Who in ASSITEJ", the Czech Bulletin, 1977 (3). Edited by the Theatre Institute, 110 01 Prague 1, Celetná 17, for the Czechoslovak Centre for ASSITEJ.

132. Juul Biography. Taken in part from "Who's Who in ASSITEJ", the Czech Bulletin, 1977 (3). Edited by the Theatre Institute, 110 01 Prague 1, Celetná 17, for the Czechoslovak Centre for ASSITEJ.

133. Kolosova Biography. Taken in part from "Who's Who in ASSITEJ", the Czech Bulletin, 1977 (3). Edited by the Theatre Institute, 110 01 Prague 1, Celetná 17, for the Czechoslovak Centre for ASSITEJ.
E-mail to Nat Eek dtd 10 January 2007.

134. Ladika Biography. Written by Ivica Simic, ASSITEJ/Croatia, sent to author by e-mail dtd 27 August 2006.

135. Lucian Biography. Ltr from Ian Lucian dtd 29 November 2006, and e-mail dtd December 2006.

136. Moudoués Biography. Taken in part from "Who's Who in ASSITEJ", the Czech Bulletin, 1977 (3). Edited by the Theatre Institute, 110 01 Prague 1, Celetná 17, for the Czechoslovak Centre for ASSITEJ.
Nat Eek, e-mail from Maryline Romain, Société d'Histoire du Théâtre, dtd 22 December 2006 and that of January 2007. Translated and edited by Nat Eek.

137. Porat Biography. Taken in part from "Who's Who in ASSITEJ", the Czech Bulletin, 1977 (3). Edited by the Theatre Institute, 110 01 Prague 1, Celetná 17, for the Czechoslovak Centre for ASSITEJ.
E-mail from Christel Hoffmann dtd 26 March 2007.

138. Rodenberg Biography. Taken in part from "Who's Who in ASSITEJ", the Czech Bulletin, 1977 (3). Edited by the Theatre Institute, 110 01 Prague 1, Celetná 17, for the Czechoslovak Centre for ASSITEJ.
Obituary taken from the *Leipzig Volks Zeitung* dtd 18 January 2006, translated by Michael Ramlöse.
Obituary of Ilse Rodenberg by Christel Hoffmannn, e-mail to Nat Eek dtd 26 March 2007, translated by Erik Eek.

139. Sats Biography. E-mail from Galina Kolosova, Moscow, Russia dtd 29 August 2006.

140. Shakh-Azizov Biography. Written by Galina Kolosova, Moscow, Russia, May 2006.

141. Snoek Biography. Taken in part from "Who's Who in ASSITEJ", the Czech Bulletin, 1977 (3). Edited by the Theatre Institute, 110 01 Prague 1, Celetná 17, for the Czechoslovak Centre for ASSITEJ.
E-mail from Christel Hoffmann dtd 26 March 2007.

142. Spencer Biography. Taken in part from "Who's Who in ASSITEJ", the Czech Bulletin, 1977 (3). Edited by the Theatre Institute, 110 01 Prague 1, Celetná 17, for the Czechoslovak Centre for ASSITEJ.
The College of Fellows 40th Anniversary Volume (1965-2005), edited by Orlin Corey with John R. Cauble, privately printed, 2005, pp. 159-160.

143. Sunyer Biography. Taken in part from "Who's Who in ASSITEJ", the Czech Bulletin, 1977 (3). Edited by the Theatre Institute, 110 01 Prague 1, Celetná 17, for the Czechoslovak Centre for ASSITEJ.

144. Tyler Biography. Nat Eek, e-mail from Gerald Tyler (son) dtd 8 November 2006.

145. *Robby Cruse*, a musical in two acts by Hans-Dieter Schmidt, lyrics by Inga Kalisch, music by Dr. Hans Sandig, presented by the Leipzig Theatr der Jungen Welt, 21 April 1975.

146. *The Story of the Deserted Doll*, a play by A. Sastre, presented by the Teatr der Freundschaft of Berlin, 19 April 1975.

147. *The Three Fat Men*, a musical in two acts by W. Rubin, presented by the Komische Oper of Berlin, 20 April 1975.

148. *Poor Konrad*, a play by F. Wolf, presented by the Theatr Junge Garde Halle, 23 April 1975.

BIBLIOGRAPHY

<u>Works Cited</u>

Adamek, Vladimir. Czechoslovakian Center, "Minutes of the Bucharest EXCOM Meeting, 1970". Child Drama Collection. Dept. of Archives and Special Collections. University Libraries. Arizona State University, Tempe, Arizona, USA.

ASSITEJ Annual, 1996/97. Ed. Wolfgang Schneider, Druckerei Heinrich, Franfurt am Main, Germany.

The College of Fellows 40ᵗʰ Anniversary Volume (1965-2005), edited by Orlin Corey with John R. Cauble, privately printed, 2005.

The Constitution of ASSITEJ (1965) and (2005).

Corey, Orlin. Complete Minutes of the Sophia EXCOM Meeting sent to the US Center EXCOM, dated 26 December 1968, and Report to the US Center. Child Drama Collection. Dept. of Archives and Special Collections. University Librairies. Arizona State University, Tempe, Arizona, USA.

Courtney, Richard. "Creativity and Theatre for Children", *the stage in Canada,* Vol. 7, No. 2, October 1972.

Eek, Nat. "Report on the Šibenik Meeting", *Children's Theatre Review* (USA) 1969.

Gilder, Rosamund. *Official Report of the Fourth International Congress of ASSITEJ,* 18-25 June 1972 (State University of New York at Albany).

Haaga, Agnes. "Report on the International Conference of Theatre for Children— May 13-21, 1964." to CTC and AETA, Mimeographed.

Hewett, Janice C. "The Development of the International Association of Theatre for Children and Young People with Particular Emphasis on the United States Participation", MA Thesis, University of Kansas, Lawrence, Kansas, USA.

Michalak, Virginia G. "Notes on the International Conference on Theatre for Children and Youth, Paris, 1965." Mimeographed.

Official Report, The Fourth International Congress of ASSITEJ, published by the State University of New York at Albany, NY, dated 18-25 June 1972.

Outstanding Plays for Young Audiences (An International Bibliography). Ed. By Patricia Whitton for ASSITEJ/USA. Funded by the Alcone Foundation, the ASSITEJ/USA Development Fund, and New Plays, Inc.

Pugh, Michael. British Children's Theatre Association, "Report on the International Conference and Festival of Theatres for Children, London, 13-21 May 1964." Mimeographed.

Regan, Frederick Scott. "The History of the International Children's Theatre Association From Its Founding to 1975." A dissertation to the Faculty of the Graduate School of the University of Minnesota, USA, July, 1975.

Ruby, Pat. CCYDA, Canadian Center for ASSITEJ, Report on the IIIrd General Assembly of ASSITEJ, Venice, Italy, 19-24 October 1970.

Sharon, Muriel. "International C.T. Meeting in Paris." *Children's Theatre News,* a Publication of Region 14, CTC, Vol. 5, No. 2, December 1965.

Shaw, Ann M. *ASSITEJ—The First 30 Years,* Manuscript.

Shaw, Ann M. *The Formation of ASSITEJ,* ASSITEJ Annual 1996/97, Ed. Wolfgang Schneider, Druckerei Heinrich, Frankfurt am Main, Germany.

Spencer, Sara. "International Children's Theatre—ASSITEJ, "Children's *Theatre Conference Newsletter*, XIV (November, 1965).

Spencer, Sara. Official Report of the USA/Canada Congress, Albany, New York, USA, 1972. Child Drama Collection. Dept. of Archives and Special Collections. University Libraries, Arizona State University, Tempe, Arizona, USA.

Tyler, Gerald. "Meeting of the Preparatory Committee held at the Cini Foundation, Isola, San Giorgio, Venice, September 1964," mimeographed.

Tyler, Gerald and Nat Eek. *History of the International Association of Theatres for Children and Young People (ASSITEJ)*, dated 1 June 1971.

"Who's Who in ASSITEJ." The Czech Bulletin, 1977 (3). Edited by the Theatre Institute, 110 01 Prague 1, Celetná 17, for the Czechoslovak Centre for ASSITEJ. Mimeographed.

References

The Encyclopaedia Britannica; Encyclopaedia Britannica, Inc., Chicago, Illinois, USA.

The World Almanac and Books of Facts (Annual). Pharos Books, Scripps Howard Company, New York, NY, USA.

Archives (Listed chronologically)

French language Minutes of the International [Constitutional] Congress of ASSITEJ, 3 pp. ASSITEJ Foundation, 1965, GS-96. ASSITEJ International Archives; Kinder und Jugend theater zentrum in der Bundesrepublik Deutschland; Frankfurt am Main, Federal Republic of Germany.

Nat Eek, notes taken of the Constitutional Meeting of ASSITEJ in Paris, France, June, 1965. Special Collections, Dept. of Archives and manuscripts. University Libraries, Arizona State University, Tempe, Arizona, USA.

Nat Eek, notes taken of the Berlin, GDR EXCOM Meeting, February 1966. Child Drama Collection. Dept. of Archives and Special Collections. University Libraries. Arizona State University, Tempe, Arizona, USA.

Nat Eek, *Report to the US Center on the Berlin Conference, 1966.* Special Collections, Dept. of Archives and manuscripts. University Libraries, Arizona State University, Tempe, Arizona, USA.

"Report of the Second Assembly of ASSITEJ" Author unknown (possibly British), 1966. Child Drama Collection. Dept. of Archives and Special Collections. University Libraries. Arizona State University, Tempe, Arizona, USA.

Nat Eek, minutes and notes taken of the Ist Congress of ASSITEJ, Prague, Czechoslovakia, May 1966. Child Drama Collection. Dept. of Archives and Special Collections. University Libraries. Arizona State University, Tempe, Arizona, USA.

Nat Eek, notes taken of the Nuremberg, FGR EXCOM Meeting, October 1967. Child Drama Collection. Dept. of Archives and Special Collections. University Libraries. Arizona State University, Tempe, Arizona, USA.

Nat Eek, "Report from the Director—Executive Committee Meeting, Nuremberg, 6-11 March 1967." Mimeographed. Child Drama Collection. Dept. of Archives and Special Collections. University Libraries. Arizona State University, Tempe, Arizona, USA.

Nat Eek, notes taken of the Moscow, USSR EXCOM Meeting in March 1968. Child Drama Collection. Dept. of Archives and Special Collections. University Libraries. Arizona State University, Tempe, Arizona, USA.

Nat Eek, minutes and notes taken and the Official Program of the IInd Congress in The Hague, Netherlands, 25-31 May 1968. Special Collections, Dept. of Archives and Manuscripts. University Libraries. Arizona State University, Tempe, Arizona, USA.

Nat Eek, minutes taken of the Šibenik, Yugoslavia EXCOM Meeting, 27 June–1 July 1969. Child Drama Collection. Dept. of Archives and Special Collections. University Libraries. Arizona State University, Tempe, Arizona, USA..

Vladimir Adamek (Czechoslovakia), minutes taken of the Bucharest, Romania EXCOM Meeting, 1970.

Nat Eek, Minutes and notes taken of the IIIrd Congress of ASSITEJ, Venice, Italy, October 1970. Child Drama Collection. Dept. of Archives and Special Collections. University Libraries. Arizona State University, Tempe, Arizona, USA.

Nat Eek, Official Minutes of the EXCOM Meeting in Bratislava, Czechoslovakia, 1971. Child Drama Collection. Dept. of Archives and Special Collections. University Libraries. Arizona State University, Tempe, Arizona, USA.

Nat Eek, Official Minutes of the EXCOM Meeting in Berlin, Leipzig, and Dresden, GDR, 1972. Child Drama Collection. Dept. of Archives and Special Collections. University Libraries. Arizona State University, Tempe, Arizona, USA.

Nat Eek, Minutes of the Bureau Meeting in Montreal, Canada, dated 13 June 1972. Child Drama Collection. Dept. of Archives and Special Collections. University Libraries. Arizona State University, Tempe, Arizona, USA.

Joyce Doolittle (Canada), Minutes taken of the IVth Congress in Montreal, Quebec, Canada, and Nat Eek (USA), Minutes and notes taken of the IVth Congress in Albany, NY, and the Official Report of the IVth Congress in Albany, NY, published by the State University of New York in Albany, 1972. Child Drama Collection. Dept. of Archives and Special Collections. University Libraries. Arizona State University, Tempe, Arizona, USA.

Joyce Doolittle, Minutes taken of the Bureau Meeting in Bordeaux, France, and notes taken by Nat Eek, October 1972. Child Drama Collection. Dept. of Archives and Special Collections. University Libraries. Arizona State University, Tempe, Arizona, USA.

Joyce Doolittle, Minutes taken of the EXCOM Meeting in London, Great Britain, dtd 29 August 1973, 11 pages. Child Drama Collection. Dept. of Archives and Special Collections. University Libraries. Arizona State University, Tempe, Arizona, USA.

Joyce Doolittle, Minutes, and Nat Eek, notes taken of the EXCOM Meeting in Madrid, Spain, April 1974. Child Drama Collection. Dept. of Archives and Special Collections. University Libraries. Arizona State University, Tempe, Arizona, USA.

Minutes of the EXCOM Meeting in Zagreb and Karlovac, Yugoslavia 3-8 February 1975, in French, apparently distributed by the Paris Secretariat, 1975. Child

Drama Collection. Dept. of Archives and Special Collections. University
Libraries. Arizona State University, Tempe, Arizona, USA.
Joyce Doolittle, Minutes, and Nat Eek, notes taken of the Vth Congress in Berlin,
GDR April 1975. Child Drama Collection. Dept. of Archives and Special
Collections. University Libraries. Arizona State University, Tempe, Arizona,
USA.

Newspaper Articles

Ann S. Hill, "At First International Session on Children's Theatre Ideologies
Submerged By Interest in Youth." *The Nashville [Tennessee] Banner*, 26 May
1964.
Ann S. Hill, *European Children's Theatre and Second Congress of the International
Children's Theatre Association* (Washington, D.C., ACTA Newsletter, 1968, p. 1.
Ann S. Hill, "*3rd Congress of ASSITEJ.*" *The Nashville Banner*, 1970. Child Drama
Collection. Dept. of Archives and Special Collections. University Libraries.
Arizona State University, Tempe, Arizona, USA.
Leipzig Volks Zeitung, "Death of Dr. Ilse Rodenberg" dtd 18 January 2006,
translated by Michael Ramlöse.

Correspondence (in chronological order)

Letter from Rose-Marie Moudoués to Scott Regan as quoted in Regan, *op.cit.* p. 11.
Letter of Michael Pugh to Sara Spencer dtd 8 September 1964.
Letters of Rose-Marie Moudoués and Nat Eek, May 1971. Child Drama Collection.
Dept. of Archives and Special Collections. University Libraries. Arizona State
University, Tempe, Arizona, USA.
Letter to the US Center Executive Committee from Nat Eek dtd 30 November
1973.
Letter from Rose-Marie Moudoués to Nat Eek dated 11 November 1974. Child
Drama Collection. Dept. of Archives and Special Collections. University
Libraries. Arizona State University, Tempe, Arizona, USA.
Correspondence of Nat Eek (USA) and Rose-Marie Moudoués (France) in 1974
and 1975. Child Drama Collection. Dept. of Archives and Special Collections.
University Libraries. Arizona State University, Tempe, Arizona, USA.
Letter from Joyce Doolittle to Nat Eek dtd June 2005.
Sara Spencer, Letter to EXCOM of ASSITEJ dated 7 April 1975. Child Drama
Collection. Dept. of Archives and Special Collections. University Libraries.
Arizona State University, Tempe, Arizona, USA.
Sara Spencer, Letter to Coleman Jennings as quoted in Regan, *op.cit.*
Jed H. Davis, Letter to Nat Eek dated 2 July 2005.
Ian Lucian, letter to Nat Eek dtd December 2007.

Interviews (in chronological order)

Patricia Snyder, interview between Snyder and Scott Regan on July, 1974.
Nat Eek, telephone conversation with Ann M.Shaw, Norman, Oklahoma, Santa Fe,
New Mexico, USA, 1 July 1996.

Ann S. Hill, interview by Nat Eek on 15-16 June 2005 in Nashville, Tennessee, USA.

Joyce Doolittle, interview by Nat Eek on 21-22 June 2005 in Calgary, Alberta, Canada.

Ann M. Shaw, interview by Nat Eek on 9 August 2006 in Santa Fe, New Mexico, USA.

Speeches

Nat Eek, Speech entitled "The Formative Years of ASSITEJ", *One Theatre World Symposium*, Seattle, USA, 10 May 10 1995.

Rose-Marie Moudoués, Speech entitled "The Birth of ASSITEJ," *One Theatre World Symposium*, Seattle, Washington, USA, 10 May 1995 as printed in *ASSITEJ Annual 1996-97*, p.92.

Nat Eek, Speech entitled "What is Children's Theatre All About?"*Vth Congress of ASSITEJ*, Berlin, GDR, April 1975.

E-mail

ASSITEJ/Serbia. E-mail to Nat Eek dtd April 2007 re: Lubiša Djoki! biography.

Doolittle, Joyce. E-mail to Nat Eek dtd 24 June 2005. Information and Personal Biography.

Hoffmann, Christel. E-mail to Nat Eek dtd 26 March 2007 re: ASSITEJ Biographies.

Kolosova, Galina. Chekhov International Theatre Festival, Moscow, Russia. E-mail to Nat Eek dtd 22 May 2006. Information and Biography of Konstantin Shakh-Azizov.

Kolosova, Galina. E-mail to Nat Eek dtd 29 August 2006. Biography of Natalia Sats.

Kolosova, Galina. E-mail to Nat Eek dtd 10 January 2007. Personal Biography.

Kulanáková, Alena. E-mail from ASSITEJ/Czech Republic dtd 13 January 2007. Biography of Vladimir Adamek.

Lucian, Ian. E-mail to Nat Eek dtd December 2006 re: Lucian Biography.

Romain, Maryline, Société d'Histoire du Théâtre. E-mail to Nat Eek dtd 20 November 2006. Biography of Léon Chancerel, translated by Nat Eek.

Romain, Maryline, Société d'Histoire du Théâtre, E-mail to Nat Eek dtd 22 December 2006 and that of January 2007. Translated by Nat Eek.

Simic, Ivica, ASSITEJ/Croatia. E-mail to Nat Eek dtd 27 August 2006. Biography of Zvjezdana Ladika.

Tyler, Gerald (son). E-mail to Nat Eek dtd 8 November 2006. Gerald Tyler (father) Biography.

Printed in the United States
108466LV00003B/67-102/P